Teaching and Learning in Preschool

USING INDIVIDUALLY APPROPRIATE PRACTICES IN EARLY CHILDHOOD LITERACY INSTRUCTION

Elizabeth Claire Venn
Paradise Valley Elementary School
Casper, Wyoming, USA

Mon
Truma
Davenport, Iowa, USA

D1534158

INTERNATIONAL
Reading Association
800 BARKSDALE ROAD, PO BOX 8139
NEWARK, DE 19714-8139, USA
www.reading.org

The International Reading Association attempts, through its publications, to provide a forum for a wide spectrum of opinions on reading. This policy permits divergent viewpoints without implying the endorsement of the Association.

Director of Publications   Joan M. Irwin
Editorial Director, Books and Special Projects   Matthew W. Baker
Managing Editor   Shannon Benner
Permissions Editor   Janet S. Parrack
Acquisitions and Communications Coordinator   Corinne M. Mooney
Associate Editor, Books and Special Projects   Sara J. Murphy
Assistant Editor   Charlene M. Nichols
Administrative Assistant   Michele Jester
Senior Editorial Assistant   Tyanna L. Collins
Production Department Manager   Iona Muscella
Supervisor, Electronic Publishing   Anette Schütz
Senior Electronic Publishing Specialist   Cheryl J. Strum
Electronic Publishing Specialist   R. Lynn Harrison
Proofreader   Elizabeth C. Hunt

Project Editor   Sara J. Murphy

Art   Cover design and Play and Learning Center Prompt Card illustrations (pp. 258–269), Linda Steere

Web addresses in this book were correct as of the publication date but may have become inactive or otherwise modified since that time. If you notice a deactivated or changed Web address, please e-mail books@reading.org with the words "Website Update" in the subject line. In your message, specify the Web link, the book title, and the page number on which the link appears.

Library of Congress Cataloging-in-Publication Data
Venn, Elizabeth Claire.
   Teaching and learning in preschool : using individually appropriate
practices in early childhood literacy instruction / Elizabeth Claire
Venn and Monica Dacy Jahn.
        p. cm.
Includes bibliographical references and index.
   ISBN 0-87207-535-4 (pbk.)
   I. Language arts (Preschool)   II. Jahn, Monica Dacy.   II. Title.
   LB1140.5.L3V46 2003
   372.6--dc22
                                                                        2003018089

Second Printing, November 2004

This book is dedicated to emergent readers everywhere but especially

to our beloved grandchildren:

Bret and Lane; and Kaitlin, Cade, and Ryan.

CONTENTS

ACKNOWLEDGMENTS

We want to acknowledge and thank many people for their support and vital help in the preparation and writing of this book. The first is our featured preschool teacher extraordinaire, Raelene Shreve. Raelene has been with our preschool program since its inception. Her enthusiasm, energy, ideas, and gift for teaching have had an impact not only on the children she has taught but also on the many new preschool educators who have observed her invigorating classroom. Raelene coauthored our first book, *All Ready Reading and Writing Preschool Guidebook* (Venn, Jahn, & Shreve, 1997), and continues to serve as our model classroom teacher. Thanks, Rae, for hanging in there through thick and thin!

We also would like to extend our sincere appreciation and admiration to our knowledgeable and energetic administrator, Christine Frude. Chris embraced our preschool efforts when she became our principal in 1996, and through the years, she not only has influenced our local preschool initiative but also has been instrumental in educating state legislators, policymakers, educators, and the public about the power of early intervention for young children and their families. She is a tireless leader and advocate for quality learning environments for all the children and teachers in her care. On a more personal note, we want to say thank you, Chris, for never giving up or letting us down when the going got tough.

Paradise Valley Elementary School in Casper, Wyoming, USA, was, and still is, our number-one preschool site. We want to express our sincere appreciation to all the Paradise Valley staff who have supported and embraced this endeavor over the years. We particularly would like to recognize the following people: powerhouse school secretary Diana Gleason, who cheerfully typed and formatted many of the documents found in the appendixes; school librarian Carol Michenzi, who helped select appropriate read-aloud books; school counselor Becky Gurtler, who provided support for chapter 4; and Kim Jennings, Donna Shepherd, Lisa Talbott, Debbie Crank, and Nancy Amend, who offered their steadfast friendship, ongoing collegial support, and encouragement. We also would like to thank Larry Regnier, our first principal at Paradise Valley, who believed in us and supported our early efforts to bring the first preschool to a public school setting in our school district. Paradise Valley Elementary School is a unique and wonderful place to be an educator because of all the dedicated and compassionate people who work there.

Throughout the Natrona County School District in Wyoming, we also have innumerable colleagues who have helped us enhance and improve our efforts to support at-risk preschoolers. Speech pathologists Bonnie Bitner and Shirla Loutas have provided invaluable knowledge and information about oral language and phonological awareness interventions for our preschoolers. We gleaned from them much of the information presented in chapter 5. Thanks, Bonnie and Shirla, for teaching us! We also would like to thank the Natrona County School District Central Service administrators and the Natrona County School Board for the unwavering financial support of our preschools. In addition, we want to thank the Casper Alliance for Children and Youth, sponsored by the Wyoming Community Foundation, for funding the early years of our preschool and supporting our belief that early intervention can and does make a difference for children. Particular thanks go to Rod Kinskey and Linda Bryce for their leadership and collaborative efforts with our preschool project. Finally, we would like to thank Pat Renton, Cheryl Selby, and Krista Hamilton for heightening in Wyoming a statewide awareness of the necessity for quality early childhood initiatives.

As our preschools have multiplied and spread throughout the state of Wyoming, we have been blessed with the opportunity to work with many wonderful early childhood educators. We want to thank all of our hardworking, enthusiastic All Ready preschool teachers—especially Marti Derringer, Stacy Butler, and Dusty Haigler—for serving as great mentors for the new teachers who we hire each year. We also would like to thank all of our amazing All Ready preschool paraprofessionals, who support and nurture our students and teachers every day in so many important ways. We want to extend a special thanks to Lynn Wilson, Patty Felch, and Nichole Bertagnole for their additional help in assisting this preschool effort.

We want to acknowledge the International Reading Association, in particular Matt Baker and Sara Murphy for their patient encouragement and expertise.

All the children and their families with whom we have worked in our classrooms, the preschools, and Reading Recovery programs are dear to our hearts and deserve special gratitude and appreciation. From them we have learned so much of what we believe about early childhood education. Our daily interactions with them continue to influence our thinking, philosophy, and passion for the wonderful world of young children and literacy learning.

Monica feels fortunate to have had the extraordinary opportunity to be a part of two remarkable schools—first Paradise Valley and now Truman Elementary School in Davenport, Iowa, USA. Truman Elementary School principal Ken Krumweide and the school staff set a high standard for collegiality, hard work, and dedication to providing the very best in teaching and learning. Thanks for your excellent models of implementing body-brain compatible, concept-based teaching and literacy instruction and for your friendship, emotional support, and interest in this book. We want to thank Arleen Lopez for her expertise in body-brain compatible, concept-based instruction and Meg Knapper for her superior music and movement knowledge. Their ideas improved our learning in these areas and enhanced this book.

Our love and thanks go to our patient and tolerant families for their help and encouragement throughout the long and sometimes arduous process of writing this book. In particular, we want to thank our husbands for their patient acceptance of erratic schedules, huge phone bills, sporadic meals, expensive plane fares, very late nights, and absent and exhausted wives. Without their continuing support and devotion, this book would not have come to fruition.

Claire wishes to express her heartfelt thanks to her parents, Ernst and Jean Sehlmeyer, for their lifelong love and support. Their unconditional love and acceptance have shaped who I am and my children after me. Thank you, Mom and Dad, for your steadfast faith in me. To my beloved children, Brian, Lindsay, and Lauren, you are my daily reminders that every child is truly a gift from God. My earnest thanks to Brian for solving all our technological problems and constructing numerous graphics in our book, to Lindsay and her husband, Rex, for blessing our family with two incredible grandsons, and to Lauren for her cheerful and positive encouragement. Finally, my deepest love and appreciation to Barry, my husband and best friend, for all you do and always have done for me.

Monica wants to thank her parents for encouraging her to be the best she can be and for instilling in her an enjoyment and appreciation of the world of books. Thanks, Mom, for giving me my love of reading and all those books each Christmas and for not being mad when I had finished one by Christmas lunch! I want to thank my dad for being an excellent writing model and tutor. He would have been so proud to see my name on a book as its author. Much love and many thanks to my children by blood and marriage: Chris and Marianne, and Jen and Eric. You have brought such joy to my life, and I am so proud of the marvelous parents and literacy teachers that you are for my beautiful grandchildren. Jen, an extra thanks for your physical education expertise. We could not have written chapter 11 without you! Most important, special thanks and all my love to my husband, Dick, for his unflagging love and support in all the things that I try to accomplish. I am truly blessed to have such a patient and understanding partner.

INTRODUCTION

We each have spent over two decades teaching children who find learning to read and write difficult. As reading specialists, early childhood educators, primary-grade teachers, and Reading Recovery teachers, we have seen firsthand the power of early intervention into a child's literacy development. Ten years ago, our work with kindergarten and first-grade children sparked our desire to help children typically labeled "at risk" begin their elementary school careers as knowledgeable as their peers were in literacy acquisition and other developmental areas. Little did we know that we were starting on a journey that would culminate in the establishment of 22 preschools in the state of Wyoming and the writing of this book. In what follows, we share some struggles from our early years and discuss our early childhood education philosophy, which has evolved through research, further education, interactions with other educators, and—most of all—our work with the children and their families with whom we have had the pleasure to teach and learn over the years.

Our first step toward our goal of establishing a preschool involved additional early childhood and literacy education opportunities. Monica pursued her master's degree in Literacy Curriculum and Instruction and became a certified Reading Recovery teacher, while Claire achieved her master's degree in Early Childhood Curriculum and Instruction along with certification in Special Education and Reading Recovery. During this time, we constructed a preschool framework, and in 1995 a grant from the Wyoming Community Foundation funded a learner-centered preschool for 3-, 4-, 5- and 6-year-olds in a Casper, Wyoming, elementary school. We started the preschool with high hopes and expectations of happy, motivated young readers and writers immersed in an appropriate, stimulating, and nurturing learning environment. However, that vision became clouded as debates among a variety of local and statewide stakeholders developed and our focus of empowering young children in literacy acquisition was prematurely labeled as an inappropriate academic approach to preschool education. Passionate discussions among local Head Start, private preschool, and public school professionals heightened our awareness of the complexities surrounding the sensitive issue of early literacy instruction.

The discussions and debates continued throughout the initial years of the preschool, necessitating the development of formal data collection and an extensive framework design. Funders and district administrators, although extremely supportive of the preschool, rightly demanded accountability and validation. University professors, Head Start and Even Start directors, our local child development center professionals, policymakers, public school teachers, private preschool owners, local school board members, and parents all brought unique perspectives to the table. At this juncture, we began to synthesize and record our beliefs as early childhood educators, which resulted in the *All Ready Reading and Writing Preschool Guidebook* (Venn, Jahn, & Shreve, 1997, 2002). The guidebook became the template for 22 new preschools funded throughout the state of Wyoming in 2003.

As we endeavored to replicate our preschool model at several additional sites, we also overcame challenges from a variety of arenas. Our savvy, articulate, and enthusiastic preschool principal, Christine Frude, took on the task of educating state legislators and political leaders about the power of early intervention, and a Wyoming state law eventually was amended to allow state funding for early childhood education in public schools. Meanwhile, the lack of early childhood educators with backgrounds in early childhood literacy acquisition was surprising to us. To fill this apparent void in preservice education, we developed our own teacher-training workshops to educate our preschool instructors about the oral language, phonological awareness, and reading and writing behaviors critical to children's early literacy learning. To spread these new ideas to other interested parties, we invited the local leaders of Head Start, Even Start, and private preschools and administrators, legislators, and Wyoming state officials to participate in our seminars. Many of them attended and expressed their realization that there had been widespread misinformation and misconceptions concerning our preschool. A new coalition of early childhood education advocates emerged to identify, delineate, and integrate existing Natrona County, Wyoming, services for young children and their families.

At about the same time as the coalition was formed, a new wave of information about early childhood education emerged. The National Research Council published *Preventing Reading Difficulties in Young Children* (Snow, Burns, & Griffin, 1998) and a follow-up book for families and educators called *Starting Out Right: A Guide to Promoting Children's Reading Success* (Burns, Griffin, & Snow, 1999). The 1998 joint position statement of the International Reading Association (IRA) and the National Association for the Education of Young Children (NAEYC) also addresses the very concerns and questions that were confronting our preschool project in Wyoming. We finally felt that we were not the only ones concerned with incorporating specific literacy elements into preschools. The literacy additions to the national Head Start standards and the mandate that all Head Start teachers must participate in 30 hours of early literacy teacher training affirmed that we needed to surge ahead. Our principal's collaborative meetings with the local leaders of Head Start, Even Start, and private preschools and the administrators, legislators, and Wyoming state officials became more productive. The coalition designed and selected joint screening tools, developed universal parental information forms, and created agreements for the electronic tracking of students from all the programs.

The following educational themes and issues central to early childhood education were ones that we encountered while realizing our dream of establishing effective learner-centered preschools. Each theme is discussed more fully in the rest of the book, but because they form the core of our philosophy, we briefly address them here.

Developmentally Appropriate Practice

We strive to provide each preschooler with *individually appropriate* guidance and instruction in the cognitive, social, emotional, and physical domains. We concur with John Pikulski's comment about the "misinterpretations of developmentally appropriate practice meaning no teaching about literacy to young children" (as cited in IRA & NAEYC, 1998, p. 1). Unfortunately, these misinterpretations have left some early childhood educators in a quandary about what is and what is not appropriate to teach across the developmental domains, especially the cognitive domain. Our philosophy encourages teachers to teach what children are ready to learn.

Play

We recognize and acknowledge play as a central activity in the development of young children. In our opinion, play opportunities encompass far more than just free-choice or dramatic play centers. We believe that play may occur in a variety of settings and may be initiated by children, teachers, or others in a variety of ways. Playful activities should permeate all the developmental domains and content areas. In addition, teachers must be skilled at delicately intervening in children's play to encourage thoughtful interactions.

Explicit Instruction

Explicit instruction is deliberate teaching designed to focus children's attention on a specific competency, or goal. Explicit instruction is clear, overt, intentional, and teacher directed. We believe that explicit teaching strategies are appropriate and necessary for at-risk children to attain many critical competencies such as self-regulation, print awareness, phonological awareness, letter knowledge, vocabulary development, and social skills. However, it is significant to note that explicit instruction for young children must be delivered within each child's Zone of Proximal Development (ZPD). (See chapter 1 for a definition and discussion of the term ZPD.)

Assessment

Authentic and appropriate assessments serve as valuable tools for identifying each child's strengths, prior knowledge, and personal interests. Expert teachers use these assessments to inform and guide their daily interactions with each child. Therefore, our preschool framework is based on a continuous cycle of sensitive observation, assessment, reflection, planning, and instruction.

Framework Foundations

Our primary purpose in writing this book is to provide preschool educators with an inclusive text that addresses all the developmental domains and content areas that have an impact on young children. We also provide an in-depth study of how literacy competencies and instruction can be fused into a general framework. We are not suggesting that our philosophy is the only way. It is one that has been successful for us and the children and families with whom we teach and learn.

Our philosophy advocates a learner-centered approach in which teachers must become expert observers of children. We continually remind our teachers that "the child is the only script." This means that instruction is based solely on each child's present performance level rather than commercially prepared programs designed to address only the "average" child. We encourage teachers to use their student observations to plan and execute daily lessons. We do not advocate a prescriptive program approach. The curriculum, outcomes, and checklists in this book are provided to assist teachers with age-appropriate expectations for their preschool students. These elements are intended as general guidelines for monitoring students' progress. Individual differences are to be expected, encouraged, and embraced as children develop according to their own maturational timelines. Therefore, we include a wide span of ages—from 3 to 6—in our developmental compendiums.

We view child development and education from a Vygotskian perspective that emphasizes the importance of social interaction and language and recognizes that learning leads development (Vygotsky, 1934/1978). These elements apply to all children, but they are essential for those preschoolers who have had limited experiences across the developmental domains. When we address the needs of the whole child, we provide the specifics of early language and literacy acquisition necessary for all children to begin kindergarten successfully. As Berk and Winsler (1995) state,

> The assumption of Vygotsky-based education—that adults can and should establish goals for children that lead to ever-higher levels of competence—is based on the notion that psychological developments of early childhood are so important that they cannot be left to chance. (p. 151)

This book is written for early childhood educators, administrators, paraprofessionals, preservice teachers, and others interested in helping young children reach their full potential. We have attempted to include current information on research and instructional practice that will be valuable for educators in a wide range of preschools as they make thoughtful decisions about their daily lessons and interactions with students. We believe that all children can benefit from the infusion of early literacy acquisition into their early childhood education setting. We also believe that it is necessary to state that, although we talk about the cognitive areas of preschool in separate chapters, we do not segment instruction into the separate areas of reading, writing, math, science, and so on. We discuss these areas in separate chapters for ease of organization only. As with most effective preschools, we encourage the integration of these content areas so children participate in activities that promote multiple learning outcomes across the developmental domains.

Chapter 1 delineates the theory behind our framework and the rationale for its need and also outlines our essential preschool components. Chapter 2 discusses three critical elements for quality preschool instruction. Chapter 3 outlines a variety of formal and informal assessments and curriculum outcomes as they relate to lesson design and instruction. Chapter 4 addresses children's social and emotional development and includes information on classroom management, self-regulation, risk taking, and dramatic play. Chapter 5 discusses the critical role of oral language development and phonological awareness in early literacy. Chapter 6 explores the different reading components of shared reading, read-alouds, ZPD groups, independent reading, print concepts, and listening comprehension. Chapter 7 focuses on the vital areas of early writing, including language experience and shared, scaffolded, ZPD, and independent writing.

In chapter 8, learning about print is the central theme, along with letter knowledge and sound-symbol correspondence. Chapter 9 describes the content areas of mathematics, social studies, and science and highlights the importance of free exploration, discovery time, literacy links, and thematic integration. Chapter 10 describes music, movement, and the creative arts as they relate to literacy. Chapter 11 covers gross and fine motor development and health and safety topics. Chapter 12 presents information about transitioning families comfortably from the home to the school culture. In our conclusion, we advocate quality preservice and inservice opportunities for early childhood educators.

The appendixes provide practical and easy-to-use preschool lesson plans and activities, assessment and student monitoring forms, and checklists, along with many other helpful early childhood education references. Appendix A includes a Preschool Lesson Plan Template, a ZPD Groups Lesson Plan Template, a generic lesson plan format, and 16 thematic literacy lesson plans that teachers can adjust to the needs of their specific preschoolers. Appendix B presents various outcomes checklists for all the developmental domains as well as reporting forms for emergent reading and writing test scores and results. Appendix C provides reproducible teacher and parent prompt cards designed to promote and instill self-regulating language and literacy behaviors in preschoolers. Appendix D offers suggestions for preschool movement games and play or learning center ideas related to literacy. Appendix E includes many suggestions for book and music resources to use with young children. Appendix F provides a reproducible parent handbook and other parent-related materials.

CHAPTER 1

Developing a Learner-Centered Preschool

• • •

One afternoon in mid-December, the mother of 4-year-old Betty came to preschool. Betty had learned to write her name just two days before and had been writing it eagerly at school. Betty's mom said, "Now that you've taught my daughter how to write her name, guess what she did? Last night, she took a heavy black marker and wrote her name on every package under our Christmas tree!"

Betty had acquired an important early literacy skill through her own effort and determination, coupled with the instruction and practice provided by a quality preschool experience. Then, she quickly and expertly applied her new knowledge to a situation that had a direct impact on her life. All young children should have the same opportunity to learn and develop in the cognitive, social, emotional, and physical domains. Preschool attendance has been shown to have a powerful impact on later school success. In fact, Snow and colleagues (1998) report that "children who have more preschool experience have higher achievement scores, fewer behavior problems, and are less likely to be retained" (p. 149). Unfortunately, many children do not have quality preschool experiences; therefore, some of these children encounter difficulties in learning to read and write proficiently. These youngsters may become struggling and below-average readers as early as the primary grades.

As reading specialists and classroom teachers in the early 1990s, we worked with struggling first- through third-grade students and endeavored to help them become strategic readers and writers. We discovered that offering more specific and intensive literacy experiences to younger children enabled them to catch up to their peers more quickly than older inefficient readers were able to. We decided to find out more about this phenomenon as we attended national and statewide conferences and workshops, read widely, and conducted research. We found that across the United States, many children in the primary grades were struggling to catch up to their peers, and our experiences were but a microcosm of a larger national problem. To clarify how we began to develop our philosophy and framework of early literacy acquisition and to explain its relationship with early childhood education, we present in the following sections highlights of the information that we gathered. The philosophy is not static; it evolves as we continue to learn more through reading research, discussions with other educators, and experiences working with children.

Early Intervention Research

Educators have long believed that children who have had many literacy experiences as toddlers and preschoolers come to school ready to learn (Allington & Walmsley, 1995). Conversely, children who enter kindergarten without these experiences may be significantly behind their peers in their knowledge of oral language development and literacy acquisition, and they will find it difficult to be successful in school. These children's opportunities for literacy-related, adult-child interactions may have been limited by single parenting, working-parent situations, poverty, and other sociocultural issues. Some children in these situations may find learning to read more difficult than their peers in less stressful environments. The joint position statement of IRA and NAEYC (1998) states, "failing to give children literacy experiences until they are school age can severely limit the reading and writing levels they ultimately attain" (p. 6). Eventually, many children who enter school lacking critical early literacy experiences are placed in special education classrooms and other supplementary reading programs.

Learning to read is a complex process that involves the integration of behaviors that Clay (1991) describes as "visual attention to print, directional behavior relating to position and movement, talking like a book, and hearing sounds in sequences of language" (p. 156). Each of these behaviors alone presents difficulties for young children who are trying to attend to and master them, but because reading and writing demand the automatic and fluent orchestration of all these behaviors, some children find these tasks overwhelming. Neuroscientist and National Reading Panel member Sally Shaywitz (as cited in D'Arcangelo, 2003), states,

> The data show that about 60–70% of children have an easy time learning to read. That sounds terrific. On the other hand, 30–40% is a very large number of children. One third to forty percent of each class is going to need help. (p. 9)

Therefore, quality early intervention programs are essential to providing at-risk children with equal opportunities to succeed both socially and academically in school. Pikulski (1994) notes that children's participation in quality intervention programs results in (a) significant reductions in special education placements, (b) lower retention numbers, and (c) fewer referrals to special programs. Barnett and Hustedt (2003) state, "Many research studies have confirmed preschool's positive effects on school readiness and school success, especially for our most disadvantaged children" (p. 57). Barnett researched numerous preschool education programs for disadvantaged children and found that "preschool programs can produce long term effects on achievement and school success for children in poverty, without school age follow-up interventions" (2002, p. 438).

In addition to their social and academic impact, early intervention programs have an economic influence on our communities. Experts claim that preschools could save $10,000 per child on remediation efforts (Klenschy & Hoge, 1991). Just one year of preschool intervention targeting 4-year-olds from low-socioeconomic-status families can have enormous economic payoffs. In addition, "Other long term benefits from preschool education include increased high school graduation rates and decreased crime and delinquency rates" (Barnett & Hustedt, 2003, p. 55). Early intervention programs can save public dollars and support the development of productive and literate citizens (Pikulski, 1994). Early intervention has proven to be a cost-effective, proactive method of intervening with at-risk children and their families.

Research confirms that children who know about books before learning to read are the most successful in literacy acquisition (Adams, 1990). The process of learning to read begins well before a child enters elementary school. Snow and colleagues (1998) report that

> a recent comprehensive review of early childhood programs for children from low income families concludes that preschool programs can produce large effects on IQ during the early childhood years and sizable persistent effects on achievement, grade retention, special education, high school graduation, and socialization. (p. 150)

They also state that

> excellent preschools can also make a difference for at risk children; excellent in this case implies providing rich opportunities to learn and to practice language and literacy related skills in a playful and motivating setting. Substantial research confirms the value of such preschools in preventing or reducing reading difficulties for at-risk children. (p. 171)

Finally, Burns and colleagues (1999) comment that

> research reveals that the children most at risk of reading difficulties in the primary grades are those who begin school with less verbal skills, less phonological awareness, less letter knowledge, and less familiarity with the basic purpose and mechanisms of reading. (p. 15)

In 1997, the U.S. Congress commissioned the National Institute of Child Health and Human Development (NICHD) to assess and evaluate reading research. The following areas were addressed: vocabulary, alphabetics, fluency, comprehension, teacher education and reading instruction, and computer technology and reading instruction. The findings of the National Reading Panel were published in December 2000 and are presently used throughout the United States to make decisions about instructional strategies and assessment instruments. In later chapters, we cite some of the study's findings as they relate to effective instructional practices for preschoolers.

Brain Research and Early Childhood Education

Another research area that has been gaining wide attention is the study of the brain's structures and functions. This study, called neuroscience, has come to the forefront of scientific study based in part on the many recent scientific and technological advances that reveal significant new information about the brain and its functions in learning. We first began reading about brain research in the 1990s when we were working on our respective master's degrees. Later, Monica learned more neuroscience information when she became a reading specialist at Truman Elementary School in Davenport, Iowa. Davenport schools mandate that educators use brain-compatible and concept-based teaching and learning methods derived from the works of Susan Kovalik and Lynn Erickson. Kovalik's work focuses on applying brain research to classroom practice, and she suggests the following essential elements for effective teaching and learning: an enriched environment, meaningful content, collaboration, movement, choices, adequate time, immediate feedback, mastery, and absence of threat combined with reflective thinking (Kovalik & Olsen, 2001). Erickson's (1995) work with concept-based teaching and curriculum encourages educators to facilitate the content learning of their students through the exploration of key facts, concepts, and generalizations. Internalization of these key facts and concepts helps children to synthesize their learning so they can construct generalizations about the world around them. (See chapter 9 for further discussion of concept-based teaching.) The Davenport Community School District provides professional development on brain-compatible instruction to all staff. Truman School, in particular, implements brain-based learning from preschool through fifth grade in all subject areas. Monica has seen firsthand how using brain-compatible, concept-based curricula and instructional strategies produces a powerful impact on teaching and learning.

> *Using brain-compatible, concept-based curricula and instructional strategies produces a powerful impact on teaching and learning.*

As new research is being conducted, analyzed, and reported, the average person is discovering the amazing capacities of the brain and the essential developments that occur in the first five years of life. For generations, parents and grandparents have marveled over the numerous milestones that young children achieve in their earliest years. However, with the explosion of interest and research into the specific functions of different brain areas, we are beginning to understand exactly how and why some of these important milestones occur.

In *Teaching With the Brain in Mind*, Jensen (1998) concisely describes the development of the brain in infants, toddlers, and young children. He states, "We now understand that the first 48 months of life are critical to the brain's development" (p. 20). The majority of the brain's infrastructure is in place by the end of the first four years, and this infrastructure assists young children in developing the many physical and cognitive skills necessary to learn to talk and eventually to read and write. For example, the vast majority of visual ability develops within a child's first year, with a growth spurt occurring between two and four months of age. Stimulation of the brain's developing visual areas is essential to developing strong visual skills, which are essential in emergent reading tasks such as visual discrimination, tracking, and directionality. Jensen also reports that the brain is ready for thinking via tactile learning by nine months of age, and some researchers hypothesize that babies "may understand basic counting principles and simple physics before age one" (p. 22).

Auditory and early language skills develop rapidly as infants explore a variety of vocalizations resulting from the stimulation of talking with their parents, singing, reading books, and listening to music. Oral language development is discussed in greater detail in chapter 5; however, we want to emphasize the importance of early and frequent oral communication with children in their first years as an essential precursor to reading success.

Motor stimulation also is vital for children's readiness to learn. Hannaford (as cited in Sprenger, 1999) states, "Children benefit when neuronal connections are made through body movement. These connections will help them develop the neuronal systems for reading when they are ready" (p. 8). Jensen (1998) strongly believes in the necessity for movement because it is associated with learning from infancy onward: "Although research in the general value of motor skills first surfaced many years ago, only today do we know about the specific value in reading, stress response, writing attention, memory, and sensory development" (p. 21).

Relevant to reading abilities in particular, Shaywitz (as cited in D'Arcangelo, 2003) reports that the following three areas of the brain are vital for reading: Broca's area, which involves articulation of spoken language; the parieto-temporal area, which involves decoding words (sounding out); and the occipito-temporal area, which involves instant word recognition. Shaywitz believes that children who have difficulty learning to read have significant underactivation of the areas in the back of the brain. She emphasizes that

> the goal of preschool, kindergarten, and first grade is to provide the experiences and the substrate that will lead to automatic reading on a behavioral level and on a neurobiological level, to begin to build the neural systems that are responsible for fluent reading. (pp. 7–8)

Most neuroscientists believe that there are sensitive periods of time (usually up to age 10) within which the brain finds it easiest to develop certain capabilities across all the developmental domains but especially in areas such as vision and language (Wolfe & Brandt, 1998). This theory does not mean that learning cannot occur at other times, only that it occurs easiest when the brain is still continuing to grow and expand its synaptic connections. Therefore, the first years of a child's life are significant in the development of strong cognitive, social, emotional, and physical capabilities.

Because the early years of children's lives are so important in establishing a strong foundation for later learning and especially for literacy achievement, we believe that it is crucial for early childhood educators to keep current on brain research, understand its relation to child development, and apply its findings to teaching and learning within the classroom. We are novices in this area, so we encourage others to read the works of respected leaders in the field of neuroscience such as Robert Sylwester, Marian Diamond, Geoffrey and Renate Nummela Caine and the authors who apply the research to educational settings such as Eric Jensen, Marilee Sprenger, and Susan Kovalik.

A plethora of information is available about brain research and studies. What is uncertain is how the studies directly apply to effective teaching and learning in the classroom. Even neuroscientists acknowledge that it is difficult to take research results definitively and apply them to classroom practice. Yet there are some findings that are universally suggested by many leaders in the neuroscience field that will positively affect learning in the classroom. The following themes appear repeatedly in brain research literature (Jensen, 1998; Kovalik & Olsen, 2001; Wolfe & Brandt, 1998):

- An enriched, stimulating environment triggers brain growth and learning.
- Emotions affect learning. A safe, secure environment promotes learning, while perceived threats prevent it. Also, meaningful, relevant experiences engage children, leading to longer lasting learning.
- The brain is a pattern seeker. It tries to make sense of and organize what it perceives while linking new information to known concepts.
- Movement enhances and cements learning.

Additional elements often mentioned in brain research literature include planning frequent breaks, changing activities to maintain student interest and attention, providing nutritious snacks and lots of water to improve brain function, using music and movement activities to help internalize new learning, and ensuring the active engagement of children in hands-on activities based on student interest and choice. Early childhood educators have incorporated these ideas into quality preschools for years, and we encourage our readers to notice the place that they have in our framework, as described in later chapters. The scope of this book does not allow us to discuss in further detail the many powerful implications that brain research offers the educational community. We hope that we have sufficiently sparked readers' interest so they will investigate neuroscience independently and apply their new knowledge to their own teaching situations.

The Theories of Piaget and Vygotsky

The information and ideas gained from our research were instrumental in helping us design a framework that would be effective for helping young children build a strong literacy foundation. Equally important was our knowledge about the theories of major constructivist theorists Jean Piaget and Lev Vygotsky, who have had an immeasurable impact on child development theories and educational practices in the 20th and 21st centuries. Every college undergraduate who wants to work with children studies Piaget's "ages and stages" philosophy, which has been a foundation of child development theory and pedagogy for decades. Piaget believed that children operate within their environment to construct their own knowledge and understandings about their world as they progress through the sensorimotor, preoperational, concrete operations, and formal operations stages, which are linked to specific ages. He thought that all children must move sequentially through each stage in order to be successful at the next stage of cognitive growth and development. McDevitt and Ormrod (2001) make the following suggestions for educators considering the implications of Piaget's theories in relation to classroom practice:

- Provide opportunities for students to experiment with physical objects and natural phenomena.
- Explore students' reasoning with problem-solving tasks and probing questions.

- Keep Piaget's stages in mind when interpreting children's behavior and developing lessons plans, but don't take the stages too literally.
- Present situations and ideas that students cannot easily explain using their existing knowledge and beliefs.
- Plan group activities in which students share their beliefs and perspectives with each other.
- Use familiar content and tasks when asking students to reason in sophisticated ways.
  (pp. 128–131)

We value the work that Piaget has given to the educational community and the impact it has had on teaching and learning for children of all ages. Some of Piaget's theories are very evident within our preschool framework, which should be apparent in the following chapters. We believe that the philosophy and framework presented in this book achieve the suggestions listed above.

Vygotsky was a contemporary of Piaget. We explain his theories in more detail than Piaget's because some readers may not be familiar with his work. Vygotsky (1934/1978) believed that cognitive development was based on an individual's social interactions within his or her environment and culture. His work progressed from the following four main points:

1. Children construct knowledge.
2. Development cannot be separated from its social context.
3. Learning can lead development.
4. Language plays a central role in mental development. (Bodrova & Leong, 1996, p. 8)

Language was particularly important to Vygotsky's work, and according to Bodrova and Leong (1996), Vygotsky emphasized that "language has two roles; it is instrumental in the development of cognition and is also itself part of cognitive processing" (p. 13). We believe that Vygotsky's theories are particularly applicable to literacy instruction because of the emphasis he places on language in both development and learning. His philosophy reveals that learning can lead development, and, therefore, it gives teachers the permission they need to intervene and teach. Ultimately, as teachers of struggling readers and writers, Vygotsky helps us understand the power of identifying and intervening at a child's actual ZPD in order to help him or her move further along the literacy continuum. Vygotsky's philosophy, as cited by Dixon-Krauss (1996), is that "instruction both precedes and leads development" (p. 14). Because we find the ZPD concept to be so powerful for our teaching, we include a brief explanation here and a visual depiction in Figure 1.

The ZPD has two boundaries. The upper boundary is termed *assisted performance* and demonstrates what a child can do in cooperation with a more knowledgeable other. The lower boundary is termed *independent performance* and shows what a child can do alone. The area between these two boundaries is the ZPD. This has been termed the *learning zone* because when teachers target instruction to a child's ZPD on a specific task and assist him or her in completing the task, new learning takes place as the child is able to link known concepts to new ones. As instruction and assisted performance continue, one can visualize the child's level of

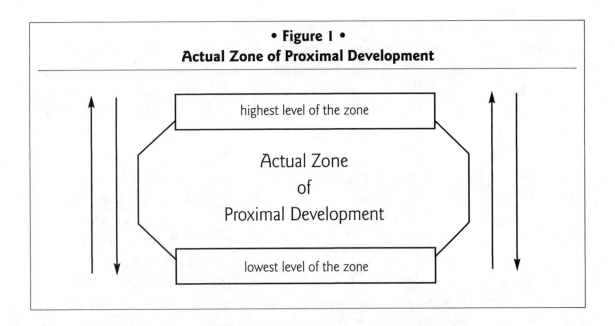

• Figure 1 •
Actual Zone of Proximal Development

highest level of the zone

Actual Zone
of
Proximal Development

lowest level of the zone

assisted performance rising closer to the upper boundary as he or she becomes more capable and can accomplish the task independently. Finally, a new ZPD is created on a new, more difficult task, and the cycle is repeated. Vygotsky believed that the most effective teaching is aimed at the higher levels of the ZPD (Bodrova & Leong, 1996). Because preschoolers come to school with varying backgrounds and experiences, there will be a variety of ZPDs among them and among the domains for each child. A skillful teacher is a careful observer who documents the ZPDs for each child in the different domains. This identification is essential for helping each child apply what he or she knows in order to learn something new. Additional information about incorporating each child's unique sociocultural experiences into daily instruction and activities is discussed in more detail in chapter 4.

Vygotsky's work also centers on the important relationship of language, mental development, and cognition. He believed that through social interactions with others, children expand their knowledge of their world, language development, and mental development. He theorized that social contexts and language directly influence learning and cognition (Bodrova & Leong, 1996). When children begin to use their own thoughts and words to describe how to accomplish a task, they use what Vygotsky termed *private speech* (Bodrova, Leong, Paynter, & Hensen, 2001). The use of private speech is essential for children in order to move from assisted to independent performance on a task so they can apply their new learning. This step is crucial to acquiring new knowledge. Private speech is also paramount in the development of self-regulation:

> One of the goals of the Vygotskian approach is to develop self-regulation of cognitive processes. Children should develop the ability to monitor, evaluate, and regulate their own thinking processes. This ability begins to emerge in first and second grade, but the foundation for it is laid in preschool. (Bodrova & Leong, 1996, p. 78)

The ability to self-regulate permeates all the developmental domains and is a foundational competency for literacy learning. Self-regulation may be witnessed in a preschool setting as children interact and monitor their own actions cognitively, socially, emotionally, and physically. As a child takes on imaginary roles in dramatic play, writes in a journal, or counts the number of beads on a string, he or she is planning and guiding his or her own behavior internally. Reading and writing acquisition requires this critical competency.

Wood, Bruner, and Ross (1976) introduced the concept of scaffolding, which is a key component to moving a child to a higher level in his or her ZPD for a given task. Scaffolding involves a teacher or expert peer giving assistance to a child so he or she can complete a task. The support is gradually withdrawn over time as the child is able to perform more of the task independently. This process works most effectively when teachers can discern the "cutting edge" of a child's knowledge—what the child is ready to take on next within a specified task. For example, Betty, from the chapter's opening vignette, entered preschool knowing some of the letters in her name. Through careful observation and interaction, Betty's teacher, Bridget Loftus, was able to help her gradually raise her level of competency until she could write her name without help.

To simplify Vygotsky's complex theories and ideas for educators, we cite the educational implications of his work as stated by McDevitt and Ormrod (2001):

- Help students acquire the basic conceptual tools of various academic disciplines.
- Present challenging tasks, perhaps within the context of cooperative activities.
- Scaffold students' efforts.
- Assess students' capabilities under a variety of work conditions.
- Provide opportunities to engage in authentic activities.
- Promote self-regulation by teaching children to talk themselves through difficult situations.
- Give children the chance to play. (pp. 139–141)

We hope that these implications are evident in our preschool framework as readers progress through the following chapters. In our view, Vygotsky's theories have great validity, especially for helping young children with literacy acquisition.

Literacy Acquisition Theories

Current literacy acquisition theories can be summarized into three general viewpoints: (1) information processing, (2) whole language, and (3) sociocultural (McDevitt & Ormrod, 2001). First, the information-processing viewpoint emphasizes the cognitive processes of reading and writing in relation to metacognition, modeling, and memorization. As a child's overall cognitive abilities grow, so will the child's reading and writing abilities. However, some behaviors—such as one-to-one correspondence, directionality, and rapid letter and word recognition—must become automatic before fluent reading and writing are possible. Second, whole-language theory proposes that reading and writing behaviors can develop similarly to the way children learn to speak—through immersion and active engagement in a literature-rich environment. Children participate in authentic literacy activities while simultaneously learning essential literacy concepts. Finally, the sociocultural viewpoint proposes the importance of social interaction that builds children's capacities to learn to read and write. Children need opportunities to observe and interact with others in literacy activities in order to improve their abilities in reading and writing.

Each theory offers valuable insights into the complexities of literacy acquisition and suggests how to help children overcome the obstacles inherent in learning to read and write. We recommend that educators employ suggestions from all three theories in planning and carrying out the instruction and assessment of their preschoolers. Our experience has shown us that there is no one best way to teach every child. Each child has his or her own unique learning requirements, and although one technique may be successful with several children, other children will need instruction, practice, and independent activities presented in a different manner. The difficulty for teachers is in determining what each child needs in order to be successful and planning how best to meet those needs.

> Our experience has shown us that there is no one best way to teach every child.

Philosophy and Framework Overview

Our experiences working with children of diverse backgrounds, ethnicities, and learning styles, along with the knowledge gained from our research and discussions, came together in the creation of our preschool philosophy and framework. The following overview gives a snapshot of the components that we believe are essential in a quality preschool. As previously noted, 22 preschools within the state of Wyoming currently use this framework. Readers who are just beginning a preschool may want to use all the components of our framework. Other readers may work in existing preschools and want to use some of the ideas, methods, and activities. We encourage all readers to think about how the ideas offered here could have a positive impact on the children and families with whom they work. This is not an all-or-nothing framework, just as there is not a finite body of knowledge that defines best-practice teaching strategies. As educators, we should continually synthesize and expand our knowledge and theories about how children learn. We believe that most quality teachers are experts at finding activities and teaching techniques that meet the individual needs of their students.

Goals and Objectives

This preschool framework is designed to give preschoolers and their families the support and guidance that they need to be successful as they enter the children's elementary school years together. The objectives of this framework are (a) to significantly increase the reading and writing acquisition of young children as they enter their formal years of education; (b) to model and provide individually appropriate practices in all cognitive, physical, social, and emotional interactions for children and their families; (c) to transition students and families comfortably into the public school setting; and (d) to increase parental awareness and support of all school activities. We firmly believe that all children can learn to read and write effectively, that all young children deserve the opportunity to be immersed in a language-rich environment, and that all children should be provided with expert instruction by a highly trained early childhood educator so they may start kindergarten as literate as their peers.

Developmentally Appropriate Practices

The National Association for the Education of Young Children defines developmentally appropriate practice as decision making that uses three kinds of knowledge: "(1) what teachers know about how children develop and learn; (2) what teachers know about the individual children in their group; and (3) knowledge of the social and cultural context in which those children live and learn" (Bredekamp & Copple, 1997, p. vii). Our framework promotes a teaching model that expands NAEYC's definition to include knowledge about explicit and implicit instruction for young children. In addition, our framework is designed primarily to meet the needs of those students who often find learning on their own difficult.

Explicit and implicit teaching of learning strategies is, in our opinion, essential for many children to reach their full potential. Instructional decisions are determined through daily observations of individual children, and then teachers use these observations to ascertain each child's ZPD on a given task. They construct or develop learning activities at the level at which the child is ready to take on new information, and they facilitate and scaffold the child's new learning. Our teachers have felt empowered by this philosophy. One of our Casper, Wyoming, preschool teachers, Rose Menghini, has worked for years within other preschool settings. She called us after teaching in our preschools for six weeks and said, "You set me free! You set me free! For so long I was told I couldn't teach this and I couldn't teach that because it was *not* developmentally appropriate! Now I have permission to teach what my children are ready to learn!" (personal communication, October 15, 2002). Not only is this framework developmentally appropriate, but it also is individually appropriate.

In our experience, we have found that some early childhood teachers have understood the definition of developmentally appropriate practice to be predominantly what a child can do independently. We believe that the term *developmentally appropriate* includes the concept of the ZPD, expanding the idea of what is developmentally appropriate to include what can be learned with assistance (Bodrova & Leong, 1996). Children need many opportunities to operate independently and with assistance, so new learning can be applied and eventually become an independent task.

Instructional Practices

The purpose of our framework is accomplished by providing a balance of varied instructional techniques that incorporate group (large, small, and partner) and independent work, choices by teachers and children, and both teacher- and child-driven activities. Daily opportunities for exploration in play and learning center activities, cooperative groups, and free-choice play centers are essential to allow children to progress in a developmentally appropriate manner in all areas. Our ZPD groups, in particular, are the cornerstones of our framework and distinguish ours from other early childhood programs. Because we strongly believe in a Vygotskian philosophy of teaching and learning, we feel that these groups offer the personalized instruction necessary to support children who find learning on their own difficult. ZPD groups are discussed in detail in chapter 6. (See Figure 2 for an example of a ZPD group at work.)

Effective instruction within a nurturing and stimulating classroom must be grounded in knowledge and understanding about three areas: (a) knowing each individual child across the domains, (b) knowing preschool curricula and appropriate developmental compendiums, and (c) knowing how to provide effective explicit and implicit instruction. Expertise in these areas enables teachers to provide appropriate instruction for each child, based on a continuous cycle of child observation, teacher planning, assisted child performance through instruction and shared tasks, and a return to observation. Thus, each child is showing the teacher what he or she is ready to learn next.

Many children require explicit instruction to become successful readers and writers. Spiegel (1999) states, "Best practice does not mean all children receive the same education. Best practice means that when a child needs explicit, systematic instruction in order to progress, the teacher provides this guidance" (p. 249). Therefore, preschool teachers need to be

• Figure 2 •
Teacher Raelene Shreve Teaches a ZPD Group

certified in early childhood education and be highly skilled in observing young children. They must be cognizant of the importance of observing children in a variety of activities and settings—large groups, small groups, and independent work—and understand the significance of identifying each child's ZPD for relevant tasks to determine daily lessons. Then, each student's instruction is linked to his or her personal background experiences as well as to the teacher's daily classroom observations. Teachers are trained to observe and record student growth and instruct or scaffold each child's learning to the next level through ongoing observations. The selection of materials and activities is based on students' individual levels of development rather than a prescribed set of events or a continuum of skills. Educators design their teaching techniques and strategies to match each preschool student's appropriate developmental level and incorporate them in a playful manner. Vygotsky's students Daniil Elkonin and Alexei Leont'ev "refined his ideas into the theory that play is the leading factor in early childhood development; it is the leading learning activity for 3–5 year olds" (Bodrova & Leong, 1996, p. 127) in terms of the ZPD. The importance of play in a preschooler's growth and development is discussed further in chapters 2 and 4.

> Each student's instruction is linked to his or her personal background experiences as well as to the teacher's daily classroom observations.

Staff Development

Employing early childhood teachers who possess sophisticated knowledge about instructional strategies, appropriate preschool environments, and effective management techniques is critical. We have firsthand experience with trying to find qualified teachers to fill preschool positions, particularly from the early years of starting our first preschool. We either found certified early childhood specialists with little or no background in early childhood literacy acquisition or certified elementary school teachers with little or no background in early childhood development. A possible solution to this problem is the implementation of more bachelor's programs designed to educate early childhood professionals with expertise in both areas.

An additional problem is that the most qualified and experienced early childhood teachers often do not seeks positions within some preschool programs because of their low compensation and benefits. As a result, the neediest children in the United States, who deserve the most qualified and experienced teachers, often have teachers who are grossly underpaid and inadequately trained in meeting students' academic needs. As educators within the public school system, we worked for several years to achieve equitable pay and benefits for our preschool teachers. They now receive the same compensation as their elementary-level peers, and therefore, our job openings attract candidates with high qualifications.

Barnett and Hustedt (2003) report, "Teachers in pre-K programs sponsored by public schools were better educated, earned higher salaries, and had lower turnover in their jobs than teachers in privately operated programs" (p. 56). We do not mean to suggest that all preschools should be housed within public schools, but we recommend that public and private preschool programs, funders, and other stakeholders work to better distribute or integrate funds for and to a variety of preschool settings. As the importance and effectiveness of quality preschool programs become more widely valued and recognized, we hope that policymakers and funders will invest in the future of our youngest students by appropriating and allocating monies that will support excellent early childhood education initiatives.

Early childhood educators also need powerful and up-to-date inservice opportunities. Snow and colleagues (1998) state, "Little systematic attention has been paid to in-service education and other options for professional development of preschool teachers" (p. 280). Therefore, staff development opportunities for teachers and paraprofessionals should focus on appropriate teacher-student interactions, individually appropriate practice, knowledge of at-risk children and families, language development, parent involvement, preschool literacy experiences, recent research, and best practices in early childhood education.

Numerous full-day workshops and ongoing site-embedded trainings are recommended so teachers have the opportunity for the in-depth examination and discussion of these topics and reflection and planning on how to incorporate their new knowledge into their teaching practices. Other staff development opportunities throughout the year, demonstration teaching by a mentor, cohort groups that read and study about specific early childhood topics, and colleague visits and partnerships help teachers stay current on best-practice methods and provide needed support and resources for the teachers involved. The effective implementation of new practice and teaching methods is highly correlated to the support of other teachers and mentors, so it is essential to develop ways to network and partner educators.

Setting

Our preschools usually have been housed in elementary schools. Each preschool typically provides one certified teacher with expertise in early childhood education, one paraprofessional, and numerous parent volunteers for up to 18 full-time students. Elementary school staff members and specialists, such as speech therapists, occupational therapists, and computer assistants, are easily accessible to preschool staff and participating families. Libraries, gymnasiums, computer labs, and lunchroom facilities are just a few of the extras provided for preschoolers within the elementary school setting. The opportunities for cross-age tutoring and peer relationships are numerous, helping to foster in the preschoolers a sense of belonging to a larger school community. This neighborhood, elementary school–based preschool concept initiates and transitions parents and their young children comfortably and smoothly into their local public school setting.

We recommend that a preschool class be limited to no more than eight or nine students per adult to ensure quality time for each student. The inclusion of parent volunteers and paraprofessionals may bring the adult-to-student ratio even lower. Children attend class for a half day, five days a week, aligning their schedules with the school district calendar. Class times are arranged to coincide with the existing kindergarten timetable. Parents or family members come into the school to pick up or drop off their preschoolers. Thus, staff and families have opportunities for daily contact to communicate information about the children that in turn fosters the development of warm and trusting relationships.

Parent Involvement

All parents want their children to succeed in school, and it is widely accepted that children are more successful in school when their families are involved in their educations. Goldenberg (2002) reports, "Considerable research suggests that skeptics [of parent involvement] are probably mistaken...schools and families can work together to help children succeed academically. This proposition is especially true in the area of early literacy" (p. 221).

However, for some family members, the school setting brings back unpleasant memories of their own academic struggles, social and emotional difficulties, or both. Therefore, a way to break the cycle of school failure is to provide families with early cognitive, social, emotional, and physical support so they become comfortable with the structure of the preschool and its activities. Parents, children, and teachers all benefit from interactions with one another at home and at school. Therefore, in our preschools, the students' parents or legal guardians are required to participate in the preschool classroom on a weekly basis. Parents or guardians must observe and interact with teachers and students within the classroom for one hour per week and may choose where they volunteer for a second hour—in the preschool or anywhere else in the school. This part of the framework is strictly upheld, even though it often can involve wide-ranging challenges for preschool educators. Parents are an integral part of preschool as they share their personal insights, experiences, observations, and interactions with their child (see Figure 3), the teacher, and other parents within the classroom. Parent and family involvement is discussed more fully in chapter 12.

• Figure 3 •
A Parent Reads to Her Daughter at Preschool

Curriculum and Outcomes

Children participating in this preschool framework focus on cognitive, social, emotional, and physical development, including reading and writing activities; oral language development; phonological awareness; music and the creative arts; and mathematics, social studies, science, and technology—all embedded in purposeful and playful activities. We referenced the *Head Start Program Performance Standards* (U.S. Department of Health and Human Services, 1998), *Building Strong Foundations for Early Learning: The U.S. Department of Education's Guide to High-Quality Early Childhood Education Programs* (Dwyer, Chait, & McKee, 2000), and the *Wyoming Department of Education Early Childhood Readiness Standards* (Wyoming Early Childhood Standards Task Force, 2002) during the development of the curriculum and outcomes. These sources provided a variety of indicators and competencies for each developmental domain and content area. We were able to review and evaluate Head Start's and U.S. Department of Education's indicators for high-quality early childhood education programs, and we refined them to reflect our beliefs about and understandings of early childhood education. Claire served on the Wyoming Early Childhood Standards Task Force, which designed the preschool standards in the state. Therefore, the outcomes and curriculum presented in this book are aligned very closely with the Wyoming Early Childhood Readiness Standards. In addition, we use an age span of 3–6 years in our outcomes and checklists for several reasons.

First and foremost, we believe that behavior is not necessarily age related. Children vary widely in their maturation, and each child reaches developmental milestones in his or her own unique way. What one particular preschooler accomplishes as a 3-year-old may take another child until age 4 to achieve. Conversely, some 4-year-olds will attain competencies in some areas that are typical for 5-years-olds. Some preschools may enroll children who are chronologically ready for kindergarten but who, for a variety of reasons, participate in preschool when they are 5 years old. Typically, age-related outcomes are based on children's average accomplishments. However, our philosophy compels us to look at children individually, not as a composite of others. The wide age span in our outcomes makes it easier to record and monitor progress for each child and then to provide appropriate instruction for each that is not always linked to chronological age.

The second reason for our age span of 3–6 years is that beginning teachers will find the range invaluable as they observe and assess their students during the challenging first years. Beginning teachers tend to be uncertain about their abilities in monitoring and accurately evaluating children's growth. The specifics of the developmental compendium provided in all areas will be essential guides for recognizing a child's current accomplishments, noting a child's achievement of previous competencies, and helping plan future instruction.

Third, although experienced teachers already are skilled at observing and evaluating the growth and development of their students, the span in ages serves as an excellent tool for tracking individual children in all tasks within one class. Within each preschool class, students have a wide variety of capabilities across the developmental domains, and teachers will be able to monitor more accurately that array with the broader span in ages that we provide.

The primary purpose of the framework is to help children grow across all the developmental domains, while building a strong literacy foundation prior to their formal schooling. Daily observations, phonological awareness activities, oral language development, social-skills development, read- and write-alouds, shared reading and writing, ZPD groups, and independent reading and writing are all components of the curriculum. Within these components, students work together with parents and teachers while exploring book-handling skills; letters names, sounds, and formations; print concepts; vocabulary development; and story frameworks. These experiences are all encompassed in a positive, risk-free, playful, and respectful atmosphere. The curriculum is designed to serve as an outline, not a prescriptive program, to guide teachers as they determine individually appropriate techniques and activities to meet children's instructional needs. We believe that we are teaching children, not curricula; therefore, we hope that our readers will find this book helpful as they observe children and then make thoughtful decisions about effective instruction for them.

Conclusion

After many years of experience working with children who have struggled unnecessarily with literacy acquisition, we enthusiastically advocate the implementation of early intervention programs that provide appropriate explicit instruction for at-risk preschoolers across the developmental domains. We have participated in many professional discussions that debate a play-oriented versus an academics-oriented approach to early childhood education. We believe that play and academics are not mutually exclusive but rather are mutually inclusive. Explicit instruction provided within a preschool setting can and always should be playful and engaging. Clay (1998) writes, "Literacy enthusiasts, through oversight and overemphasis are in danger of narrowing the interpretation of what contributes to school progress, while early childhood educators are in danger of setting literacy aside until children get to school" (p. 1). We endeavor to avoid these pitfalls as we try to bridge the theoretical and practical gaps that exist between preschool and elementary school.

We have constructed our preschool framework to infuse literacy instruction into a playful preschool setting. For years, early childhood educators have created a warm, nurturing, and affirming environment in which children have participated in open-ended, play-based activities. We endeavor to sustain these important attributes, while enhancing instructional strategies for early literacy learning. These instructional strategies include teacher expertise in the execution of both implicit and explicit language and literacy instruction in a learner-centered preschool. Chapter 2 discusses the importance of implicit and explicit teaching in the context of authentic situations and profiles.

Using Individually Appropriate Instruction in Preschool

• • •

We had a sign on the bathroom door—one side was red, and the other was green for *stop* and *go,* respectively. Alexa went to the bathroom and left the sign on green. Kyle got up and flipped it to red for her. She opened the door and flipped it back to green. Kyle flipped it back to red. This continued for three or four more times. Finally, Alexa came out with her hands on her hips and said, "This is green, and it means go, and I have to *go!*" (D. Haigler, personal communication, December 10, 2002)

Every child brings his or her own unique cultural and familial experiences to the classroom setting. It is the teacher's responsibility to observe, value, and acknowledge this wonderful diversity and then provide a supportive bridge between the home and school cultures. Expert teachers use this knowledge to enhance and scaffold each child's learning to the next level, linking known information to new. Alexa's schema in relation to the class bathroom routine and the concept of *go* are very obvious as a result of this interchange. She definitely knows that green means *go,* but her understanding of *go* in the context of the bathroom is different from Kyle's and different from what the teacher had intended. Alexa's teacher, given this new insight into Alexa's understandings, may now appropriately intervene and clarify any confusion that may affect Alexa's bathroom use in the future. The stoplight metaphor of green meaning the bathroom is available and red meaning the bathroom is occupied also may become a first step for Alexa in learning the important concept of analogy. The principle of analogy, cited humorously in this tale, is also a significant strategy in literacy acquisition as children use what they know about a known word to decode a new word. This vignette provides a realistic opportunity for a knowledgeable teacher to mediate and facilitate new understandings for young children based on daily observations and deliberate, planned instruction.

Quality preschool instructors must be astute child observers and strategic planners, using what they know about human development coupled with an intimate knowledge of children as learners. Simply stated, the children are and should be the only script in an individually appropriate preschool classroom. Having said that, we encourage an array of materials such as references, literature, resources, assessments, and curricula to support teachers in lesson design and development. We caution teachers that although prescriptive programs may serve as valuable resources, they should not control or determine classroom instruction. We firmly believe that preschool teachers need to be well trained and serve as early childhood education experts, designing appropriate instruction for individual students. In addition, preschool teachers should endeavor to follow each child's lead, identify his or her ZPD, and then carefully plan playful, engaging activities that move the child along in his or her individual learning progression.

This instructional approach typically triggers the big question, How do we know *what* to teach if we don't have a teacher's manual? Our answer is always the same: Teachers need three critical teacher competencies:

1. knowing and understanding each individual child across the developmental domains

2. knowing preschool curricula and appropriate developmental compendiums

3. knowing how to provide appropriate explicit and implicit instruction

In this chapter, we delineate and clarify each of the three critical teacher competencies by citing specific student examples and supplying helpful resources for teachers.

Knowing and Understanding Each Individual Child Across the Developmental Domains

The preschool teacher's first challenges are getting to know each child as a learner, acknowledging the child's special interests, and celebrating his or her unique qualities. These tasks may be approached in a number of ways, including home visits; family conferences; one-on-one assessments; and purposeful, daily teacher observations and anecdotal records.

Home Visits

Home visits provide teachers with a wealth of information about the child and his or her home environment. We encourage preschool teachers to make at least one home visit early in each child's preschool experience. During a home visit, teachers may share pertinent preschool information with parents and perhaps read aloud a story to the child. This effort conveys to parents the teacher's genuine interest in home-school collaboration. It often is helpful to have a list of questions or topics to discuss during the visit. For example, soliciting information about unique family traditions and hobbies may provide valuable information for planning future lessons and also may serve as a mechanism for involving parents in particular thematic units or events. Teachers may secure valuable information about the literacy and language resources that the child has available—or lacks—in the home. All this information empowers preschool teachers as they individualize instruction and make thoughtful decisions about their students' needs.

Family Conferences

In our experience, many parents become uncomfortable with or disinclined to fill out even the simplest surveys when asked, so we encourage our preschool teachers to confer casually with parents and families to elicit pertinent, insightful information. Parent or family conferences at the preschool or by phone provide communication opportunities that often strengthen the home-school connection. Conferences may be formally scheduled or spontaneous in nature. During these conversations, teachers may ask parents about their goals and aspirations for their children and learn about any special interests the children may have. Parents and teachers may generate collaborative plans to enhance social interactions and academic growth. Teachers' anecdotal notes about families' talents and interests also may facilitate class field trips, guest speaker choices, and thematic unit decisions at a later date.

One-on-One Assessments

One-on-one assessments provide invaluable information about a child's strengths and weaknesses across the developmental domains. The developmental and phonological awareness screenings, literacy assessments, and social and emotional surveys addressed in chapter 3 secure valuable information about students. This information may be compiled, along with student-generated artifacts and parent comments, into individual student portfolios that guide preschool teachers as they plan their instruction. The assessment process is ongoing as teachers are encouraged to develop and hone their skills as capable observers and assessors of children throughout the year.

> Watching children closely to identify what they know and what they need to know next is at the heart of good teaching in any classroom.

Teacher Observations and Anecdotal Records

Teacher observations and anecdotal record keeping are imperative to document and target a child's ZPD across the developmental domains. Techniques for observing children effectively and recording anecdotal excerpts are studied in depth in chapter 3, and the Preschool Outcomes Checklist can be found in Appendix B, page 241. Watching children closely to identify what they know and what they need to know next is at the heart of good teaching in any classroom. It is a skill that we believe separates expert teachers from their less-skilled peers. To explain and clarify this complex process further, we have provided the following examples.

During a home visit, one teacher from our preschool wrote in her anecdotal notes that 4-year-old Kirstan was using regular past-tense verbs correctly in casual conversation but mispronounced several irregular past-tense verbs (for example, using *maked* for *made*, *falled* for *fell*, and *growed* for *grew*). In Kirstan's portfolio, the teacher targeted irregular past-tense verbs as the child's next oral language competency. The teacher checked the language development and literacy section of the Preschool Outcomes Checklist to verify that irregular past-tense verbs were a 4-year-old skill, and this fact coupled with Kirstan's daily oral language communications affirmed that the child was, in fact, ready to take on this new concept.

In our second example situation, 3-year-old Rebecca was observed writing a letter in the post office play center while using an inappropriate pencil grip. As she wrote, Rebecca's hand was curved into a hook position. Her teacher recorded this behavior in Rebecca's portfolio and later asked the school district's occupational therapist for suggestions to promote and facilitate an appropriate pencil grip. The occupational therapist explained that sometimes when young children write on a table with the paper lying horizontally in front of them, they exhibit this improper grip. The occupational therapist suggested that Rebecca be encouraged to write in settings that provided a vertical positioning of the paper, such as standing at a chalkboard or an easel. This accommodation helped to rotate her pencil grip naturally into the appropriate position, with her wrist and elbow lying below her fingers as they grasped the pencil.

A third student, 5-year-old Daniel, demonstrated competencies in rhyming and word segmentation (clapping words in sentences) on the phonological awareness screening. The teacher noted these accomplishments in his portfolio and targeted compound word and syllable segmenting and blending (*cow...boy, tooth...brush, com-pu-ter*) as Daniel's next accomplishments to increase his phonological awareness. Once again, the teacher checked the Preschool Outcomes Checklist and other phonological awareness resources (e.g., Adams, Foorman, Lundberg, & Beeler, 1997; Floyd & Yates, 2001; Paulson, Noble, Jepson, & van den Pol, 2001) to verify that syllable blending and segmenting were an appropriate next step for Daniel. Based on his actual development level in this area, she proceeded with this goal.

These three examples all describe how expert preschool teachers identify individual students' learning zones in several different developmental domains and content areas and then prepare appropriate instruction. This lesson-design process involves the following four systematic procedures for any task in any of the developmental domains:

1. Carefully observe and assess student performance,

2. identify the student's ZPD,

3. refer to developmental compendiums to determine the student's next step for new learning, and

4. plan appropriate instruction to scaffold the new learning.

Knowing Preschool Curricula and Appropriate Developmental Compendiums

After identifying a child's ZPD for a particular task, the next challenge for preschool teachers is to know about human development, developmental compendiums, and curricula to determine each student's actual point of development and discern what to teach next. To enhance a teacher's knowledge in this area, we have developed a Preschool Curriculum Framework (see Appendix B, page 235) and corresponding Preschool Outcomes and Preschool Outcomes Checklist (see Appendix B, pages 236 and 241, respectively) that delineate the developmental domains and content areas of study for students ages 3–6. This curriculum aligns closely with many state preschool standards, including the *Wyoming Department of Education Early Childhood Readiness Standards* (Wyoming Early Childhood Standards Task Force, 2002). Teachers may want to attach the curriculum, checklist, or both to the inside of their lesson-plan books to help them in developing class activities and lessons. The Preschool Curriculum Framework, Preschool Outcomes, and Preschool Outcomes Checklist are collectively designed to serve as a guideline, not a prescriptive program, to help preschool teachers as they determine individually appropriate instructional techniques and activities to meet students' individual needs. Teachers are responsible for planning and designing themes and activities that are directly relevant to the diverse cultures, background experiences, and specific interests of their students. (See Figure 4 for a student engaged in an activity designed at his ZPD level.)

The Preschool Outcomes (see Appendix B, page 236) are outcomes and indicators with age-appropriate expectations that will support teachers as they tailor personalized lessons for their students. The outcomes on the list are intended as a general guideline to monitor student progress. The purpose of these indicators, or outcomes, is to provide teachers with general goals, accomplishments, or both for young children. Teachers may glean useful information about which important concepts, strategies, and skills a child may be ready to learn next, always taking into consideration what the child already knows. Referring back to our previous student examples, we can demonstrate this process more clearly.

Rebecca's fine motor skills development, Daniel's progress in phonological awareness, and Kirstan's oral language development could be recorded easily and documented on the Preschool

---

• Figure 4 •
Soni Matches Letters to a Muffin Tin Template

Outcomes Checklist. Then, new learning or skills to be learned next may be identified and targeted for future personalized lessons. For example, Kirstan may be ready to increase the complexity of her conversational sentences by using her newly acquired, irregular past-tense verbs. Rebecca may be ready to write some recognizable letters from her name on the chalkboard or easel, and Daniel, having mastered clapping two smaller words within compound words, may be ready to orally segment multisyllabic words. New skills to be taught to these students and others may be selected from a continuum of developmental competencies such as our Preschool Outcomes (see Appendix B, page 236), and for recording students' progress teachers can use the Preschool Outcomes Checklist (see Appendix B, page 241). (See also Venn, Jahn, & Shreve, 2002, pp. 57–62.)

Individual differences always should be expected and encouraged as children develop according to their own maturational timelines. This compendium purposefully refrains from delineating grade-level or yearly age-level expectations for the skills of 3–6-year-olds. We believe that teachers should be familiar with typical, sequential patterns of development and also acknowledge and embrace individual differences that may not fit the normal chronological age boundaries. For this reason, we propose a developmental continuum that lists general 3- and 4-year-old indicators in regular typeface and 5- and 6-year-old indicators in boldface type. Both two-year spans are purposefully designed to encourage teachers to focus on each child's individual growth and development rather than relying too heavily on age expectations.

To support our proposed two-year spans, we cite Jensen's (1996) statement that in the typical classroom there may be from a one- to a three-year difference in the maturation of students' brains: He reveals that "30% of children have lesser maturation, 35% are most typical, and 35% have greater maturation" (p. 12). In addition, Jensen cautions that "statewide curriculums and frameworks which include specific grade-level performance standards are biologically inappropriate" (p. 12). Our experience working with fragile readers and writers mirrors Jensen's findings. We have found that our at-risk readers and writers are frequently the children who do *not* follow the traditional age-appropriate norms. Teachers may have several 4-year-olds accomplishing competencies of 6-year-olds, while other 4-year-olds may demonstrate the competencies of 2- or 3-year-olds. Therefore, we have provided a preschool compendium that not only provides for two-year age spans but also encompasses four years of expected outcomes (3-year-old through 6-year-old skills) to provide, we hope, for the wide variance that preschool teachers surely will observe in student performance. Inevitably, preschool teachers will find numerous occasions where even this four-year span will not be adequate, and they will need to append this developmental compendium to serve children performing developmentally below 3 years of age or above 6 years of age, and we certainly encourage that they do so.

Knowing How to Provide Appropriate Implicit and Explicit Instruction

The third and final challenge that preschool teachers need to address in their training is knowing how to provide both implicit and explicit instructional opportunities within each child's ZPD. As previously stated, Vygotsky believed that a child's ZPD is activated through social interactions and play (Bodrova & Leong, 1996). These early childhood basics provide natural contexts for implicit and explicit instruction. Our definition of implicit instruction is learning embedded and modeled within the context of realistic experiences. Conversely, explicit instruction is defined as deliberate teaching designed to focus students' attention on a specific competency or goal. Explicit instruction also is characterized as clear, overt, and intentional teacher-directed instruction.

Implicit Instruction

For preschool-age children, implicit instruction occurs in many contexts, such as field trips, read-alouds, and recess, but the leading context is play centers. Well-planned and purposeful play centers are a priority in a quality preschool. A daily pursuit should be providing young children with a variety of realistic free-choice activities. Play centers provide children with the chance to discover and explore all the developmental domains and content areas. Art, computer, water-table, science, math manipulative, block, writing, library, listening, fine motor, and dramatic play centers are just some of the center opportunities we encourage in preschool. The dramatic play center may reflect real-world settings such as hospitals, homes, banks, restaurants, post offices, bakeries, and greenhouses. The centers should change frequently and be based on students' interests, offering purposeful, challenging new themes. See Figure 5 for a student participating in a free-choice play center.

• Figure 5 •
Bradley Experiments With Sand Manipulatives

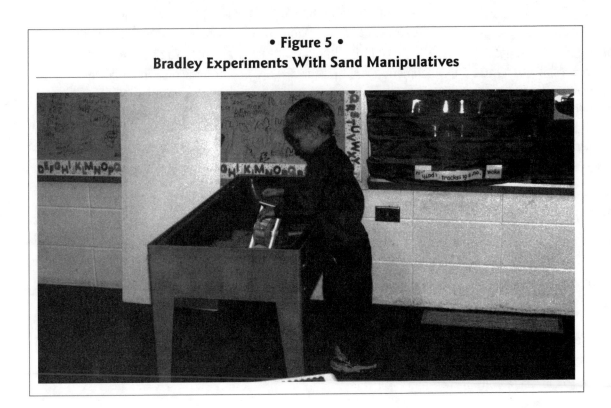

As literacy advocates, we encourage teachers to provide reading, writing, and environmental-print materials that implicitly teach their students literacy competencies through a variety of center themes. Construction books may accompany the block center, road signs may appear in the race car center, cookbooks may be in the household center, checkbooks and pens may support the bank center, and menus may adorn an Italian restaurant center. Authentic literature is everywhere in the adult world and may be emulated and modeled in the young child's world.

Explicit Instruction

We also believe that explicit instruction needs to precede most play center situations. Many children do not understand the purpose of cookbooks, menus, road signs, and so on. Too often, it is assumed that children have some prior experience or knowledge about the artifacts and materials provided in play centers. Explicit instruction, modeling, prompt cards, and role-playing will enhance and enrich the pragmatic learning that occurs in these centers.

We also stress the importance of viewing play centers as authentic opportunities to meet each child's ZPD through both implicit and explicit instruction. Specific centers should be set up to incorporate a variety of individual student abilities and interests. For example, Kirstan's teacher may provide a book browsing center, a computer game center, and a listening center that reinforce Kirstan's correct usage of irregular past-tense verbs. The story of Little Miss Muffet, who *sat* on a tuffet, is a good example of an appropriate listening center choice for Kirstan. An easel paint center or a chalkboard drawing center may facilitate additional opportunities for Rebecca to write so she can practice her appropriate pencil grip. At the listening center, Daniel may listen to environmental sounds on an audiotape and play "guess the sound" to support and enhance his phonological awareness skills. Play centers can and should provoke thoughtful teacher planning to promote student development. Expert teachers know how to provide and enhance personalized implicit instructional opportunities for their students. Samples of play center cards with helpful adult teaching prompts may be found in Appendix C, pages 256–269.

> We also stress the importance of viewing play centers as authentic opportunities to meet each child's ZPD through both implicit and explicit instruction.

Explicit instruction in early childhood education is and will continue to be a hotly debated topic in preschool classrooms. As veteran teachers who have worked for more than two decades with children who find learning to read and write on their own difficult, we want to leave no doubt about our position on this critical topic. Explicit instruction, particularly in literacy acquisition, is imperative in the early years for most children to achieve school success. For some children, exploration and discovery opportunities in a literature-rich environment are sufficient, but the majority of children need more individualized instruction that links their prior knowledge to new learning.

Pianta and La Paro (2003) have spent years researching the quality of early childhood settings and teaching practices. They observed over 2,000 pre-K to first-grade classrooms in their most recent study, and they report the following observation that is consistent across the grade levels:

We can characterize these early childhood environments as socially positive but instructionally passive. Despite being generally well-organized, busy places, these classrooms appeared low in *intentionality*-directed, designed interactions between children and teachers in which teachers purposefully challenged, scaffolded, and extended the children's skill. Factors commonly used to regulate classroom quality—such as teacher education or class size—bore little relation to these observations of quality. (p. 28)

Explicit instruction may be offered in a variety of settings and groupings. The ones most commonly practiced are one-to-one lessons, small-group instruction, and whole-class activities. Expert teachers seize the teachable moments when they catch a child on the verge of new learning. Kirstan's teacher cites an example of a one-on-one conversation they had when Kirstan came to school one Monday morning, ran to her bean plant, and exclaimed, "My plant grew when I was home!" Her insightful teacher acknowledged and rejoiced in Kirstan's discovery and then restated her appropriate use of the irregular past-tense verb *grew*. The teacher said, "Good job, Kirstan. I like the way you said that. Today your bean may *grow* some more. Over the weekend it *grew*, and today it may *grow* even more!" It was a great opportunity for the teacher to target and reinforce Kirstan's oral language development. Later that day, the teacher went to recess with Kirstan and played catch with a small group of her similarly developing peers. They used the words *threw* and *throw* as they played together. Kirstan received explicit instruction in both a one-on-one and a small-group setting to enhance her oral language ZPD. She received explicit instruction in the use of irregular past-tense verbs several times that day to enhance her understanding of the concept. Focused and recurring explicit instruction such as this is an effective approach when supporting young learners.

Whole-class activities also may provide great opportunities for explicit instruction. Remember Daniel, who was ready to learn syllable segmenting and blending? Whole-class circle time is a great time for Daniel's teacher to practice counting the number of syllables in everyone's names: "Daniel Olsen, you're first. Let's say your name slowly and count the number of parts. *Dan-iel Ol-sen.* How many parts did you hear?" The children inevitably provide a variety of answers. Then, the teacher says, "Let's check it. Put your hand under your chin, and let's count together how many times our chins drop as we say his name. *Dan-iel Ol-sen.* Good, I counted four, too! Rebecca Thompson, you're next!" This lesson is just one example of a whole-class activity designed specifically for Daniel to scaffold his phonological awareness development to the next level. Inevitably, other children in the group also will benefit from this activity.

As another example, Rebecca may participate in a small group with other children ready to learn some early letter formation strategies. Together with their teacher, they may practice their gross and fine motor skills by writing invisible circles and lines in the air, on the rug, and on the chalkboard. Putting lines and circles together, they may form the *a* and *b* in Rebecca's name or the *d* or *p* in someone else's name. This activity highlights the simple manner in which explicit instruction and reinforcement can be offered to individual students and their similarly developing peers.

Conclusion

We believe that quality preschool instruction emanates from teacher expertise and experience. Teacher-training programs that encourage and educate preservice and inservice teachers to teach children and not curricula are unusual commodities in colleges and classrooms today. In the past, state-funded bachelor programs in early childhood development often were sponsored in the College of Agriculture's Department of Family and Consumer Sciences rather than in conjunction with the College of Education. This situation is changing at the University of Wyoming and other universities as these institutions reconfigure early childhood degree programs. The previous structure prevented teacher certification and classroom internship opportunities for many educators who work with the youngest and neediest children. Training teachers who understand human development across the developmental domains, early childhood literacy competencies, and effective interventions for the most at-risk populations is imperative for early childhood education programs today. Our conversations with recent early childhood program graduates reveal satisfaction with their preparation in human development but an overwhelming concern about the lack of training they have received in teaching early literacy skills, managing small-group activities, and designing specific interventions for at-risk children.

As we have delineated in this chapter, quality preschool instruction requires three critical teacher competencies: (1) knowing and understanding each individual child across the developmental domains, (2) knowing preschool curricula and appropriate developmental compendiums, and (3) knowing how to provide appropriate explicit and implicit instruction. We believe that expert preschool instructors methodically incorporate and execute these components smoothly and efficiently every day. In accepting the theoretical framework that "the child is the only script," teachers first must identify each child's ZPD on any and all tasks in order to plan daily and weekly instruction and themes. This type of individualized instructional planning typically begins with the important teacher proficiencies of astute student observation and appropriate assessment. Ongoing student observations, anecdotal records, parent and teacher surveys, developmental screenings, and literacy assessments all contribute to this deliberate instructional-planning and lesson-design process. The study of observation and assessment in a preschool setting is a complex and integral part of learning to teach all children in an individually appropriate manner. This important topic is explored in depth in chapter 3.

Knowing Preschoolers as Literacy Learners

• • •

During a recent site visit at one of our preschools, we were told by the classroom teacher, "In the beginning, I thought I was a great preschool teacher because I was fun and entertaining. I was always center stage, and I liked that. I thought the kids did, too! Now, I know I wasn't helping my kids like I could have. By using the literacy checklist, a developmental compendium, and identifying what my kids need to know, my teaching is more deliberate. Now, I'm more focused on them, rather than on me."

Assessments and student observations, such as the checklist mentioned in the vignette, often provide efficient and productive vehicles to personalized student instruction. Relevant assessments used to inform instruction can be very powerful tools to focus a teacher's attention on individual students' strengths and needs, rather than on age- or grade-level expectancies. However, assessing children from birth to age 6 is very different from assessing older children or adults. The assessment tools and administration even may differ remarkably from one year to the next because of the rapid change in the developmental capabilities of young children. For our purpose, we will discuss formal and informal assessments and observation tools that we have found to be helpful as we endeavor to work with 3- to 6-year-olds and their families in a preschool setting. Assessments of particular interest focus on literacy acquisition and oral language development. We want to underscore the importance of ongoing assessment for all children to ensure that daily instruction is tailored to meet the individual development of each child.

For many years in the United States, formal and informal assessments were given every quarter, every semester, or every year to measure student growth and to determine if students were progressing typically. It was a kind of "wait, watch, and evaluate" approach to see if children were developing normally. A more recent system of ongoing assessment has emerged, and we believe that it augments the early intervention initiative. This proactive approach uses assessments to guide and direct instruction, thereby personalizing and enhancing lessons for young children. Ultimately, we believe that this method of continually assessing a child's progress and readjusting instruction for him or her accelerates the learning curve for most children. Many assessments exist that can be used to determine what a child knows and that also provide information about what skills need to come next. We believe that experienced educators employ these assessments—along with sensitive, systematic observations—to determine a child's ZPD and inform their teaching of that child.

Formal Assessments

Two types of formal assessments used with preschool-age children are norm-referenced tests and criterion-referenced tests. Norm-referenced tests are standardized and compare one child's performance to that of a group of students, typically measuring ability, achievement, or personality traits. A standardized test has precise content and procedures for administration and scoring and offers normative data for interpreting the scores. Criterion-referenced tests are used to describe an individual's performance on a specific set of objectives. Developmental and diagnostic assessments and screenings often used during the preschool years are criterion referenced. Developmental screenings are used as a gauge or checkpoint for children who are developing typically. However, they also are critical for flagging those children who may have some developmental delays and will benefit from special services or interventions.

Numerous developmental screenings are available for early childhood educators to use. We selected the Brigance Preschool Screen and Brigance K–1 Screen to use with our preschoolers because the screens are norm referenced and criterion referenced in addition to being very simple to administer. It takes approximately 12 minutes to complete one of the screenings with a cooperative child. These screenings assess a child's knowledge of personal data, body parts, gross and fine motor skills, vocabulary, oral language, visual motor skills, number concepts, and so on. They also provide a cutoff chart for detecting children likely to have developmental disabilities or delays. Children who fall below these cutoff scores should be referred immediately to a child development center or a special education program for further evaluation. Trained specialists will be able to give more extensive standardized assessments such as the Wechsler Preschool and Primary Scale of Intelligence (WPPSI-III) or the Test of Language Development (TOLD). These assessments and others will provide helpful, in-depth information about the child's cognitive, social, emotional, physical, and language development.

Informal Assessments

Informal assessments appraise a child's performance on tasks or samples of work that are directly related to the school's curriculum or the teacher's educational objectives. (See Figure 6 for two students engaged in an informal assessment.) Although they often are not standardized, these assessments provide valuable information about the knowledge that a child can construct independently. Informal assessments are helpful to teachers because they measure and demonstrate development over time, complement a portfolio approach to data collection, and facilitate authentic performance record keeping. Although literacy acquisition in young children is

Jackie and Logan Demonstrate Their Number Sense in a Fun and Creative Assessment

the primary focus of this book, we feel strongly that early childhood educators need to monitor closely the development of the whole child; therefore, we suggest a variety of assessments throughout the chapter to ensure that all the developmental domains are addressed.

An informal literacy screening that we highly recommend is the Emerging Literacy Screening found in *Building Early Literacy and Language Skills* (Paulson et al., 2001). This screening incorporates print awareness, language usage, and phonological awareness in one 20-minute assessment. All three characteristics analyzed in the screening have been determined to be significant predictors of later reading and writing success. The print awareness skills assessed include the following:

- book awareness (is aware of the front and back of the book, that print carries a message, that the left page comes before the right, and one-to-one correspondence between voice and print),
- symbol identification (recognizes environmental print, alphabet letter names, and letter sounds),
- print development (creates scribbles, mock letters, random letter strings, and semi-phonetic spellings),

- identification of his or her own name in writing, and
- knowledge of the Alphabet Song.

The language usage skills assessed include

- awareness of rhythmic patterns;
- knowledge of concepts such as top, bottom, first, and last;
- relating a past event;
- speech sound intelligibility; and
- syntax and sentence usage.

The phonological awareness skills assessed include

- rhyming identification,
- rhyme production,
- blending syllables,
- blending sounds or phonemes,
- segmenting syllables, and
- segmenting sounds or phonemes.

The format and one-on-one delivery of this assessment provide teachers with a list of the critical competencies that young children need to be successful readers and writers, and they also expose the children's current understandings in an authentic and meaningful context. Once a child's ZPD is determined in each area through this screening, his or her teacher can design appropriate lessons. Paulson and colleagues (2001) provide numerous activities to develop these critical skills and facilitate lesson design.

To assess individual student literacy development, we also have used three subtests from Clay's *An Observation Survey of Early Literacy Achievement* (1996). The Concepts About Print subtest helps teachers determine a child's book-handling skills, directional behaviors (where to start, which way to go, return sweep or tracking print from left to right and returning to the left, and the concepts of first and last), and hierarchical concepts (word and letter boundaries). The Letter Identification subtest reveals a child's letter knowledge (names, sounds, or labels), and the Writing Vocabulary subtest allows children to demonstrate their writing skills. Clay's informal assessments show pertinent information about a child's literacy development over time, and this information also can be used to determine appropriate follow-up lessons. We have found these subtests to be very helpful in providing common expectations and language between public school teachers and preschool instructors because so many of Wyoming's public schools have adopted the Reading Recovery program or are familiar with Clay's work.

In addition, we have found Floyd and Yates's (2001) phonological awareness screenings for kindergartners and preschoolers to be very effective in evaluating phonological skill development.

The screenings delineate the skills of rhyming, segmenting, blending, isolating, and deleting, in addition to some print awareness competencies. Floyd and Yates's screenings have helped to focus teachers on the phonological awareness skills that are imperative for young readers and writers to attain. Both screenings are easy to administer (approximately 5–8 minutes each) and clearly demonstrate a child's growth over time.

Informal assessments of young children also can be conducted through parent or teacher surveys. The Ages and Stages Questionnaire (ASQ; Bricker & Squires, 1999) has several age-related subtests that are relatively simple and a concise developmental survey that examines the social, personal, communication, problem-solving, and physical growth of young children. Completed by a child's parents either independently or in collaboration with a teacher, the ASQ subtest offers age-appropriate expectations and helps teachers monitor student growth in these areas. We recommend that parents complete the appropriate age-related survey at the preschool so questions and confusions can be addressed immediately by the child's teacher. Some examples of questions from the ASQ subtest for a child of 42 months are as follows:

1. When she is looking in the mirror and you ask, "Who is in the mirror?" does your child say either "Me" or her own name? (yes, sometimes, not yet)
2. When you ask, "What is your name?" does your child say both her first and last names? (yes, sometimes, not yet)
3. Show your child how to make a bridge with blocks, boxes, or cans. Does your child copy you by making one like it? (yes, sometimes, not yet)
4. When drawing, does your child hold a pencil, crayon, or pen between her fingers and thumb like an adult does? (yes, sometimes, not yet) (Bricker & Squires, 1999, pp. 3–6)

Checklists

For years, developmental checklists have served as the template for early childhood observation, assessment, curriculum matching, and instructional planning. The outcome or success of early intervention is highly dependent on sensitive, systematic observations and subsequent teaching by expert teachers. In our opinion, the careful, intentional observation of young children is the most effective way to understand and monitor student growth. Checklists provide teachers with behaviors on which they need to focus during their daily observations, and checklists with rating scales (e.g., Mastered, Developing, Not Applicable) also serve as informal assessments or records of student progress over time. In addition, checklists may reflect curriculum expectations and, therefore, inform instruction. The checklists discussed in this chapter have been designed to address the previously mentioned areas of literacy acquisition, phonological awareness, social and emotional development, fine and gross motor skills, and overall development.

The Preschool Outcomes Checklist (see Appendix B, page 241) addresses the whole child and mirrors the Preschool Curriculum

> The outcome or success of early intervention is highly dependent on sensitive, systematic observations and subsequent teaching by expert teachers.

Framework (see Appendix B, page 235). Teachers use the Preschool Outcomes Checklist as an informal assessment to monitor and document the growth and development of their individual students. Once again, we want to reiterate that developmental checklists serve only as guides, not the sole determinants or references for necessary preschool accomplishments. Individual differences should always be expected and encouraged as children develop across the domains. The Preschool Outcomes Checklist purposefully refrains from delineating single grade-level or yearly age-level expectations (see chapter 2 for explanation).

Checklists, although comprehensive and specific by nature, can be a daunting task for teachers with large numbers of children to assess. Often, these checklists are over 10 pages per student. To condense the checklist process, we encourage teachers to use one checklist for the whole class. In other words, the same outcomes or competencies are listed horizontally on a spreadsheet with the class members listed vertically. In addition, each domain is listed on one page. This method leaves teachers with one long checklist to complete, not 20. The Preschool Comprehensive Quarterly Report in Appendix B, page 255, is a sample of a comprehensive class checklist.

To support teachers' observations in the area of literacy development, we present separate Preschool and Kindergarten Literacy Checklists in Appendix B, pages 249 and 250, respectively. The kindergarten checklist is included for those preschoolers who exceed preschool expectations. These checklists incorporate phonological awareness, book handling, directional behavior, oral language concepts and vocabulary, writing, hierarchal concepts, printed language, and letter identification. Teachers frequently place a laminated copy of one of the checklists in the front of each student's literacy folder so they can check off mastered competencies. Work samples, photos, audiotapes, and anecdotal notes are kept inside the folder to document student progress. The literacy checklist provides a systematic way for teachers to monitor literacy acquisition in their students. We suggest that teachers closely observe and record their observations with these checklists during their ZPD groups. If one child is targeted in each group every day, then every child in a class of 20 will be carefully observed at least once a week, given that there are four groups. We have found that systematic observations in which teachers set out to watch specific behaviors, identify and record a child's ZPD, and scaffold new learning are the most effectual in advancing student achievement.

Anecdotal Records

Anecdotal records are written descriptions of a child's behavior during an observation. A record may recount a specific incident, and it typically will include the language and behavior exhibited by the child. A teacher may record separately an interpretation of the incident. Anecdotal records commonly are described as nonsystematic or incidental observations. However, these nonsystematic records may provide the impetus for determining what a teacher needs to observe systematically. For example, 5-year-old Jordan is "writing the room" (see Figure 7). She has a clipboard, paper, and a pencil. She stops at the word wall and copies all the names of her

• Figure 7 •
Jordan, Ethan, and Chandler Write Names From the Word Wall

classmates that begin with the letter A—Ashley and Abigail—using her right hand. Then, she turns to a classmate and says, "I can write everyone's name. You want me to help you? I will! My name starts with J. But, I have an a, too! It's just different!" Her teacher writes the following notes:

> Jordan is ready to look at capital and lowercase letters, beginning particularly with those in her name. An uppercase/lowercase letter-matching game may be fun to do together tomorrow in a ZPD group. Try J and j and O and o, for Jordan.

Anecdotal records provide a valuable mechanism for effective student observations. As mentioned previously, they often help teachers to target a student's behaviors that they need to monitor more closely, while also providing a burgeoning script or portrait of a child. Anecdotal notes may contain any number of interactions, occurrences, personality traits, or special interests that are observed. This brief observation of Jordan revealed not only her writing abilities and letter knowledge but also a lot about her personality. She is a helper and a nurturer. She wanted to include her classmate in her writing practice and was willing to enable that occurrence. Anecdotal records also may divulge useful information about unique interests that may motivate new learning or generate a new class theme. We encourage teachers to take anecdotal notes on at least one or two children each day. This practice allows teachers to observe every child up to twice a month in a class of 20 children.

Taking anecdotal notes should be simple and routine in a quality preschool setting. We recommend that a teacher wear an apron with large pockets to house small notepads or index cards for taking notes. Some teachers have one small notepad for each student; others carry index cards and file them in a small file box at the end of the day. We also have seen some teachers take notes on large computer labels, which they then adhere to full-sized sheets of paper so up to 12 labels fit on one page.

Knowing each student as comprehensively as possible is the goal of keeping anecdotal records. Reviewing these notes frequently and reflecting on their content will provide invaluable insights and enhance teacher-child relationships and instructional interactions.

Portfolios

Any previously mentioned checklist or informal assessment may be incorporated into a student's portfolio. Portfolios may include a comprehensive collection of a child's work, teacher assessments, and other artifacts that contribute to a picture of a child's progress. Portfolios can be housed in a variety of ways. The most common housing is expandable file folders, but other ideas include hanging folders, large envelopes, plastic crates or baskets, shoe boxes, or envelopes made by stapling together two large poster boards. A developmental approach to organizing a preschooler's portfolio may prove to be the most reasonable. Dividing the portfolio into cognitive development, literacy and oral language development, social and emotional development, and motor and physical development may be an efficient methodology. The contents of the portfolio may be teacher, parent, or student directed or any combination of the three. Portfolios are a wonderful way to show parents the progress that their children have made throughout the year. Several checklists and assessment forms displayed in Appendix B, pages 241–255, may be added to a student portfolio.

> Portfolios may include a comprehensive collection of a child's work, teacher assessments, and other artifacts that contribute to a picture of a child's progress.

Program Evaluation

It is important to evaluate general program effectiveness in addition to monitoring and assessing student progress. There are a variety of ways to obtain this important data. First, kindergarten teachers may be surveyed to ascertain pertinent information about students' cognitive, social, emotional, and physical capabilities. The kindergarten-teacher survey should be conducted three to four weeks after the school year begins to give kindergarten teachers some time to get to know their students so they can respond to the survey questions with assurance. The teachers' responses on the survey may offer valuable information about each child's level of competency across the developmental domains and background of experiences, including any preschool attendance (e.g., Head Start, Even Start, private preschools, special education child-development centers, public school preschools, or any combination of these programs). A second program evaluation method may incorporate state- or districtwide norm-referenced or criterion-referenced assessments that are conducted as children enter kindergarten. Two of these assessments are the Brigance K–1 Screen and Clay's *An Observation Survey of Early Literacy Achievement* (1996). As readers select tools for program evaluation, we would like to caution that

> assessments must be used carefully and appropriately if they are to resolve, and not create, educational problems. This means using each assessment in the way in which it was designed and intended. To use assessment as a blunt instrument, in which one type of assessment is expected to perform the functions of others, squanders resources and places children at risk for school difficulties. (Bowman, Donovan, & Burns, 2001, p. 259)

Another program evaluation, the *Early Language and Literacy Classroom Observation (ELLCO) Toolkit* (Smith & Dickinson, 2002), provides program information regarding the overall literacy environment, classroom observations, and teacher interviews. The ELLCO toolkit also provides a literacy activities rating scale. In addition, we have designed the informal Preschool Environment Checklist (see Appendix B, page 251) that both teachers and evaluators may use to identify and monitor key components and indicators in quality preschools.

Perhaps the most notable measure of success may be the documentation of the number of special education referrals and placements. Paradise Valley Elementary School has experienced a substantial decrease in the number of special education students since the implementation of the preschool. Specifically, the percentage of special education students has declined from 14% to 5%. Although there are inevitably several other factors having an impact on these figures, we believe that tracking these data is a reliable way to verify a preschool program's effectiveness.

Early literacy assessments currently mandated in our school district for entering kindergartners also have supplied other relevant data that we use for our preschool evaluation purposes. Our districtwide literacy assessments provide raw scores for every kindergartner in the following areas: concepts about print and letter identification (see Clay, 1996) and letter-sound association. The letter-sound association component assesses if kindergartners can link one appropriate sound to each of the 26 letters in the English alphabet. Any appropriate sound is accepted for letters with multiple sounds (long and short vowel sounds and the soft and hard sounds of *c* and *g*). Over the past several years, we have collected and analyzed these kindergarten data, comparing our preschool participants to all nonparticipating students. Although some preschool studies may choose to compare their preschool participants only to other socioeconomically deprived children, we wanted to see how our former preschoolers' early literacy competencies compared to the other kindergartners in their classes (economically advantaged and disadvantaged), so we compiled the data accordingly. The assessment results and data that we have analyzed about our students and other beginning kindergartners are extremely validating. The graphs in Figures 8, 9, 10, and 11 illustrate how well our preschoolers perform on these literacy assessments and how they compare with their peers who have not participated in our preschool program.

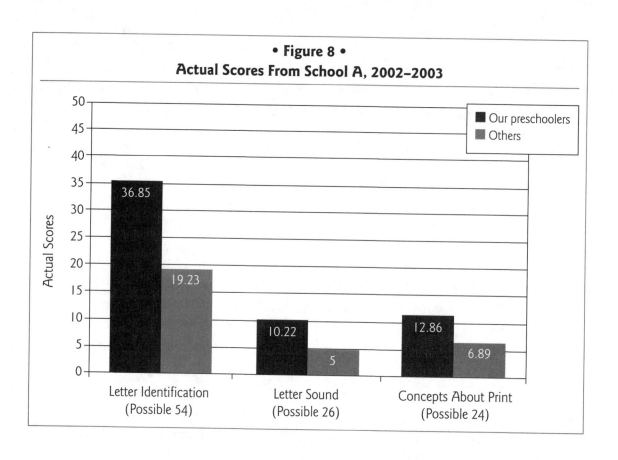

• Figure 8 •
Actual Scores From School A, 2002–2003

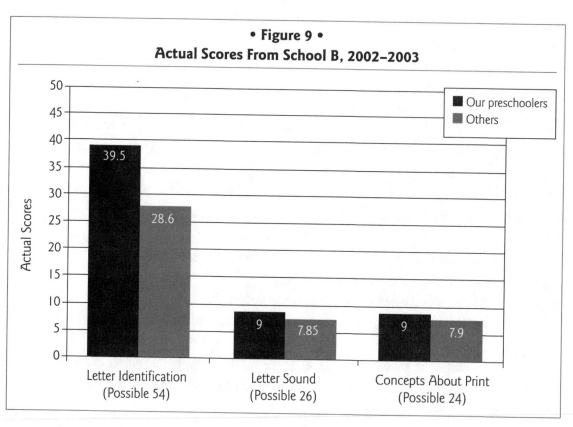

• Figure 9 •
Actual Scores From School B, 2002–2003

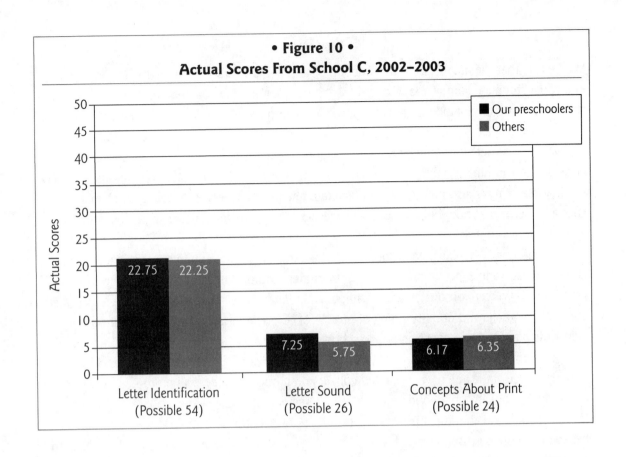

• Figure 10 •
Actual Scores From School C, 2002–2003

- ■ Our preschoolers
- ■ Others

Letter Identification (Possible 54): 22.75, 22.25
Letter Sound (Possible 26): 7.25, 5.75
Concepts About Print (Possible 24): 6.17, 6.35

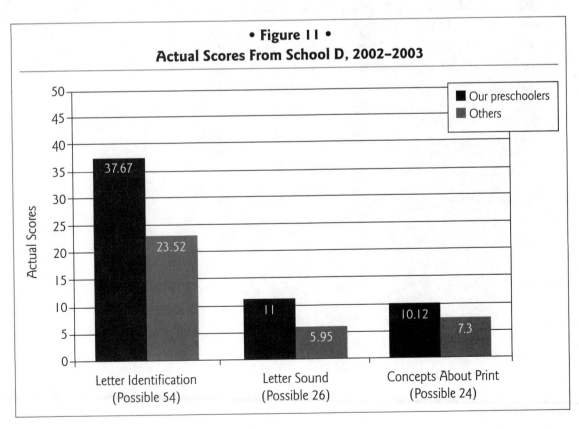

• Figure 11 •
Actual Scores From School D, 2002–2003

- ■ Our preschoolers
- ■ Others

Letter Identification (Possible 54): 37.67, 23.52
Letter Sound (Possible 26): 11, 5.95
Concepts About Print (Possible 24): 10.12, 7.3

Conclusion

We believe that the most significant function of assessment is to inform instruction for individual students. Formal and informal assessments can provide parents, teachers, and other stakeholders with valuable insights into and information about a child's world. This information can be used to help teachers and parents make critical decisions about when and how to intervene. Class activities, small-group instruction, explicit teaching, and modifications in the classroom environment or arrangement are just a few of the instructional interventions that may result. Assessments also may prompt or facilitate referrals to speech or language therapists, special educators, school nurses, or other specialists, thus providing more aggressive and intensive interventions.

In addition, when aligned to local state standards and benchmarks, assessments facilitate common goals and expectations across communities, counties, and states in preschool programs. The inception of statewide readiness standards in the United States has promulgated a common language and understanding of preschool competencies. These early childhood standards have had an impact on public schools, child development centers, Head Start and Even Start programs, private preschools, day-care facilities, and families in numerous ways. Most important, the standards have facilitated collaboration opportunities and promoted universal expectations for early childhood organizations, classrooms, and providers. Therefore, families transitioning between programs, moving into the public school system, or doing both may experience more consistency and less uncertainty. The standards have specified *what* needs to be taught without mandating *how* to teach it. This structure allows teachers to be creative and innovative in the manner in which they provide instruction for their students, with assessments and observations providing the critical channel between standards and instruction. These standards and assessments cover all the developmental domains, including cognitive, social, emotional, and physical areas. Throughout the following chapters, we will refer back to the information presented here as we document student development across the curriculum.

CHAPTER 4

Linking Literacy Learning With Social and Emotional Development

• • •

Colter came to preschool every morning after an hour drive from his home on a small ranch just west of town. He always wore his Wrangler jeans, western belt buckle, cowboy boots, and western shirts. His language was subtly different from the language of the other children in the class. He frequently substituted *done* for *did* and *is* for *was*, and he related most of his experiences to his rural lifestyle. In Wyoming, Colter's lifestyle is certainly not unique; however, in his preschool, he was the only "ranch kid."

As early childhood educators, we need to acknowledge, value, and understand the sociocultural environments from which our students come. Each child brings to school a unique background of experiences, social rules, and expectations. These sociocultural behaviors may manifest themselves in a child's oral language, nonverbal communication, interactions with peers and adults, attitudes and interests, and preferred modes of learning. A quality preschool environment promotes an atmosphere of warmth, trust, and acceptance of each child's individual sociocultural conditions to ensure his or her positive social and emotional development. The social and emotional curriculum should incorporate self-care competencies, appropriate interactions for self and others, and appropriate family and community relations. Multiple modes of learning should be embraced and enhanced by preschool staff, including motivation and curiosity, reasoning and problem solving, attention to task and continuance, and representational and symbolic thinking. Modes of learning—along with cognitive, social, emotional, and physical development—all work in concert to orchestrate an intricate ensemble of mutually dependent human characteristics. This chapter provides concrete methods for explicitly and implicitly incorporating social and emotional support and instruction for young children in a preschool setting.

Transitioning From the Home Culture to the School Culture and Back Again

Preschools located at an elementary school setting provide a unique opportunity for young children and their parents to begin school together. When parents not only are encouraged but also are expected to come to school with their children, some incredible changes often occur. Parents are present both to explain subtle nuances that may perplex or bewilder their children as they begin school and to support them in their adjustment. In addition, parents help teachers to understand their children's unique personality characteristics and interpret unclear communications.

Children develop and form new attachments more confidently with their parents beside them. The preschool model that we advocate encourages parents to translate the language of home to the language of school and vice versa. Ongoing involvement allows parents to engage in a variety of activities that parents typically do not experience at their children's schools. For example, parents fulfilling their volunteer hours may have opportunities to accompany their children to the cafeteria for lunch or to the library, gymnasium, computer lab, or recess. These experiences familiarize the parents with the supplementary staff and the daily routines that their children encounter. This firsthand knowledge of routines and supplemental educators empowers parents as they engage in before- and after-school conversations with their preschoolers and plan their academic futures.

The preschool environment should be designed to reflect both the home and school environments. According to Kovalik and Olsen (2001), "Given the primacy of emotions to drive attention and thus memory, problem-solving, and virtually every other aspect of learning and performance, the number one job of a teacher is creating and maintaining an environment free from threat" (p. 28). We recommend including couches, rocking chairs, computers, beanbag chairs, lamps, rugs, plants, toys, tables, and so on in the preschool classroom to replicate the comforts of the home setting because they promote the safe and secure atmosphere that brain research says is necessary for optimal learning conditions. (See Figure 12 for a homelike setting in

• Figure 12 •
Seana-Lyn Pretends She Is Cooking at Home

the preschool classroom.) Snack time and convenient restroom facilities also should be provided. The surroundings should be warm and welcoming to stimulate and motivate students' well-being and interests. Whenever possible, the preschools should be housed in large, easily accessible classrooms with plenty of natural light. Teachers should be encouraged to display student creations, rather than commercial bulletin boards, as much as possible. Children should be given the opportunity to bring family artifacts from home to share with the class, and they also should be encouraged to share their personal histories and experiences during small-group discussions in order to facilitate a strong sense of community and belonging.

We encourage preschool teachers to build positive partnerships with their students' parents. Developing a positive rapport with parents takes time and effort, but teachers who build an atmosphere of trust and belonging typically find that the parents are more cooperative and supportive in problem-solving situations. Teachers who know and use their parents' special interests and talents also reap enormous educational benefits for their students. Chapter 12 provides an in-depth study of home-school partnerships.

Self-Care Competencies

A child with good self-care skills demonstrates a positive sense of self. Common indicators of high self-esteem often include the ability to separate from family members and adjust to new situations, express one's emotions and feelings, stand up for one's rights, and have confidence in a variety of personal accomplishments. Good self-esteem allows children to become risk takers, accepting new learning and challenges more readily as they mature. Verbal praise is the most efficient path to building a child's good self-concept. Parents are typically the first and primary source of positive reinforcement; however, teachers also can provide this important support.

Research shows that all too often the children who need the most praise receive the least. Hart and Risley (1999) have seen "the powerful dampening effects on development when relatively more of the children's interactions began with a parent-initiated imperative ('Don't,' 'Stop,' 'Quit') that prohibited what a child was doing" (p. 147). They also discovered that

> professional parents gave their children affirmative feedback every other minute, more than 30 times per hour, twice as often as the working class parents gave their children affirmative feedback and more than five times as often as parents in welfare families gave their children affirmative feedback. The children in welfare families heard a prohibition twice as often as they heard affirmative feedback. (p. 126)

Regrettably, this study affirms the parent behavior patterns that we observe all too often in our preschool families. As early childhood educators, we can use this information to validate the positive reinforcement strategies that we employ and work to increase the number of positive reinforcement statements that children hear every day in our classrooms. We need to reflect the 6 to 1 ratio of encouragements to discouragements that Hart and Risley have recorded in the homes of professionals and their children. A can-do attitude that is cultivated and nurtured in children during their early childhood years pays high dividends later as they become productive, confident adults.

Excellent self-care competencies include the ability to self-regulate one's behavior. Self-regulation indicators include having a sense of self-direction and independence, taking responsibility for one's well-being, respecting and caring for one's environment and materials, following rules and regulations, and maintaining appropriate attention to tasks. Self-regulation is a life skill that traverses all the developmental domains, promoting social relationships, self-control, a positive work ethic, and systematic problem-solving abilities. When children are able to self-regulate, they can work and play independently, competently, and happily without continuous adult assistance (see Figure 13). Self-regulation may be nurtured in a variety of ways: (a) scaffolding new learning and behaviors through adult-child social interactions, (b) offering explicit instruction and demonstration of desired behaviors, and (c) providing opportunities for young children to be responsible.

Nurturing and developing self-regulation in young children begins with adult-child interactions. The adult initially provides substantial support and then gradually encourages the child to accept responsibility for more and more of the task. In young children, we frequently observe this phenomenon in their physical development as they take on the independent task of

• **Figure 13** •
Rylie and Katarina Self-Regulate Their Behavior as They Role-Play Being Parents

walking. Adults support this accomplishment by holding a child's hands or standing him or her up by a couch as the child begins to learn to walk. Eventually, the child no longer requires adult assistance and walks independently. Adults also provide the pragmatics that children need socially and emotionally to interact appropriately with others and express their feelings, needs, or wants. An example may be a parent modeling the word *please* to request a turn or a toy from someone else. Eventually, children take on the language of their mentors and self-regulate their social interactions.

Teaching and nurturing self-regulation is an essential focus for early childhood educators. As children learn to control and monitor their own actions, they become more confident and self-reliant. In a classroom setting, these capabilities are vital to securing a safe and high-quality learning environment. Teachers need to explicitly teach, encourage, demonstrate, and acknowledge self-regulation. Articulating and modeling for children what this behavior looks like and providing oral prompts for them are helpful.

Self-regulation is one of the critical precursors for early readers and writers as they begin to problem solve independently with text. Prompts that encourage preschool children to self-regulate in reading may sound like the following:

- You checked the pictures to tell the story. Good job!
- You saw the fox hiding behind the rock. Good noticing!
- You know where to start reading. Great!
- You know how to turn the pages. Good work!
- You found a *T* in our storybook. Good, Travis!
- *Red* does rhyme with *Ted*. Good job!

Once children are able to regulate their own behaviors, they are able to function productively on their own, and the teacher is free to enhance and vary his or her instruction and interactions. Dorn, French, and Jones (1998) explain that

> when a child becomes a self-regulated learner, he uses his current skills, strategies, and knowledge at a new level of cognitive activity; that is, he plans and guides new learning and uses existing knowledge for solving new problems in a variety of situations. (p. 11)

Self-regulation is significant in the development of early literacy learning competencies. Before children can learn early literacy behaviors and strategies, they must be able to self-regulate their behaviors. We cannot overemphasize the importance of this critical, foundational skill. Teachers must be aware that self-regulation is the number-one precursor to literacy acquisition.

More and more children come to school each year without this critical self-care competency. Children in today's society have fewer opportunities to be responsible contributing participants within their family structure. Hart and Risley (1995) suggest that the values of work, cooperation, and accomplishment are no longer taught through chores on the family farm or for the family business. Instead, today's parents endeavor to teach these values through sports, creative arts, and other similar activities. Assigning appropriate classroom tasks and duties for children to do every day gives them a sense of importance and ownership in the school community. These classroom jobs may be as simple as line leader, office messenger, clean-up crew member, table setter, teacher's helper, pledge-to-the-flag leader, shared-reading pointer, playground monitor, weather watcher, or calendar helper. Ultimately, the child who is responsible and who self-regulates efficiently will be much more fruitful in his or her pursuits. By addressing and improving this competency early in a child's development, teachers will significantly increase the likelihood of the child's later school success.

Appropriate Interactions for Self and Others

As experienced educators, we know that young children who have experienced few positive interactions with peers often struggle with social interactions into and beyond adolescence. Learning to interact appropriately and express emotions effectively and developing effective social pragmatics are fundamental to successful social relationships. Indicators that children are developing appropriate social behaviors include playing well with other children, making friends, acknowledging and responding to the feelings of others, sharing with and respecting the rights of others, and engaging in problem-solving strategies to resolve conflicts. Each of these indicators may be systematically observed, taught (explicitly and implicitly), and practiced with young children.

Teaching appropriate social interactions may be most easily facilitated through structured dramatic play centers, large- and small-group role-playing, teacher modeling of appropriate behaviors, and read-aloud and shared-reading sessions. Dramatic play centers provide an ideal setting for social interaction experiences because children are involved naturally in small-group communications that allow them to practice and hone their interpersonal skills. Teachers may intervene and model proper interactions when appropriate. An ideal moment for teacher modeling may arise over the issue of two children sharing a favorite race car in the racetrack play center. The teacher may intervene by stating the problem, "Tyler, I can see you want to play with the red race car, too!" Next, the teacher may model an appropriate interaction such as, "Tyler, try asking like this: 'Joshua, may I share the red race car with you? We can take turns.'" Then, the teacher may model an appropriate response for Joshua: "Joshua, you can say, 'Here, I have room for you to sit down and play with me right here. We'll take turns driving this car, OK?'" Practicing these social communications in the context of real situations makes the learning opportunity both meaningful and appropriate for young children.

Large- and small-group role-playing helps children to rehearse the social interactions that they may encounter at home or with friends. Acting out fairy tales and folk tales is a wonderful format for discussing desirable social skills with young children. For example, *The Little Red Hen* (McQueen, 1987) is a great precursor to a discussion about helping one another. Performing nursery rhymes such as *Little Miss Muffet* (Collins, 2003) or "Humpty Dumpty" (dePaola, 1985a) gives children an opportunity to think about and produce the different emotions that these characters might be feeling. Acting out different emotions and having the children guess the emotion is another great way to enhance student awareness of others' feelings. An example of this role-play may include the teacher asking one student to be a clown making happy, sad, or angry faces while the audience selects from an assortment of face cards to match each of the clown's emotions.

Read-alouds and shared reading provide wonderful opportunities for children to hear about and discuss the emotions and social interactions of the characters in books. The storybook *Duck on a Bike* (Shannon, 2002) depicts a variety of emotions in each of the farm animals as a duck proudly rides past them on a bike. The illustrations clearly reflect each animal's reaction—jealousy, disgust, indifference, or admiration—to the duck's unusual behavior. *There's a Nightmare in My Closet* (Mayer, 1968) is ideal for encouraging children to express their bedtime fears. *Frog and Toad Are Friends* (Lobel, 1970) provides a great model for discussions about friendships and getting along with others. *The Enormous Turnip* (Parkinson, 1987) may encourage a discussion about helping one another. The Berenstain Bears (Berenstain & Berenstain, 1997, 2000) solve numerous problems of their own making, and *Leo the Late Bloomer* (Kraus, 1994) and *This Is the Place for Me* (Cole, 1986) also provide children with models of good problem-solving strategies. *Alexander and the Terrible, Horrible, No Good, Very Bad Day* (Viorst, 1987) presents an opportunity for children to relate their own experiences of sad and frustrating emotions. After presenting one of these books as a read-aloud or shared reading, a teacher may follow-up with activities that allow children to practice the targeted behavior. Citing the characters' interactions in the context of real activities or experiences often internalizes socialization concepts for young children.

> Read-alouds and shared reading provide wonderful opportunities for children to hear about and discuss the emotions and social interactions of the characters in books.

Family and Community Relations

As young children become more aware of the world around them, they identify similarities and differences between themselves and others. They become able to characterize their own and others' families by family compositions, personal characteristics, last names, and even unique family traditions or cultural differences. Preschoolers begin to develop an awareness of people's jobs and some of the tasks involved. In addition, preschoolers begin to understand the concepts and language that relate to the geographies of their homes, schools, neighborhoods, and communities.

Young children's understanding of these concepts is enhanced in a quality preschool setting in a variety of ways. For example, play centers typically replicate the community at large by providing the artifacts necessary to emulate community helpers—such as police, firefighters, doctors, and sales clerks—and their responsibilities. Children "play" at these professions, extending their own ZPDs by exploring and practicing the language and rules of the jobs that they are performing. For example, a group of children may be playing in the grocery store center and pretending to be clerks and shoppers using a cash register, calculators, money, and other items that extend their vocabulary and understandings beyond their ordinary levels of conversation.

Role-play also affords young children a unique opportunity to modify their actions in order to emulate the person whom they are portraying. For example, when a child pretends to be a doctor writing a prescription for a patient, he or she automatically self-regulates his or her behavior and language based on personal knowledge about doctors and prescriptions. During a recent visit to a preschool, a child approached us and asked if she could check our ears, heart rates, and blood pressures. After acting out the procedures, she scribbled on a blank piece of paper and said, "Take this to the store. You'll feel better!" This child is already learning that she can and should change her behavior and language based on new surroundings, circumstances, and stimuli. The ability to self-regulate one's actions and behaviors is a fundamental learning competency for young children.

Field trips to community businesses and special events help to further facilitate and extend the vocabularies and geographical understandings of young children. Trips to a grocery store, restaurant, bakery, hospital, fire station, police station, museum, zoo, greenhouse, farm, ranch, law office, bank, and so on all serve to expand and enhance a child's repertoire of background experiences. Each outing expands a child's fundamental knowledge, experiential base, and geographical understandings. In turn, that foundation supports listening and reading comprehension capabilities as children get older. As literacy educators, we concur with Keene and Zimmermann (1997) that

> when applied to reading, schema theory provides direction and focus for helping children to enhance their comprehension. It has been known for some time that one of the most effective ways to improve comprehension is to activate mental files before reading. (pp. 50–51)

If the content of a text is familiar to the reader, his or her reading comprehension is hastened, and if the text's content is unfamiliar, the reader's comprehension is more laborious. As mentioned in chapter 1, brain research suggests that the more hands-on life experiences we can provide for young children, the more connections they will be able to make later to new learning.

Read-alouds and shared and guided readings about families, communities, and different cultures also broaden a child's experiences, knowledge base, and geographical understandings. Books such as *The Black Snowman* (Mendez, 1991), *Hershel and the Hanukkah Goblins* (Kimmel, 1994), and *Tikki Tikki Tembo* (Mosel, 1988) all reflect different cultures from around the world. *Home Lovely* (Perkins, 1995), *Are You My Mother?* (Eastman, 1960), *Peter's Chair* (Keats, 1998b), and *The Biggest House in the World* (Lionni, 1987) all help children learn about how different families function. Literature is a wonderful way for children to experience the world without leaving the classroom or their living rooms.

Modes of Learning

Motivation and curiosity, reasoning and problem solving, attention to task and continuance, and representation or symbolic thinking are the four modes of learning that need to be addressed in a quality preschool setting. Because learning is such a vigorous and challenging process, educators and the general public must invest early in the lives of children. Our own experiences as educators tell us that learning begets learning and that early intervention has lasting effects on this vital process. The love of learning is a life skill that we can see clearly in young children, and we must endeavor to continue and enhance this characteristic.

Children are naturally curious about the world around them, and that curiosity motivates them to explore and experiment with the materials in their surroundings. As preschool teachers, we want to provide a stimulating, challenging, and changing classroom environment that activates our students' natural curiosity. Unusual artifacts, diverse thematic units, dramatic presentations, guest speakers, science discovery centers (see Figure 14), math manipulatives, open-ended questioning techniques, picture-book displays, computer centers, writing centers, small-group interactions, and a variety of dramatic play centers all contribute to a stimulating and compelling preschool environment.

The ability to reason and problem solve permeates every developmental domain. Traditionally, educators have associated problem solving with the content areas of math, science,

• **Figure 14** •
Soni, Alex, and Zack Explore in the Science Discovery Center

and language arts when, in fact, social interactions may provide some of the most challenging problems to overcome. Teaching children a systematic process for problem solving is a valuable—if not an essential—life skill. For young children, this process may reflect the following steps suggested by our school counselor (B. Gurtler, personal communication, March 26, 2003):

1. Identify the problem.
2. Think about different solutions or choices.
3. Select the best option.
4. Try the selected option.
5. If the option works, that's great. If it does not, try another option.

A picture chart with children actually working through this process in a variety of situations may be the easiest model for children to imitate. Teachers should think aloud about this process to model for children as they work on developing this competency. For example, a teacher might think aloud the following scenario just before snack time one day:

> I have a problem. 1. It is snack time, and I can't open my milk carton. 2. I see that my teachers are busy, so they can't help me, but I see that Robbie was able to open his milk carton. Maybe he'll help me. 3. Yes, I'll ask Robbie to help me. 4. Robbie, can you help me open my milk carton? 5. [Robbie successfully opens the carton.] "Thanks, Robbie!"

Thinking aloud these simple problem-solving situations just before a timely event facilitates and activates the independent problem-solving skills that we hope to develop in our students. Dramatic, enthusiastic teachers make these presentations fun and memorable for their students. Soon, children have a repertoire of problem-solving experiences to draw from and use on their own. A final note on this topic is the importance of maintaining a judgment-free atmosphere in which children have no fear of failure and trying out their thoughts and ideas.

Attention to task and continuance are learning modes that support children as they decipher and explore the perplexities in their world. In early childhood education, on-task behavior at times may seem to be the most difficult competency to cultivate in students. We hope to supply teachers with a few practical ideas to facilitate and enhance this skill in their students. Brain research suggests that planning appropriate activities that allow for movement and active engagement is the key (Jensen, 1998). Teachers should keep reasonable time limit expectations on sedentary activities. They should think about segmenting the day into "up and down" and "inside and outside" activities or moving from large-group to small-group activities and back again. Teachers also should make all lessons and activities playful and engaging and change the setting or delivery mode of instruction to support and enhance children's attention spans. The old adage that variety is the spice of life certainly applies here.

To maintain a child's attention to task, transitioning between activities is necessary. Teachers can capitalize on these transitions and make them attention getting, active, meaningful, and relevant. If the theme for the week is numbers, the teacher can dismiss students for recess by their ages or phone numbers. If the theme is body parts, students can play Simon Says. When students are moving to play centers, the teacher can encourage them to walk like elephants or pretend to swim like fish. During a fire-station unit, the teacher can encourage children to move quickly like a firefighter on his or her way to the fire. Even though these activities are brief, they help children to practice attending to a desired task.

Setting goals and defining parameters helps children to focus their attention and work toward task completion. Teachers should use think-alouds to model and furnish the language that children need to set and accomplish goals. For example, a teacher might begin a modeling session by saying, "I want to draw a T-Rex dinosaur in the art center today. I'm thinking it will be brown and green, so I will need those colors." The teacher models and verbalizes locating and preparing the colored markers and then says, "I also think that I need a picture of a T-Rex to help me think about what it looks like." The teacher goes to the library center to search for a dinosaur book and brings one back to the art center. He or she remarks, "I see that the T-Rex has a pretty long neck, sharp teeth, and short forearms. I'll think about those features as I draw my picture." Through the think-aloud process, the teacher articulates the goal, demonstrates the necessary steps, and models continuance and completion. This modeling gives children a concrete example of what they are expected to do and prevents confusion.

> Teachers should use think-alouds to model and furnish the language that children need to set and accomplish goals.

When a child states a similar intention to begin a project, such as "I am going to build a tall building with the blocks today," the teacher may restate the goal if the child becomes distracted and help him or her follow through with the appropriate steps. Open-ended questions also will allow teachers to guide and facilitate this independent goal-setting process. For example, the teacher might say, "Today you said that you wanted to paint a picture of a caterpillar. Tell me how you are going to do that. What do you need? How will you start?" The teacher also should acknowledge and praise the child's perseverance after he or she has finished with the project.

Representation and symbolic thinking are critical learning modes that evolve as young children move from the three-dimensional world into the two-dimensional world of texts. These modes of learning are easily viewed in playful activities as children use objects to represent, or symbolize, something else, such as a pencil for a wand, a stick for a horse, or a block for a building. Children also use speech and actions to imitate the roles or circumstances that they wish to emulate. Think back to our last student example of a girl who pretended to be a doctor and write a prescription. Her conversation and actions mirrored the language and events that she had encountered in her own medical experiences. Children who play symbolically develop the capacity for manipulating and using symbols efficiently, and they eventually are able to visualize representations mentally without the concrete object being present. The girl playing doctor became a teachable moment for the child's innovative preschool teacher who spent a few moments talking with "the doctor" about her prescription, implanting the language that the child needed to scaffold her learning to a new level. Then, during read-aloud time the teacher extended the child's learning once again by reading the songbook *Five Little Monkeys Jumping on the Bed* (Christelow, 1998) and engaging the class in a discussion about what the doctor might prescribe for the five little monkeys after they fell off the bed. This activity became the impetus for the teacher's writing lesson that day, and everyone wrote a prescription for the five little monkeys. The teacher used her observation to scaffold the child's symbolic play into a meaningful writing experience.

Drawing, scribbling, and writing provide teachers with a wonderful window into a child's representational thinking. Observing a child's drawings over time allows the teacher to note what the child notices. As a child becomes more and more observant, or more particulars are discussed and emphasized at home and at school, the drawings begin to reflect those budding details. In addition, the teacher's suggestion of one or two additional details in a drawing can help to scaffold the child's new learning and understandings. Writing mirrors the drawing process. As a child's scribbles begin to look more and more like conventional alphabet letters, teachers are privy to his or her actual development in writing. Maintaining a portfolio of each child's drawings and writing artifacts allows teachers to analyze, plan, and scaffold systematically the critical capability of symbolic and representational thinking. In addition, drawing, scribbling, and writing allow children to experiment with symbolic representations of their world that eventually lead into more conventional writing behaviors (Clay, 1975).

Dramatic or Imaginary Play

Berk and Winsler (1995) note that

> Vygotsky viewed play as a major developmental activity for preschool-age children. His theory suggests that make-believe play supports the emergence of two complementary capacities: (1) the ability to separate thought from actions and objects, and (2) the capacity to renounce impulsive action in favor of deliberate and flexible self-regulatory activity. (p. 54)

In other words, Vygotsky believed both that dramatic play provides the ideal conditions for children to use concrete artifacts in an abstract manner and that the covert and inherent rules of imaginary play to which children voluntarily adhere lay the foundation for their later compliance with the overt rules of society. These two critical competencies—symbolic thinking and self-regulation—have an impact on development across the developmental domains.

Many parents and teachers view dramatic play as fruitless but fun entertainment. Bodrova and colleagues (2001) emphasize that "play provides a unique context in which children are motivated to act. At the same time, they can develop the ability to self-regulate their behavior" (p. 20). For their cognitive, social, and emotional development to thrive, children must acquire oral language, the ability to think symbolically, and the ability to self-regulate. Dramatic play is a logical and proven means to facilitate these critical skills.

The big question is not *whether* children should participate in dramatic play in preschool but *how* that play should manifest itself. Should play opportunities be child initiated, teacher initiated, environmentally stimulated, socially mediated, independently engaged in, small-group centered, large-group centered, inside or outside, on campus or off campus? Our answer is all of the above. Play in a quality preschool program should occur all day long in any and all of the modes previously mentioned. The amount of time spent in child-initiated versus teacher-initiated play, small-group versus large-group play, and so on should be determined by the cognitive, social, emotional, and physical needs of the children in each preschool.

For many years, developmentally appropriate play has mirrored developmentally appropriate practice. As we state in chapter 1, developmentally appropriate practice has been interpreted by some preschool teachers as what children can do independently. We believe it may and should be expanded to include what can be learned with assistance (Bodrova & Leong, 1996). Children need many opportunities to operate both independently and with guidance so their new learning can be applied and they eventually can complete independent tasks. This definition of developmentally appropriate practice speaks to the idea that dramatic play may exist and even flourish in a variety of settings, groupings, and interactions. Haight (2003) observes, "When children pretend with their caregivers, the play is more complex, more elaborated, and also more extended than when they play by themselves. They also use ideas that parents initiate in their subsequent pretending" (p. 1). Teachers must embrace the philosophy that play is a powerful channel for the education of young children and exploit its magnetism throughout the preschool day in a variety of ways.

> The amount of time spent in child-initiated versus teacher-initiated play, small-group versus large-group play, and so on should be determined by the cognitive, social, emotional, and physical needs of the children in each preschool.

Classroom and Behavior Management

Classroom management models can and should vary from one preschool to another. Ultimately, the student population in a classroom should shape the classroom community, atmosphere, and physical arrangement. As we often state throughout this text, the child is the only script. With that idea in mind, we attempt to provide some general classroom management and arrangement guidelines to support teachers as they plan for the social and emotional well-being of their preschool students. In Appendix A, pages 202–233, we provide a generic preschool schedule and 16 specific lesson plans that may help overwhelmed beginning teachers as they embark on their early childhood teaching careers. However, we want to state clearly that the order in which activities are listed on the sample schedule and the specific activities themselves are not mandated in any of the preschools that we serve.

Several factors have an impact on and facilitate excellent classroom and behavior management. These factors are routine, structure, organization, clear expectations, consistency, flexibility, proactive discipline, and positive reinforcement. All children—particularly young children—feel safe and comfortable in a predictable environment. Teachers may want to spend the first four to six weeks of preschool modeling and teaching expectations to their preschoolers for positive social interaction and learning. Taking the time upfront to teach and model appropriate school decorum is imperative.

Providing classroom management systems or processes that are both reasonable and predictable sets the stage for the entire school year. Many of our preschool teachers use *The Stop and Think Social Skills Program: Teacher's Manual for PreK–1* (Knoff, 2001). This social skills program provides numerous activities and cue cards to teach and support specific social skills such as following directions, accepting consequences, ignoring distractions, sharing with others, and dealing with anger. Figure 15 lists the basic 5-step process that Knoff advocates for the self-regulation of student behavior. We encourage our teachers to post Knoff's Stop and Think Behavior Chart to illustrate the appropriate actions. Consistent teaching, modeling, and monitoring of this proactive approach to social skills instruction yields positive classroom and behavior management outcomes.

We have found, however, that it is not only the children in our programs who benefit from this type of social skills modeling and training but also many of our teachers and parents who struggle with the delivery of consistent and appropriate discipline. Over the years, several of our teachers and parent volunteers have exhibited less-than-desirable adult-child social interactions. A typical undesirable interaction is "Stop now!" or "Don't do that!" expressed to a child in a harsh, discomforting fashion. To preempt inappropriate adult-child interactions and implant desirable disciplinary discourse, we provide a teacher and parent intervention prompt chart adapted from Knoff's (2001) original (see Figure 16). Several of our preschool teachers have enlarged this chart and posted it for parents' and teachers' reference. They have commented that it has provided a common language for all the adults in the preschool, and from it the children have learned the consequences for inappropriate behavior. Many parents also have expressed their appreciation for the modeling and training that they have received and have discussed the changes that they have made at home based on their experiences in the preschool.

The physical organization of the preschool classroom is dependent on a variety of factors, including the size of the room, the available furniture, the play artifacts, the storage space, the

---

• **Figure 15** •
Stop and Think Behavior Chart

What Should I Think and Do?

1. Stop and think!

2. Are you going to make a good choice or a bad choice?

3. What are your choices or steps?

4. Do it!

5. Good job!

Source: Reprinted from Knoff, H.M. (2001). *The stop and think social skills program: Teacher's manual for PreK–1.* Longmont, CO: Sopris West. Used with permission.

• Figure 16 •
Stop and Think Prompt Chart

What Should I Say and Do?

1. Stop and think!

2. Speak quietly and firmly.

3. "I can tell you are feeling (sad, angry, frustrated, etc.)."

4. You are (state the inappropriate behavior).

5. You may choose to (state desired behavior or task), or go to the thinking chair!

6. Repeat number 5 if necessary, and follow through!

Adapted from Knoff, H.M. (2001). *The stop and think social skills program Teacher's manual for PreK–1*. Longmont, CO: Sopris West.

---

restroom facilities, and the flooring material. However, we make some general recommendations to all our teachers. First, make your preschool environment aesthetically pleasing and welcoming for young children. Second, display children's art and writing projects whenever possible. Third, provide for a community or whole-class meeting area that provides adequate seating for all. Fourth, place noisy, active play centers apart from more sedentary, quiet play centers. Fifth, provide furniture that matches the physical needs of the children. Finally, assemble books, materials, and manipulatives in a manner that is organized and easily accessible to the children.

Conclusion

The great question in preschool education today seems to be, Should early childhood educators support a social and emotional approach, emphasizing independent exploration and discovery, or should they support an individually tailored cognitive approach with a focus on cognitive development? We believe that the answer is a simple one: We must provide both. As professional early childhood educators, we are responsible for educating the whole child. The cognitive, social, emotional, and physical development processes of young children are all integrated and addressed appropriately and individually in a quality preschool. It is not an either-or decision. Teachers should consider a variety of management systems that allow them to integrate all four developmental domains and the content areas in a playful, active, nurturing, and stimulating environment.

One of the basic principles guiding the Vygotskian philosophy is that human development cannot be divided from the social context. Vygotsky believed that social mediation is fundamental to cognitive construction. Bodrova and Leong (1996) further elaborate that "for Vygotsky, the social context influences learning more than attitudes and beliefs; it has a profound influence on how and what we think. The social context molds cognitive processes, while it is also a part of the developmental process" (p. 9). Vygotsky's theory underscores the importance of social competencies and language to achieve cognitive outcomes. Social and emotional development and extensive oral language opportunities in a preschool setting are imperative to nurture the whole child. Chapter 5 further explores social pragmatics in oral language development and phonological awareness and their central role in ensuring later literacy success.

An Incredible Connection: Oral Language, Phonological Awareness, and Literacy

• • •

Ian was a 5-year-old kindergartner in our preschool. He was unable to orally segment or blend individual sounds in words. The teacher assessed Ian with a phonological awareness screening that our local speech pathologist, Shirla Loutas, recommended, and she determined that Ian could orally segment compound words (*cow...boy*) and syllables (*el-e-phant*), but he was unable to blend or segment individual phonemes orally (*c-a-t*). Once we had determined his ZPD in phonological awareness, Shirla suggested that the next step would be to work with "continuant" phonemes in words such as *M-o-m*. It worked. Ian could hear the *m-m-m-m* and *o-o-o-o* phoneme sounds that could be sustained for longer periods of time. Eventually, after many weeks of instruction and practice, he began to hear and segment "stop" phonemes that cannot be sustained for longer periods of time, such as those in *c-a-t*.

Ian's story is one of many that verify the incredible connection between oral language, phonological awareness, and literacy. For years, it has been universally accepted that fundamental oral language competency is a critical antecedent to literacy acquisition. Burns and colleagues (1999) report,

> During the first months and years of life, children's experience with language and literacy can begin to form a basis for their later reading success.... Research consistently demonstrates that the more children know about language and literacy before they arrive at school, the better equipped they are to succeed in reading. Main accomplishments include: oral language skills and phonological awareness, motivation to learn and appreciation for literate forms, and print awareness and letter knowledge. (p. 8)

Both oral language development and phonological awareness instruction are vital components in quality early childhood education programs. Throughout the chapter, we investigate these two skills and their significant relationship to literacy acquisition.

• Figure 17 •
Oral Language Terms and Definitions

- **Phonology** is the study of the speech sounds of a language and the rules used to put sounds together into meaningful syllables, words, and speech.

- **Morphology** refers to the rules of word formation and units of meaning.

- **Semantics** is the study of the development and changes in word meanings.

- **Syntax** refers to the rules of word ordering in grammatical form.

- **Prosody** is the inflection, rhythm, pitch, and volume of speech.

- **Pragmatics** refers to the rules that children learn for using language in specific situations.

• Figure 18 •
Phonological Awareness Terms and Definitions

- **Phonological awareness** is the explicit awareness that words have a structure (syllables, sounds, etc.).

- **Phonemic awareness** is the manipulation of the smallest units of sound (c-a-t).

- The **Alphabetic Principle** is an understanding of the letter-sound relationship.

A number of technical terms that we find essential in our work with preschool children relate to oral language development and phonological awareness and may be helpful to other preschool teachers. Our primary reference for the definitions in Figures 17 and 18 is *Building Early Literacy and Language Skills* (Paulson et al., 2001), a resource and activity guide for preschool and kindergarten.

Oral Language Development

As we previously mentioned, oral language development is the foundation for a preschooler's literacy acquisition. For the purpose of this book, we attempt to explain the basic elements of oral language and divide them into some workable parts that will enhance language development and instruction in early childhood programs. First and foremost, it is important to understand that oral language is typically categorized as receptive language (listening) or expressive language (talking). Both are important oral language competencies that often develop naturally in young children. Receptive and expressive language may be further delineated into the following observable and teachable components: semantics, pragmatics, oral language structures and syntax, and prosody. Experiences and competencies in each of these areas empower young children as they begin their formal school educations. (See Figure 19 for a preschooler using expressive language.)

• Figure 19 •
Robby Shares His Story With His Class

Receptive and Expressive Language

Although receptive and expressive language opportunities are common occurrences in preschools, researchers have documented that these language activities most often occur independently of one another in classroom settings. Extensive conversational opportunities, particularly those between adults and young children, are essential to enhance children's vocabulary development and articulation of speech sounds and allow them to practice various sentence structures. The reciprocal process of speaking and listening in conversation develops a child's flexible use of semantics, pragmatics, oral language structures and syntax, and prosody. Snow and colleagues (1998) reference the Bermuda Day Care Study of Phillips, McCartney, and Scarr (1987) that "showed that the quality of conversation (both receptive and expressive) in the classroom and the amount of one-on-one or small-group interactions that children engaged in were highly related to language measures" (p. 148). Clay (1991) states,

> The preschool child's language development is vital to his progress in reading. We are concerned not only with the development of his vocabulary, but with the range and flexibility of the patterns of sentences that he is able to control. His development in this behavior is critically dependent on the preschool opportunities he gets to converse with an adult. (p. 37)

Our experience mirrors the Bermuda Day Care Study and Clay's observations. When completing annual teacher surveys, our preschool instructors frequently comment that they have trouble holding the attention of their students during whole-class discussions. Our typical response is to ask, Are you in a large-group setting, and are you doing most of the talking?

To support reciprocal conversations and language usage in our preschools, we discourage overuse of large-group activities and encourage the use of small-group or one-on-one interactions as much as possible.

Numerous experts (e.g., Snow et al., 1998) have verified that the amount of dialogue or oral language in which a child engages daily correlates directly to his or her vocabulary growth. In a recent study revealing the language experiences of children from birth to three years of age in welfare, working-class, and professional homes, Hart and Risley (1995) conclude, "The most important difference among families was the amount of talking that went on" (p. 192). They also state that

> the strength of the relationships revealed by the longitudinal data between the amount of children's expressive and receptive experience and their later accomplishments convinced us whatever the heredity of less advantaged children, more experience could not be irrelevant or wasted. (p. 194)

Semantics. Semantics, commonly referred to by educators as vocabulary development or word-knowledge building, traditionally has been addressed in preschool through implicitly embedded activities. Numerous read-aloud opportunities, show and tells, field trips, and realistic play centers—including science exploration, math manipulatives, social role-play, fine and large motor activities, and creative arts—have traditionally been central to this goal. Many preschools also have incorporated nonfiction read-alouds and guest speakers from a variety of professions to further the realistic and implicit word-knowledge-building agenda. Each activity is wonderful, but for many children the activities are not enough.

Activity-embedded vocabulary development is helpful, but explicit, intentional vocabulary instruction is imperative to ensure that young children enter school with optimum language skills. There are numerous ways to provide explicit word-knowledge instruction and increase children's language experiences appropriately in a preschool setting. First, teachers should select themes and topics that introduce new vocabulary and provide for a variety of language structures. Too often, the same traditional holiday themes of Halloween, Thanksgiving, Christmas, and Easter are repeated every year, particularly in multiage preschools, with little or no new knowledge or language for children to assimilate. Although these holiday themes are fun and meaningful, teachers may wish to reflect carefully about how many weeks are devoted to these familiar, repetitive themes and how to embellish the language outcomes cited in the Preschool Outcomes Checklist (see Appendix B, page 241).

> • • • • • • • • • • • • • • • •
> Activity-embedded vocabulary development is helpful, but explicit, intentional vocabulary instruction is imperative to ensure that young children enter school with optimum language skills.
> • • • • • • • • • • • • • • • •

Second, themes of study should be experiential, emergent, relevant, and intentional to match and augment the cognitive, social, emotional, and physical development of individual preschool populations. To determine and initiate different themes, we suggest beginning with multiple-genre read-alouds such as folk tales, fairy tales, nursery rhymes, nonfiction, realistic fiction, poetry, how-to books, multicultural stories, and resource texts (e.g., newspapers, telephone books, and cookbooks) to solicit unique student interests. When teachers observe their students closely during new literature presentations, they are able to target students' special interests. The length of thematic units should be based on children's attention and motivation. Once a theme is selected and introduced, the teacher models and presents the new language repetitively in multiple contexts. Initially, it is helpful to create pictorial semantic maps using photos or large posters that relate to the theme. Name and label the features and items in the pictures in order to extend student's vocabulary about the new topic. Collect, label, and display related artifacts that children can manipulate at a play center. These activities help children to absorb and use the new language and vocabulary more naturally. Revisiting these pictorial semantic maps often may encourage and enhance student's abilities in automatic object naming. Snow and colleagues (1998) state,

> To our knowledge, only five kindergarten prediction studies have included confrontation naming measures in the predictor battery, but the magnitude and consistency of the results of those studies suggest that naming vocabulary is a reliable predictor of future reading ability. (p. 109)

These studies confirm the importance of explicit daily vocabulary instruction for preschoolers. Vocabulary lessons and activities may be augmented with numerous visual props and concrete examples to enhance student comprehension. We encourage teachers to be thoughtful and intentional about the new vocabulary opportunities that they are providing for their students.

Third, and most significant in our experience, are the one-on-one and small-group adult-child interactions. Adult-child interaction before, during, and after play and content learning centers, field trips, and guest speakers all facilitate and encourage vocabulary development. During these exchanges, adults may model new words, facilitate extended conversations, and ask open-ended or higher-level questions. For example, after a field trip to the fire station, one teacher asked Ricky, "Why do the firemen wear those hard hats?" That question initiated an extensive conversation about the different types of hats people wear and hats' unique features and functions.

Raelene Shreve, our most experienced preschool teacher, has implemented play centers in her classroom that encourage the retelling of stories and folk tales heard during read-aloud time. She provides costumes (usually masks) and props, along with scenery transparencies that the children and adult helpers manipulate on the overhead projector to reenact a story. In another play center, puppets and a puppet stage also advance expressive language usage through imitation and role-play. Still another play center may facilitate a small group of five children and one adult as they use five marionette monkeys and a toy bed to retell *Five Little Monkeys Jumping on the Bed* (Christelow, 1998; see Figure 20). These playful, small-group activities provide for explicit, relevant, and motivating vocabulary growth in young children.

Show and tell is perhaps the most traditional preschool activity used to target expressive language usage and vocabulary development. In our opinion, however, show and tell provides very limited expressive language opportunities. Typically, one child presents while the rest of the class listens, making show and tell predominantly a receptive language activity. To maximize the

• Figure 20 •
Claire and Her Students Perform
Five Little Monkeys Jumping on the Bed **(Christelow, 1998)**

number of conversation (receptive and expressive) opportunities for preschoolers, we suggest using show and tell in small groups so everyone shares and everyone listens (see Figure 21 for a small-group show and tell). Each group may be facilitated by an adult such as a teacher, aide, parent, principal, or older student. Small-group show and tell promotes rich conversations and discussions that are initiated by the children's personal interests. We encourage daily small-group show and tells to provide for optimal language exploration and usage by our preschool participants. After implementing this simple change in her preschool classroom one of our teachers, Erin Jackson, commented,

> Thank you for telling me about the small-group show and tells. We had three different groups share today, and we were able to have great conversations. I was able to listen and respond to each child in my group, rather than spending my time keeping everyone else on task. I had enough adults for two for each group. I didn't have to spend the whole day on it. (personal communication, November 12, 2002)

In addition to using the small-group setting, we encourage children to present new show and tell items or share experiences that match class themes, thus expanding their existing vocabulary knowledge. Too often, children stagnate by constantly regurgitating old, familiar information and vocabulary, such as discussing Beanie Babies or Matchbox cars. Experienced teachers interact thoughtfully in these show and tell conversations to model new and appropriate language structures and vocabulary without making the experience an inquisition. For example,

in one preschool classroom, Tyler said, "I got dinosaur." The teacher responded, "I can see that you have a Tyrannosaurus Rex to show us. Wow, he looks mean!" Her response modeled new vocabulary, embellished Tyler's syntax usage, and expressed positive enthusiasm for the topic. Then, the teacher followed up with a few *why* and *how* questions to elicit and maximize Tyler's language usage. Modeling, responding, and attending are the most effectual teacher actions during show and tell. This small-group discussion about dinosaurs was relevant and motivating for all participants.

Although vocabulary development has been shown to be critical in language development and reading achievement, it is not sufficient on its own. Positive self-image and an extensive number of opportunities to practice oral language structures, syntax, prosody, and pragmatics also have been cited as significant contributors to future literacy learning (Snow et al., 1998). Modeling and practicing appropriate social discourse with children are potent interventions that may be integrated easily into a variety of contexts throughout the preschool day.

Pragmatics. Pragmatic knowledge of words is a skill that takes many people a lifetime to acquire. Pragmatics is the ability to choose appropriate language to communicate one's desire or intent clearly in a specific situation. Choosing socially acceptable language when requesting a favor or soliciting a response is a social competency that develops over time with frequent opportunities to talk with others. Subtle nuances that facilitate and promote positive social interactions, including words and phrases such as *please, excuse me,* and *thank you,* often need to be modeled repeatedly in preschool settings to support children's development of this skill.

Participating effectively in conversations and group discussions requires the ability to listen and respond politely and appropriately. The choice of words, phrases, sentences, or a combination of the three to promote this type of discourse evolves with plenty of conversational opportunities and experiences. The give-and-take of reciprocal discourse and conversational etiquette is critical to the development of oral language competency. The adjustments that we make in our voice tone, word choice, explanations, and questioning are all pragmatic skills that we learn as we communicate orally. Providing preschool children with continuous models and opportunities for the practice of appropriate social interactions in a variety of settings is vital. Play centers, field trips, dramatic play, small-group discussions, show and tell, snack time, recess, and class discussions all provide wonderful opportunities for children to practice this competency. To support teachers, aides, and parents as they model pragmatics for young children, we provide in Appendix C, page 257, the Show and Tell Prompt Card with conversation starters and sustainers and the Reading Prompt Card to encourage discourse during story reading. Prompts such as "This story reminds me of…" or "I wonder…" model for children and parents the art of conversation and the development of social pragmatics.

> The give-and-take of reciprocal discourse and conversational etiquette is critical to the development of oral language competency.

When young children develop an understanding of social pragmatics, the skill directly correlates into reading and writing pragmatics later. The ability to understand an author's meaning, tone, dialect, language structures, and inferences in a text depends on what children already know about the rules of language. Ultimately, the development of these oral language competencies leads to effective reading comprehension in later years. This correlation is also true in writing. Children eventually write with the audience in mind, determining the content based on the perceptions that they have about what the reader will need or want to know. Knowledge of the societal rules of language (i.e., pragmatics) has an impact on a child's ability to initiate and receive communication effectively throughout his or her life.

Oral Language Structures and Syntax. Additional oral language abilities that have been found to be particularly relevant to early reading success include language structure flexibility, speech, sound articulation capability, positional word understanding (e.g., *up, around,* and *behind*), correct pronoun usage, correct irregular past-tense verb usage, morphology usage (e.g., using prefixes and suffixes that change word meanings), and finally, acquisition of complex sentence structures (sentences with five or more words). To promote these competencies, our preschool teachers are trained to identify each child's ZPD in each area and teach accordingly. Identifying and targeting immature oral language structures and syntax are most easily accomplished through ongoing formal and informal language assessments, in addition to daily anecdotal student records (see chapter 3). Once a child's ZPD has been determined, teachers model desired language usage and plan activities to facilitate student practice opportunities. Knowing each student's level of personal language acquisition is not enough. Teachers also need to acknowledge and incorporate the various structures and syntax of oral language that vary from one culture to another, one region to another, one socioeconomic group to another, and one text to another.

Language structure experience and flexibility are powerful communication skills that enhance reading, writing, and speech acquisition. Children must be exposed to and assimilate a variety of oral language structures to communicate effectively in the world today. For example, simple communications relating to mealtimes may be syntactically dissimilar depending on the geographical region in which one is reared in the United States. Someone from the southeast may say, "Come and eat, y'all!" while someone from the west may say, "Soup's on! Come and get it!" and someone from the northeast may say, "Dinner is served!" These three statements are semantically comparable but structurally distinct. Young children will advance their oral language usage and flexibility when language structure coaching accompanies field trips, presentations, and read-alouds, especially when these activities involve unfamiliar cultures or situations. Teachers should serve as the link between a child's personal language structures and the ones presented in new experiences or texts, guiding and supporting children as they learn different language structures.

Perhaps the most efficient way to advance language structure flexibility in a preschool setting is through multicultural and multigenre read-alouds. Clay (1991) describes this preschool behavior as learning to "talk like a book" (p. 77). The knowledge and imitation of various "book" language structures empower children as they explore the world of literacy and support their understanding of the language structures of dissimilar cultures and disciplines.

Most preschool teachers implicitly incorporate a variety of language structures during storytime, but they often are unaware or make little use of the available teaching possibilities. Recognizing and providing explicit instruction for young children about predictable or repetitive language structures may enhance their future reading comprehension and fluency skills. Teachers may consider providing explicit instruction in timeless language structures such as "Once upon a time" or "Once there was...." The instruction may be accomplished easily through multiple shared-reading experiences of traditional fairy tales. For example, the teacher may prompt children by saying, "This is a fairy tale. It begins like *The Three Bears*, which we read last week. Do you remember how it started? Many fairy tales start the same way." Or before reading a poem, the teacher may remark, "This is a poem. You can tell because many of the words rhyme." As we expand and incorporate the number of language structures that children experience, they become more flexible in and knowledgeable about the world around them and the literature that they encounter. Children who have not heard or understood oral language structures such as "Once upon a time" inevitably stumble when encountering them later as early readers.

Standard or conventional syntax knowledge also empowers beginning readers. As first-grade Reading Recovery teachers, we frequently observed beginning readers' syntactic or structural miscues, such as using incorrect irregular past-tense verbs (e.g., *maked* for *made*, *comed* for *came*, or *growed* for *grew*), making positional word errors (e.g., confusing *behind* and *over*), and misusing pronouns (e.g., confusing *her* and *she*). These early reading miscues are frequently the result of a child's inexperience with conventional oral language structures. Attention to these competencies during the preschool years may eliminate the future necessity of reading support or special education services for the child.

The following examples and activities support explicit teaching in language structure flexibility and conventional syntax knowledge. This instruction may occur in a variety of one-on-one, small-group, or whole-group settings. Read-alouds, shared reading, independent reading, and ZPD group sessions (which will be discussed in depth later in the chapter) provide positive learning conditions that enhance language structure flexibility. Through these four daily activities, much of the explicit oral language instruction occurs, including language structure flexibility, sound articulation capability, positional word understanding, correct pronoun usage, irregular past-tense verb understandings, and complex sentence structures.

A read-aloud and subsequent retelling or play-acting of *We're Going on a Bear Hunt* (Rosen, 1989) provide numerous occasions to teach positional words such as *under*, *over*, and *through*. An obstacle course of pretend ponds, grass, woods, and mud can be constructed to solicit student participation and solidify new understandings. *Rosie's Walk* (Hutchins, 1968) and *Five Little Ducks* (Raffi, 1999) are additional titles that are frequently used to teach these directional concepts. In our preschool, children act out the stories by climbing up, over, and down a prefabricated hill with hidden stairs behind it.

A shared reading of *Little Miss Muffet* (Collins, 2003) and other nursery rhymes allows children to receive explicit instruction and practice using irregular past-tense verbs. The teacher may read through the rhyme first and revisit the text later to teach *sit* and *sat*, *come* and *came*, or *eat* and *ate*. After the shared reading, the teacher may ask, "What did Miss Muffet *eat*?" Together, the teacher and children should respond, "She *ate* curds and whey." Or the teacher may ask, "What did Miss Muffet *sit* on?" Together, the teacher and students should respond, "She *sat* on a tuffet." In this activity, children always are given the opportunity to echo the teacher and practice appropriate past-tense verb usage. To reinforce proper past-tense verb usage, we often sing a little jingle with our students: "Today, I sit.... Yesterday, I sat.... Tomorrow, I will sit."

Independent-reading browsing boxes and play centers promote child-generated, open-ended storytelling. Wordless books can be particularly effective in promoting oral language structure and syntax practice as children create their own words to match the illustrations. To ensure quality story development from students in our classes, we always model our own version of a wordless tale before asking the children to do the same. Some great wordless books are *Peter Spier's Rain* (Spier, 1982), *Amanda's Butterfly* (Butterworth, 1991), *Carl Goes Shopping* (Day, 1989), and *Look Up, Look Down* (Hoban, 1992).

Prosody. A wonderful teaching tool for modeling the concept of interactive conversation and prosody to young children is *White Dynamite and the Curly Kidd* (Martin & Archambault, 1989b). The entire book is a conversation between a bull rider and his young daughter during a rodeo. Folk tale plays and puppet shows, as previously mentioned, also are frequent occurrences in quality preschools to teach complex sentences, prosody, and syntax construction. The children emulate the dialogue presented in familiar tales such as *Red Riding Hood* (Marshall, 1993) and *Goldilocks and the Three Bears* (Cauley, 1992). Dramatic lines such as "Not by the hair of my chinny, chin, chin!" or "Someone's been eating my porridge, and it's all gone!" promote children's use of longer sentences and development of new vocabulary. Our preschoolers are captivated by the stories and intrigued by the voice impersonations portrayed dramatically by their teacher.

In summary, optimal oral language development occurs when children have frequent opportunities to converse with adults and other children in one-on-one and small-group settings. As documented by Hart and Risley (1995), the more conversations a child has, the more vocabulary growth he or she usually has. The reciprocal language experience that is enhanced through numerous and varied adult-child conversations is invaluable in a child's education and its benefits are often irretrievable if a young child misses these opportunities. The unmistakable message for all early childhood educators and parents of young children is that you cannot talk to a child too much.

Phonological Awareness

Phonological awareness is not necessary to communicate orally, but it is critical to the acquisition of reading and writing skills. Stanovich and Adams (as cited in Stahl, 2002) "suggest that a child's phonological awareness ability is a better predictor of success in reading than IQ or even knowledge of the alphabet" (p. 341). Phonological awareness, as we defined earlier in this chapter, is the channel through which children discriminate the sounds of language and integrate them into meaningful print. Paulson and colleagues (2001) state that

> research shows that young children's phonological awareness abilities are excellent predictors of their later reading and spelling performance levels; children with poor phonological awareness abilities often experience greater difficulty learning to read. In addition, early emphasis on phonological awareness appears to put children in a better position to take advantage of later literacy instruction. Research further suggests that children need some minimal level of phonological awareness before they can gain much benefit from letter-sound instruction. (p. 116)

Phonological awareness provides a foundation for later instruction in phonics. We believe, and many researchers have verified, that explicit instruction in phonological awareness for preschoolers is a powerful steppingstone to later reading success.

Many experts have identified the phonological awareness competencies that 2- to 4-year-old children typically acquire, which are rhyming, alliteration, and blending and segmenting (Paulson et al., 2001). Each competency may be addressed in an array of preschool classroom settings—one-on-one, small-group, and large-group—while always considering each child's ZPD in phonological awareness. Relevant activities should be fun, dynamic, and developmentally appropriate for young children. Children with notable language delays should be referred to certified speech or language pathologists for further evaluation as soon as possible.

Rhyming

Rhyming is a fundamental component of phonological awareness. Teaching rhyme recognition frequently begins with repetitive nursery rhymes, songs, and finger plays such as "Old King Cole" (dePaolo, 1985b), *Little Miss Muffet* (Collins, 2003), and *Little Rabbit Foo Foo* (Rosen, 1990). Young children seldom have difficulty reciting and recognizing the rhyming words in these simple rhymes after numerous chanting or singing opportunities. The next level of rhyming is rhyme completion. After hearing a chant or rhyme several times, a child may volunteer to fill in the missing word that rhymes. An example may be "I know an old lady who swallowed a fly, perhaps she'll ____?" or "Brown Bear, Brown Bear what do you see? I see a white dog looking at ____." The third level of rhyming development is rhyme production. In our preschools, we like to introduce this skill with a simple little chant: "Rhyming words end with the same sound; sit down, stand up, turn around!" Then, we solicit a rhyming word from the children by saying, for example, "Now say the color that rhymes with *bed!*" A way to personalize rhyme production and make it more meaningful is by using the children's names. The teacher may sing to the tune of "London Bridge," "I'm thinking of a name that rhymes with *Pyler*, rhymes with *Pyler*, rhymes with *Pyler*. I'm thinking of a name that rhymes with *Pyler*...." The children respond, "*Tyler, Tyler, Tyler!*" Another song to sing and act out to the tune of "London Bridge" is "What's the rhyme you hear in *green*, hear in *green*, hear in *green*? What's the rhyme you hear in *green*? *Een, een, een!*" Other rhyming activities may include bringing rhyming objects to show and tell (e.g., a coat and boat or a pear and bear) or playing I Spy with rhymes (e.g., "I spy something on the wall that rhymes with *dock*" [the clock]). These phonological awareness activities and many more can be found in *Building Early Literacy and Language Skills* (Paulson et al., 2001).

Great read-aloud texts to teach rhyming include traditional nursery rhymes; songbooks such as *Twinkle, Twinkle, Little Star* (Trapani, 1994), *I'm a Little Teapot* (Trapani, 1997), *Down by the Bay* (Raffi, 1990), and *Five Little Monkeys Jumping on the Bed* (Christelow, 1998); and narratives such as *Green Eggs and Ham* (Seuss, 1960a), *One Fish, Two Fish, Red Fish, Blue Fish* (Seuss, 1960b), *Good Night, Moon* (Brown, 1991), *Is Your Mama a Llama?* (Guarino, 1997), *Jump, Frog, Jump* (Kalan, 1989), *Mary Wore Her Red Dress, and Henry Wore His Green Sneakers* (Peek, 1985), and *To Market, to Market* (Miranda, 1997).

Alliteration

Alliteration is another important phonological awareness competency. Children between 3 and 4 years of age typically can identify, repeat, and produce words with the same initial sounds. For example, they may be able to identify classmates whose names all begin with the letter or sound of *J*: Jacob, Joshua, Jordan, John, and Jessica. An understanding of alliteration often is a prerequisite to onset (hearing the initial sound of a word) and rhyme. Children generally hear and segment the initial sounds in words before the medial or ending sounds. Once again, to the tune of "London Bridge" the teacher can sing, "What's the first sound that you hear, that you hear, that you hear? What's the first sound that you hear in *Jacob, Joshua, Jordan?*" Many wonderful read-alouds also exist that model alliteration, such as *Animalia* (Base, 1987), *Eating the*

Alphabet: Fruits and Vegetables From A–Z (Ehlert, 1989), *A My Name Is Alice* (Bayer, 1992), *Alphabears: An ABC Book* (Hague, 1999), and *Matthew A.B.C.* (Catalanotto, 2002).

Blending and Segmenting

Blending and segmenting skills are generally used together as children decode and encode print. We recommend that teachers begin by having children orally blend compound words. For example, the teacher may say, "Guess this word: *cow...boy, jump...rope,* or *shoe...lace.*" When a child is able to blend compound words orally, the next step is to blend multisyllable words such as *com-pu-ter, di-no-saur,* or *kin-der-gar-ten.* Modifying the game Duck, Duck, Goose is also a fun way to allow children to practice this skill. The children all sit in a circle while one child walks around tapping each child's head and saying someone's segmented name—*Jor-dan, Jor-dan, Jor-dan*—and finally saying *Jordan* as he taps one child. The child who is tapped when the name is blended chases the other child around the circle to find the vacated seat. Then, the game continues with a new child and a new name.

Children typically segment one-syllable words in sentences (for example, *I—love—you*) and syllables in words (*com-pu-ter*) at about the same time in their development. To avoid confusion when we help our preschool children distinguish words and syllables, we encourage our teachers to "stomp" words in sentences and "clap" syllables in words. We also help children with syllable segmentation by modeling a hand placed under the chin with the explanation that each time our chin drops, we are saying another syllable. Counting syllables in students' names is fun and meaningful for preschoolers. One child (Jordan) comes to the front of the class, and everyone puts their hand under their own chin and says and counts the syllables in Jordan's name. Together, the class discovers that *Jordan* has two syllables. Using chin drops rather than or in addition to hand claps helps our preschoolers to understand the basic concept of syllable segmentation. A syllable segmentation card game also may be played by a small group of students with animal or picture cards. A child draws a picture card with a tiger, for example, segments it into *ti-ger,* and declares that the word has two syllables. Then, he or she gets two markers, chips, or blocks. The next child draws a picture of an antelope, segments the word, and declares that it has three syllables. That child gets three markers, chips, or blocks. The game continues in the same fashion until all the cards are gone. The child with the most markers, chips, or blocks at the end of the game is the winner.

Phonemic Awareness

Phonological awareness typically precedes phonemic awareness. This order is significant because in regard to learning the alphabetic principle, a child's understanding of phonemic awareness upon entering school is thought to be the strongest determiner of the success that he or she will experience in learning to read (Adams et al., 1990; Stanovich, 1986). According to Wallach, Wallach, Dozier, & Kaplan (as cited in Adams et al., 1998), "Poorly developed phonemic awareness distinguishes economically disadvantaged preschoolers from their more advantaged peers" (p. 2).

Once children master segmenting and blending syllables in words, the next step is blending and segmenting continuant phonemes in words. This competency reflects the beginning stages of the alphabetic principle. Continuant sounds are the letter sounds, such as the consonants *m*, *f*, and *s* and all the vowel sounds, that can be sustained orally for longer periods. In contrast, stop sounds, such as *p*, *b*, *t*, and *k* are much more difficult for children to hear because they cannot be sustained for long periods. (A complete list of stop and continuant sounds may be found in chapter 8, page 131.) For example, it is often much easier for a child to blend words with continuant sounds, such as *m-o-m* or *f-i-sh*, than it is to blend words with stop sounds, such as *c-a-t* or *t-o-p*. For preschoolers and kindergartners who are ready for this level of instruction, games such as guessing whose name is being pronounced (*S-a-m* or *M-o-ll-y*) are a fun way to begin. Our preschool teachers also have observed that many children practice and perfect the alphabetic principle while writing in their journals. Encouraging children to say words slowly and record the initial, medial, and ending sounds that they hear is a meaningful and strategic way to enhance their phonemic awareness.

Texts for read-alouds that facilitate blending and segmenting competencies in young children include *The Doorbell Rang* (Hutchins, 1986); *Polar Bear, Polar Bear, What Do You Hear?* (Martin, 1997); and *The Very Hungry Caterpillar* (Carle, 1994). Each text provides numerous character, animal, or food names to segment and blend together. Words from these stories may be segmented into sentences (e.g., *What—do—you—hear?*) or syllables (e.g., *grand-ma*), or initial sounds may be segmented or blended from the rest of the word (e.g., *a-pple*).

Explicit Instruction of Phonological Awareness

Explicit instruction in phonological awareness competencies is delivered in a variety of whole-class, small-group, and one-on-one settings in quality preschools. However, we have found ZPD groups to be the most efficient method for providing phonological awareness instruction in each child's ZPD. These small-group interactions allow teachers to tailor their instruction to meet each child's individual level of development. Part One of the *Report of the National Reading Panel* (NICHD, 2000) states that "when children were taught phonological awareness in small groups, their learning was greater than when they were taught individually or in classrooms" (pp. 2–4). Most of our preschool teachers work with a total of 18 children. Given these numbers, they typically find it helpful to conduct a minimum of four ZPD groups each day. There are usually 3–5 children per group, and each group session lasts approximately 7–12 minutes. Children are placed into the same group based on their common instructional needs. For example, one group may be learning to recognize rhyming words, while a second group is segmenting syllables, a third group is working with alliteration, and a fourth group may be listening for initial sounds in words.

> We have found ZPD groups to be the most efficient method for providing phonological awareness instruction in each child's ZPD.

Our ZPD groups generally share a common literacy theme or a particular book that the entire class has read together in a shared-reading session. Each lesson typically targets one oral language or phonological awareness skill, one print awareness competency, one letter identification activity, and one writing activity, all encompassed in the context of a meaningful text. For the purpose of the sample ZPD group lessons that follow, we have selected the familiar nursery rhyme "One, Two, Buckle My Shoe." We provide four authentic oral language and phonological awareness lessons that were used recently by one of our preschool teachers, Raelene Shreve. Raelene designed her lesson plans for ZPD groups to follow a shared reading of her teacher-made Big Book based on the chosen nursery rhyme. Her ZPD group lessons included the following phonological awareness activities:

> Group I: Say and act out the rhyme together. Stomp the number of words in the first sentence, and then manipulate one object for each word.
>
> Group II: Say and act out the rhyme together, then ask, "Do these words rhyme: *two* and *green*? *Four* and *door*? *Six* and *mix*? *Eight* and *bait*? *Ten* and *jump*?"
> Guess the word: *door-knob, shoe-lace, num-ber, buc-kle*.
>
> Group III: Retell the story in the past tense. (What did you do? I buckled my shoe, or I opened the door.) Think of the number words that rhyme with *shoe, door, sticks, gate,* and *hen*.
>
> Group IV: Segment the onset and rhyme with two different colors of blocks. Children push one block forward for the onset and the second for the rhyme: for *cat*, students would move block 1 for *c* and block 2 for *at*.

These lessons are short and concise but give children the guided practice that they need at their particular developmental level.

Conclusion

Recent research verifies that phonological awareness should be explicitly taught in early childhood education programs to ensure future reading success. According to Paulson and colleagues (2001),

> It is especially important for young children with risk factors such as language delays and limited exposure to literacy to receive training in phonological awareness; to reduce the risk of reading disabilities, children need to receive this training during their preschool years. (p. 121)

Bradley and Bryant's 1983 (as cited in Stahl, 2002) study "found that preschool and kindergarten children given training in categorizing sounds in spoken words were significantly better readers by the end of three years" (p. 341). Stanovich (1991) calls phonological awareness one of the major contributions that psychology has made to the pedagogy of reading over the past 25 years.

We have discovered and implemented numerous phonological awareness activities well beyond those mentioned in this chapter. They all encourage children to play with and enjoy language. Teacher-initiated rhymes, alliteration, and blending and segmenting games are frequently emulated by children in free-choice play centers and at home with their family members. The transfer of these important phonological abilities from playful preschool experiences to later reading and writing competencies is cited frequently by kindergarten and first-grade teachers. Four excellent resources for phonological awareness activities are *Curriculum-Aligned Thematic Phonological Awareness Treatment* (Floyd & Yates, 2001), *Building Early Literacy and Language Skills* (Paulson et al., 2001), *Fall Phonemic Awareness Songs and Rhymes, Vol. 2340: Fun Lyrics Sung to Familiar Tunes* (Jordano & Callela, 1998), and *Phonemic Awareness in Young Children: A Classroom Curriculum* (Adams et al., 1997).

Oral language development and phonological awareness for second-language learners is another hot topic that is vigorously debated by many experts in the field. Burns and colleagues (1999) state that specifically for learners of English as a second language,

> the initial instructional priority should be developing the children's oral proficiency in English. Print materials may be used to support the development of English language skills. But formal reading instructions in English should be postponed until an adequate level of oral proficiency in English has been achieved. Insuring this proficiency will require extremely rich and well-adapted oral language environments. (p. 132)

In Geva and Wang's work (as cited in Gersten & Geva, 2003),

> a less well-known finding is that the awareness of individual speech sounds in one's native language correlates with awareness of individual speech sounds in a second language. Phonological awareness in Spanish or Korean, for example, transfers to phonological awareness in English. This awareness can also predict reading and spelling development in both languages, even when the two languages are very different from each other. (p. 44)

According to Thompson, Vaughn, Hickman-Davis, and Kouzeknanai, and Geva (as cited in Gersten & Geva, 2003), "New research suggests that with appropriate instruction, English learners can learn phonological awareness and decoding skills in English as rapidly as native English speakers can" (p. 44). This research underscores the benefits of oral language development and phonological awareness for second-language learners in a preschool setting.

Finally, we want to emphasize the incredible connection between oral language, phonological awareness, and literacy acquisition. We believe that the oral language and phonological awareness foundation skills are so critical to children's later reading achievement that we recommend that every preschool enlist the services of a certified speech or language pathologist to model interventions that the classroom teacher can implement daily. We further encourage preschools to provide these specialists on a weekly basis to observe and support the students, model skills for them, and ensure that all the students have the opportunity to develop appropriate early language competencies. See chapter 6 for a list of oral language and phonological awareness indicators that highlight the important competencies and that we suggest preschool teachers incorporate appropriately into their classroom instruction. Additionally, the Preschool Outcomes Checklist, the Preschool Literacy Checklist, and the Kindergarten Literacy Checklist may be found in Appendix B, pages 241, 249, and 250, respectively. Receptive and expressive language center ideas, including suggestions for activities in a phonological awareness center, are included in Appendix D, pages 270–271. For additional information and services, readers may visit the American Speech-Language-Hearing Association at www.asha.org/proserv.

Having documented the critical nature of oral language development and phonological awareness to later reading achievement and school success throughout this chapter, next we explore their incredible connection to literacy learning in the preschool environment. Chapter 6 extends the concepts of oral language development and phonological awareness into more specific literacy learning through activities in the modes of reading. Read-alouds, shared reading, ZPD groups, and buddy and independent reading provide the structure for children's exploration and acquisition of early literacy competencies.

Preschoolers as Readers

• • •

During a recent hallway discussion at school, three early childhood educators talked about management issues that they had experienced with their ZPD groups. The two preschool teachers commented that ZPD groups were feasible in their classrooms because they always had aides and parents to supervise the children who were not involved in the ZPD lessons. The kindergarten teacher voiced her concern about monitoring the rest of the class without a paraprofessional to help. We asked if the teachers felt that there was another way they could reach each of their students within their ZPD in literacy acquisition every day. All three responded, "No way!" They indicated that there is not enough time in the school day to ensure this personalized instruction in any other way and that whole-class teaching just does not do the job. One teacher said, "With a skilled aide to monitor the rest of the children, ZPD groups really work well, and I feel like I know what all of my kids can do."

The use of ZPD groups is one of the most important elements in our preschool framework, and, as such, it also sets our framework apart from other early childhood frameworks. We have heard other educators say that young children should not be grouped for instruction in any way. We firmly disagree because we believe that small-group instruction and activities offer the following elements that are critical in the early childhood education of all children: opportunities for adult-child conversations and children's oral language development, active engagement and participation of all children, instruction at the child's ZPD level, increased individual attention to each child, and careful and frequent assessment and observation. We more fully discuss ZPD groups later in the chapter.

Enjoyment of Books

First, we want to emphasize that the aesthetic appreciation of books and literature is at the very core of reading with preschoolers. One can see the excitement and wonder on the faces of children as they attend to the storyline in a great book. They are captivated by the language that they hear and the pictures that they see, and these sounds and images provoke natural comments and feelings that are spontaneously shared. Ensuing conversations further enhance children's understanding and enjoyment of the text.

Children's interactions with text can begin early in life with infants listening to simple, patterned stories or rhymes read by their parents at bedtime. As previously mentioned, this home atmosphere is replicated as much as possible within a preschool situation so preschool reading experiences will underscore and expand children's enjoyment of the stories and situations. The skillful teacher is the foremost reading model as he or she appropriately uses enthusiasm, drama, inflections, and fluency to heighten the children's involvement and enjoyment. Well-chosen texts are geared to the appropriate developmental level and personal interests of each classroom of young children to mirror and extend the children's experiences. Well-written books are ones that children will ask to revisit again and again whether independently, in shared readings, or in read-alouds. Morrow (2001) states, "One of the first goals in early literacy development is the nurturing of positive attitudes toward reading. Those attitudes usually result in voluntary readers" (p. 163).

Rationale for Teaching Early Reading Competencies in Preschool

The joint position statement of IRA and NAEYC (1998) states, "The ability to read and write does not develop naturally, without careful planning and instruction. Children need regular and active interactions with print" (p. 7). Therefore, we believe that it is imperative that early childhood educators make thoughtful, skillful, and appropriate decisions about the activities in which children participate in preschool, while understanding and implementing knowledge about the fundamentals of early literacy acquisition. The components of oral language development, phonological awareness, and all the reading modes that we present in this chapter become part of the three cueing systems that children will use when they begin to read continuous text formally: systems of meaning (semantics), structure (syntax), and visuals (print). These systems are essential for the navigation of printed materials, and children must be skilled in using all three systems in concert to become thoughtful and competent readers. The components that we describe in the following section provide the vital underpinnings needed for their effective use.

Modes of Reading

The modes of reading identified in this chapter are labeled with terms commonly used in elementary school settings. We use them in our framework to help establish between early childhood and primary-level educators and between educators and families a common language regarding quality literacy interactions with young children. Although most of the terms are the same as in elementary usage, we want to emphasize that the lessons or activities within each area are remarkably different from those at the grade school level. For example, a shared-reading lesson in first grade may have the same purpose as one in fifth grade, but the activities are very different at these grade levels because of the differences in students' ages and knowledge and desired outcomes. In what follows, we discuss how the reading activities suggested for each succeeding component are accomplished very differently for preschool children.

In the preschool framework, the modes of reading that we suggest to support literacy acquisition are read-alouds, shared reading, ZPD groups, and buddy and independent reading. Each mode has specific purposes and activities that help preschoolers understand more about oral language, phonological awareness, literacy, and their world.

Read-Alouds

Read-alouds provide total teacher support to children as the teacher reads an entire text aloud to the class (see an example in Figure 22). Only the teacher has a copy of the text, but interactive discussions and activities may occur. Notably, read-alouds enhance the early development of listening and reading comprehension strategies and understandings. They give children numerous opportunities for hearing and enjoying quality literature. Children's oral language, vocabulary development, and phonological awareness expand with every text as they hear vivid vocabulary and a diversity of simple and complex language structures.

Books chosen for read-alouds need to be of the highest possible quality; diverse in gender and multicultural perspectives; and from multiple genres such as storybooks, poetry, nonfiction,

• Figure 22 •
Teacher Raelene Shreve Reads Aloud to Her Students

songbooks, how-to books, and nursery rhymes. Using multiple genres for read-alouds helps children begin to understand the different characteristics inherent in each genre and become more aware of how books work—their structures, layouts, and language. Selected materials for read-alouds should relate to the personal interests and experiences of the children as well as to the themes and concepts used within the preschool. Such texts help children to operate within the upper ends of their ZPDs because each read-aloud session is stimulating and packed with new discoveries about language, literacy, and the world.

The read-aloud opportunity, when interactive, is particularly beneficial for building children's schema and background knowledge in a variety of topics without children ever leaving the classroom environment. During an interactive read-aloud, children are not only listening but also responding to the teacher and one another before, during, and after the reading of the text. The teacher may intersperse predictions, inferences, questions, and connections throughout the reading to keep children engaged with and thinking about the story. Providing manipulatives (e.g., flannel pieces, pictures, or miniature figures) for children to sequence or use to respond to questions will hold their attention and promote vigilant listening and thinking. Claire likes to read aloud "The Lost Button" chapter from *Frog and Toad Are Friends* (Lobel, 1970) while the children determine which button in their prepared bag of buttons is Toad's lost one. The children eagerly attend to the story (see Figure 23), carefully listening to the descriptions of each button that Frog and Toad stumble upon before returning home to find "Toad's white, four-holed, big, round, thick button" (p. 37).

• **Figure 23** •
Preschoolers Listen Eagerly as Claire Reads About Toad's Lost Button

Calkins (2000) suggests that children should "partner talk" at intervals during read-alouds to encourage their involvement in the text and to support the development of listening comprehension strategies. Calkins also states,

> We teach children to think with and between and against texts by helping them say aloud, in conversations with us and with others the thoughts they will eventually be able to develop without the interaction of conversation. The great Russian psychologist Lev Vygotsky helped us realize that by giving our students practice in talking with others, we give them frames for thinking on their own. (p. 226)

Therefore, through interactive read-alouds, children are exposed to innumerable subjects and life experiences that extend their current understandings and encourage them to share their thinking and personal connections to the text. This activity allows for the social interactions and adult assistance that Vygotsky recommends to scaffold new learning at the upper end of a child's ZPD.

The *Report of the National Reading Panel* (NICHD, 2000) cites research that shows the importance of storybook reading for preschoolers' incidental learning in vocabulary development. Rereadings and child-initiated talk also are noted in the report as effective in improving vocabulary. We recommend that this type of interactive read-aloud be used once a day, in addition to two to three conventional read-alouds. Some books and poetry that teachers may want to consider for read-alouds are listed in Figure 24.

Shared Reading

Shared reading is a whole-class or small-group, teacher-led activity for which Big Books often are used so all children can see and interact with the text. Holdaway (1984) originated the concept of Big Books and shared reading because he wanted to emulate within the school environment the "lap reading" occurrences that children typically experience at home. His idea of enlarging the text into Big Books makes it easier for preschool children to view the text and participate in the reading when they are unable to sit one-on-one with the teacher.

We encourage teachers to approach this activity just as they would a lap reading experience if they had a child or grandchild of their own. This activity is intended to be a wonderfully warm, intimate, and collaborative effort. The teacher draws the children into the essence of the story while explicitly modeling the intricacies of the reading process. The children all have a bird's-eye view as the teacher shares his or her personal connections, predictions, and observations and solicits theirs.

The shared-reading experience is intended to be an elaborate, interactive conversation between the teacher and children about the text. Teachers often begin by modeling a prediction that they might have about a story based on its title or the illustrations. Next, they might read the story aloud while making personal connections to the pictures. The children's interactions and responses are encouraged and facilitated through strategic dialogue between teacher and children. Following the shared reading, the teacher might model a retelling of the story. A concrete way to demonstrate *beginning, middle*, and *end* is to use green, yellow, and red cards, respectively, to symbolize the sequential retelling concept. Then, children may use the cards to support their own retellings. This activity is an example of representational thinking or a mental model, which helps children internalize their thinking.

Teachers need to make careful decisions about what elements they will highlight in their before-, during- and after-reading activities that will increase the enjoyment and engagement of their students. Also, teachers must consider their students' schema (prior knowledge) about each text—its structure, themes, language structures, and vocabulary—in order to support the children's understanding of the text and their emotional connections to it. Finally, educators must decide how best to maximize the opportunities that one text offers to enhance and extend appropriate early literacy learning concepts, such as directionality and one-to-one correspondence, as well as content learning concepts in other curricular areas.

Typically, the before-reading activities include arousing the children's interest, connecting the text to the children's schema, explaining or modeling any unusual or unfamiliar language structures or vocabulary, and setting a purpose for listening. During-reading activities keep the children involved and engaged in the text by having them make predictions and share their own reactions to and feelings about the story. After-reading activities allow children to discuss and deepen their understanding of the story and their responses to it. More specific suggestions for each of these areas are given in the next sections. Also, specific thematic literacy lessons that follow this lesson design are given in Appendix A, pages 203–233.

The Big Book format enables the children to see the teacher using appropriate book-handling skills such as reading the title, deciding where to start and which way to go, turning pages, recognizing that the print carries a message, and so on. The print is enlarged in Big Books so teachers can point to the words as they read, modeling one-to-one correspondence and left-to-right and top-to-bottom directionality skills. Teachers might revisit the smaller features of print after the first reading to point out meaningful words, letters, or punctuation, but they always should model that reading is first and foremost about eliciting meaning from the text. The following list contains many elements that teachers may choose to model and teach during shared reading:

- front of the book
- print contains a message
- title, author, and illustrator
- title page
- one-to-one correspondence
- page turning
- book etiquette
- picture clues
- left page before right page
- which way to go when reading
- return sweep
- concepts of first and last

We encourage repeated readings to help children explore a text's meaning, language, sequence, print details, and much more. One rereading may target the language structures used, while another reading may emphasize relevant social and emotional concepts inherent in the text. Teachers need to be thoughtful as they make decisions about the discussion topics that they will address for their particular preschool population and carefully select the shared-reading texts that match their students' needs and interests. In addition, preschool teachers may take a moment to focus children's attention on the details of print through an activity such as counting the words or letters in the title of the book to refine the children's understandings of word and letter boundaries. In our preschools, we frequently play a punctuation game to act out the purpose of different punctuation marks. We model that a period means *stop* when we are at the end of a thought. We have the children gesture with one hand to demonstrate that it is time to stop. When we come to a comma, we all take a breath and pause; when we come to an exclamation point, we all throw our arms up in the air and look excited; and when we come to a question mark, we put our index fingers to our temples and pretend to be thinking of an answer. This activity is a fun and playful way to teach punctuation through representational thinking and role-playing.

Shared reading does not have to be conducted with commercially made Big Books. Teacher-made Big Books are a common phenomenon in many preschools, and we frequently make our own nursery rhymes. We type a small version of the text on a computer and enlarge it on a photocopier so we have one Big Book and several standard-size copies to use for ZPD lessons. We laminate these teacher-made Big Books so children can use dry-erase markers to create their own illustrations and perhaps circle known words and letters.

Shared reading also may be facilitated with chart-size poems or songs. We have typed numerous poems and songs on the computer and enlarged them on the photocopier to use for this activity. Short excerpts from newspapers or magazines also may be copied onto an overhead transparency and shown on a large screen to create a similar effect. Shared reading should included multiple genres, and read-alouds and materials are limited only by one's imagination. Some popular books for shared reading are listed in Figure 25.

As a final thought, shared reading is truly intended to imitate the home experience of lap reading. If the children become distracted or uninterested, change the direction of the conversation, finish reading the story quickly, and move on to another activity just as a parent would at home.

• Figure 25 •
Recommended Books for Shared Reading

Brown, M.W. (1991). *Good night, moon.* Ill. C. Hurd. New York: Harper.

Carle, E. (1994). *The very hungry caterpillar.* New York: Scholastic.

Cowley, J. (1992). *The hungry giant.* Bothel, WA: Wright Group.

Cowley, J. (1999). *Mrs. Wishy-Washy.* Ill. E. Fuller. New York: Philomel.

Crews, D. (2003). *Freight train.* New York: Mulberry Paperbacks.

Fox, M. (1989). *Night noises.* Ill. T. Denton. San Diego: Harcourt.

Guarino, D. (1997). *Is your mama a llama?* Ill. S. Kellogg. New York: Scholastic.

Hutchins, P. (1986). *The doorbell rang.* New York: William Morrow.

Martin, B., Jr. (1983). *Brown bear, brown bear, what do you see?* [Board book]. Ill. E. Carle. New York: Henry Holt.

Mayer, M. (Ill.). (1968). *There's a nightmare in my closet.* New York: Dial.

McQueen, L. (Ill.). (1987). *The little red hen.* New York: Scholastic.

Numeroff, L. (2000). *If you give a mouse a cookie.* Ill. F. Bond. New York: HarperCollins.

Rosen, M. (1989). *We're going on a bear hunt.* Ill. H. Oxenbury. New York: Margaret K. McElderry.

Seuss, Dr. (1960). *Green eggs and ham.* New York: Random House.

ZPD Groups

We believe that small-group literacy instruction is critical to ensuring that every child receives personally tailored literacy instruction within his or her ZPD every day. This component, which we refer to as ZPD groups, is perhaps the one that most notably sets our framework apart from other preschool frameworks, philosophies, or models. We believe that these strategically planned teacher-child interactions are vital to ensure that all preschoolers are challenged at the upper end of their literacy ZPDs every day. As teachers plan for these lessons, we encourage them to consider the following suggestions. First, form small, flexible ZPD groups of three to five children based on mutual student needs, strengths, and interests (the teacher observations and assessments addressed in chapter 3 may assist with these grouping decisions). Second, embed the lesson in the context of a meaningful text or activity. Third, target one phonological awareness or oral language skill, one print awareness competency, one letter knowledge activity, and perhaps one writing activity. And fourth, carefully plan for an individually appropriate setting in which to deliver the lessons based on the group members' attention spans; personal interests; and physical, social, and emotional needs (see Figure 26 for an example of a ZPD group setting).

This activity is typically the only time during the preschool day that we recommend children be grouped with other children at approximately the same developmental level in their literacy acquisition. Frequently, these groups reflect the chronological ages of the preschoolers, but age is not the primary determinant. One group may have two 4-year-olds, a 3-year-old, and a 5-year-old, while another group may have only 3-year-olds. The groups should not be static and

• **Figure 26** •
Stacy Butler Selects the Floor as the Appropriate Setting for Her ZPD Group Literacy Lesson

will very likely change on a daily or weekly basis. The major goal is to identify, plan, and deliver explicit literacy instruction for each child at the high end of his or her ZPD in an appropriate and playful manner.

The Preschool Literacy Checklist presented in Appendix B, page 249, may serve as an ongoing assessment tool and provide an individualized roadmap for planning ZPD group lessons. Weekly maintenance of the checklist informs teachers of each child's literacy development, providing a picture of what a child knows in oral language, phonological awareness, print awareness, letter identification, and reading comprehension and what he or she needs to learn next. The ability to identify the next skill to be taught in each area and bring together children with similar competencies and needs is an ongoing, significant challenge for even the most experienced, expert teachers. In addition, teachers are expected to make these ZPD lessons fun, engaging, manipulative, active, and appropriate. Specific lesson plans for each day's ZPD group literacy session are suggested to serve as teacher guides and ensure thoughtful, differentiated instruction for all children. For teachers who prefer to use anecdotal records (see chapter 3) to monitor student growth, the lists in Figure 27 may help to tailor the lesson plans for ZPD groups. These lists are by no means exhaustive or sequential, but we hope that they will be helpful to teachers as they contemplate and plan their ZPD group lessons.

The texts or materials used during ZPD lessons normally mirror the classroom themes currently in use. Book selections are made thoughtfully by teachers to entice and motivate students' enthusiasm and interest and meet their individual developmental strengths and needs. Texts may include familiar favorites, nursery rhymes, nonfiction books, poems, songbooks, and so on. Quite often, the shared-reading text or Big Book is the springboard to the ZPD lessons. Children are provided with a "little book" version of the shared-reading text, which allows them an opportunity to practice "reading" in a text to which they have already been exposed in a shared experience. Many of the ZPD group materials that we use may be purchased commercially, and others are teacher made. Some trade books that we have purchased in multiple small-book sets of six to eight copies for ZPD lessons are listed in Figure 28. Nursery rhymes and songs such as "Patty Cake, Patty Cake," "Days of the Week," "One Potato, Two Potato," "Five Little Speckled Frogs," and "One, Two, Buckle My Shoe" are some examples of Big Books and ZPD books that our teachers have made.

One, Two, Buckle My Shoe is an example of a teacher-made ZPD book that many of our preschool teachers have used during their nursery rhyme or number thematic units. Preschool teacher Raelene Shreve shared an entire day's lesson plan that incorporates this text. Although she used a sample lesson template (see Appendix A, page 200), she redesigned her ZPD lessons to meet the specific needs of her individual students. We want to reiterate that this template and others displayed throughout this book are only samples of one way to organize a preschool day, and we are not suggesting that they are the only way. We always advocate and encourage teachers to arrange their daily schedules and times to support the cognitive, social, emotional, and physical needs of their students. We have intentionally refrained from suggesting time frames for the daily activities, knowing that each preschool population has its own unique needs.

• Figure 27 •
List of Competencies for Teachers to Reference While Planning ZPD Group Lessons

ORAL LANGUAGE AND PHONOLOGICAL AWARENESS

- Isolates (segments) words in a sentence
- Recognizes, completes or predicts, and produces rhymes
- Segments compound words
- Segments syllables
- Blends syllables
- Alliterates
- Distinguishes between different environmental sounds
- Uses prepositions, conjunctions, adjectives, pronouns
- Speaks in a fully intelligible manner
- Asks questions
- Uses simple past-tense and irregular past-tense verbs correctly
- Uses compound and complex sentences (four to seven words)
- Understands categorization
- Understands and follows oral directions
- Discriminates phonemes
- Imitates phonemes
- Isolates initial and final sounds of phonemes
- Blends and segments phonemes

READING

- Demonstrates appropriate book-handling skills
- Imitates reading
- Makes text-to-self connections
- Correctly answers questions about stories read aloud
- Makes predictions about texts

- Uses picture clues
- Uses the presented pattern to predict text
- Notices when simple sentences fail to make sense
- Retells stories in sequence
- Reads own name
- Reads familiar signs and labels
- Knows that print carries a message
- Matches voice to print (one-to-one correspondence)
- Reads left to right, top to bottom, and left page to right page with return sweep
- Understands the concepts of first and last
- Knows letter boundaries
- Knows word boundaries
- Locates known words in context
- Blends letter sounds to decode words
- Understands meanings of period, exclamation point, and quotation marks

LETTER IDENTIFICATION

- Identifies letters in own name
- Discriminates between different shapes
- Knows letters by name
- Knows letters by formation
- Knows letters by sound
- Knows letters in context
- Knows letters by label
- Understands the alphabetic principle
- Discriminates between different letters
- Can identify 10 or more known letters

• Figure 28 •
Recommended Books for ZPD Groups

Adams, P. (Ill.). (1989). *There was an old lady who swallowed a fly.* Swindon, UK: Child's Play.

Ahlberg, J., & Ahlberg, A. (1999). *Each peach pear plum.* New York: Penguin.

Bang, M. (2003). *Ten, nine, eight.* Glenview, IL: Scott Foresman.

Cauley, L. (2001). *Clap your hands.* New York: Putnam.

Christelow, E. (1998). *Five little monkeys jumping on the bed.* Boston: Houghton Mifflin.

Fleming, D. (Ill.). (1998). *In the small, small pond.* New York: Henry Holt.

Guarino, D. (1997). *Is your mama a llama?* Ill. S. Kellogg. New York: Scholastic.

Martin, B., Jr. (1983). *Brown bear, brown bear, what do you see?* [Board book]. Ill. E. Carle. New York: Henry Holt.

Melser, J. (1988). *Sing a song.* Bothel, WA: Wright Group.

Peek, M. (Ill.). (1985). *Mary wore her red dress, and Henry wore his green sneakers.* New York: Clarion.

Raffi. (1990). *Down by the bay.* Ill. M.B. Westcott. New York: Crown.

Raffi. (1990). *Shake my sillies out.* Ill. D. Allender. New York: Crown.

Raffi. (1999). *Five little ducks* [Board book]. Ills. J. Aruego & A. Dewey. New York: Crown.

Trapani, I. (Ill.). (1993). *The itsy bitsy spider.* Watertown, MA: Charlesbridge.

Trapani, I. (Ill.). (1994). *Twinkle, twinkle, little star.* Watertown, MA: Charlesbridge.

Trapani, I. (Ill.). (1997). *I'm a little teapot.* Watertown, MA: Charlesbridge.

Trapani, I. (Ill.). (1999). *Row, row, row your boat.* Watertown, MA: Charlesbridge.

Trapani, I. (Ill.). (2003). *Mary had a little lamb.* Dallas, TX: Whispering Coyote Press.

Ward, C. (1988). *Cookie's week.* Ill. T. dePaola. New York: Putnam.

However, ZPD group lessons should be relatively brief, lasting approximately 7–12 minutes each. We encourage teachers to be flexible, always considering the attention, interests, and motivation of their students.

The following sample of a daily schedule (see Figure 29) provides for four learning centers—mathematics, art, motor and physical, and a ZPD group. The first three centers may address any of the developmental domains or content areas and may vary weekly depending on student interest and class themes. The fourth center is always a teacher-directed ZPD group, which is intended to provide explicit ZPD instruction in phonological awareness, oral language, print awareness, letter knowledge, and writing within the context of meaningful, high-quality literature. Teachers are encouraged to begin each ZPD group with a fun child-initiated or interactive rereading of the entire text. As indicated in Raelene's plans, each group may "read" the text a little differently. For example, one group may act it out, another may read it chorally, a third may echo the teacher as he or she reads, and the last group may cuddle up on the beanbag chair or couch with the teacher and listen to the story. In addition, sometimes the same text is used for all four ZPD groups, while at other times different texts may be used for the different groups. These reading decisions should be made by the teacher based on his or her intimate knowledge of the students' learning strengths and preferences.

ZPD lessons should and do look very different in a preschool than small-group reading activities do in a first-grade classroom. The teaching prompts about book handling, letter knowledge, phonological awareness, and writing should be purposeful, explicit, and brief but set in a meaningful, nurturing, and playful context.

After the teacher and students have enjoyed the story together, the teacher incorporates some fun, brief activities to teach the targeted literacy skills. The oral language and phonological awareness lessons may have one group "stomp" the number of words in the title to practice segmenting words in sentences. Other groups may work separately on rhyme recognition, past-tense verbs, or hearing phonemes in words. In our example (see Figure 29), all these activities are related to the teacher-made ZPD book *One, Two, Buckle My Shoe* but allow for different levels of development. The activities are brief, fun, and designed to target the learning zone of each participant. The print awareness activities also vary from one group to another. Some children are just learning how to hold books and turn the pages, others are ready to learn about word boundaries and matching voice to print, and still others are learning the concepts of first and last. The letter knowledge lessons include sorting letters visually and tactiley, recognizing and locating known letters in context, and learning to identify letters written or typed in multiple fonts. Writing activities include brief instruction in letter formation, name writing, and writing from left to right.

Teachers have amazed us with the creative ways that they have found to facilitate their ZPD groups. This portion of the day is perhaps the most challenging in terms of classroom management, so we want to share some organizational secrets that we have observed. Keep in mind that all of our preschools have one teacher, an adult aide, and approximately 18 children. Parents are required to spend one hour of their two-hour volunteer commitment in the preschool each week, so one or two parents are frequently, but not always, available to facilitate one of the learning centers. Some preschool sites are very roomy, and others are half the size of a regular public school classroom.

We always have a ZPD group as one center and usually have a mathematics center during learning center time. The other two centers fluctuate regularly, encompassing all the content areas of study such as science, social studies, music and movement, creative arts, physical health, social and emotional skills, computer use, writing, language, and reading. The centers normally follow the current class theme. The center activities described in Raelene's lesson follow the number theme that she developed: The mathematics center focuses on the concept of number, the art center provides an opportunity for the children to experiment with numbers and different art media, and the motor and physical activity center allows children to practice their hand-eye coordination while tracing numbers.

In our preschool classrooms, each center is monitored by an adult or older student helper whenever possible (see Figure 30), and students' time at each center ranges from 7–12 minutes. Students in Raelene's room may choose which of the non–ZPD learning centers they wish to

• **Figure 29** •
Teacher Raelene Shreve's Lesson Plan

Theme: Number Nursery Rhymes and Songs

I.   Welcome, attendance, and community building

II. Independent and/or buddy reading: Book boxes are personalized at this time with each child having his or her own favorites and "known books" to read alone, with a parent, or with a buddy.

III. Opening and calendar activities

IV. Shared reading: *One, Two, Buckle My Shoe*

    A. Teacher reads entire text to students

    B. Teacher and students count letters and words in title (discuss author and illustrator)

    C. Teacher and students focus on looking at print, particularly at punctuation

    D. Teacher and students clap syllables in number words to transition into centers

V.   Learning Centers

    A. ZPD Groups: Each group interacts with *One, Two, Buckle My Shoe* student books in small ZPD groups.

       1. ZPD Group 1 (cuddle on the couch together while the teacher reads the rhyme aloud)

         a. Reading: Teacher and students say the rhyme together

         b. Phonological awareness: Students stomp the number of words in one sentence

         c. Print awareness: Teacher models book handling (front and back, getting hands ready to turn the pages)

         d. Letter knowledge: Students match magnetic letters to own name templates

         e. Writing: Students make round eggs and tall sticks for graphic practice

       2. ZPD Group 2 (lie on stomachs on the floor together)

         a. Reading: Students echo the teacher as she reads the rhyme in a fun, dramatic fashion

         b. Phonological awareness: Do these words rhyme: *Two* and *green? Four* and *door? Six* and *mix? Eight* and *bait? Ten* and *jump?*

         c. Print awareness: Teacher models appropriate directionality and one-to-one correspondence

         d. Letter knowledge: Students sort round (*o, c*) and stick letters (*x, k, l*)

         e. Writing: Students write own names with colored chalk on the chalkboard

(Recess and snack break)

       3. ZPD Group 3 (sit on the floor together)

         a. Reading: Teacher and students chorally read the rhyme, pointing to each word together

         b. Oral language: Students repeat or retell the story in past tense
           (Ex.) What did you do? "I buckled my shoe" or "I opened the door."

         c. Print awareness: Students put a marker or poker chip on each word on the first page to enhance one-to-one correspondence

         d. Letter knowledge: Students find and circle the letters *s* and *f* with pipe cleaners

         e. Writing: Teacher writes *shoe* interactively with students who are saying the word slowly

(continued)

• Figure 29 (continued) •
Teacher Raelene Shreve's Lesson Plan

    4. ZPD Group 4 (sit at a table together)
       a. Reading: Students read rhyme with buddies, while pointing to words in own texts
       b. Phonemic awareness: Students push a different colored block forward for each sound in a word (e.g., *t...e...n, p...e...n,* and *m...e...n*)
       c. Print awareness: Students underline the first and last word on a page
       d. Letter knowledge: Teacher provides individual letter cards that separately display the letters *a* and *g* in several different fonts. Students sort the cards into two piles: one for the *a*'s and one for the *g*s.
       e. Writing: Teacher and students interactively write *big fat hen* on dry-erase boards

  B. While not with their teacher in a ZPD group, children are heterogeneously grouped in the following centers:

    1. Mathematics center: Students sort, sequence, or do both to the numerals 1–10 or 1–20 in muffin tins

    2. Art center: Students paint three or more animals or figures at the easels

    3. Motor and physical activity center: Students race around masking tape numerals on the floor with matchbox cars

VI.   Break into small group show and tells.

VII. Read aloud *Ten Black Dots* (Crews, 1986).

VIII. Interactive and scaffolded writing: Teacher and students interactively write and illustrate the numeral *3* and word *three* for the number-word class chart; illustrate and display.

IX.   Each student independently writes a "play plan" in journal, showing at which center the child will play.

X.   Free-choice and role-play centers: Students model number use by counting in the restaurant center with receipts and a cash register.

XI.   Closing

attend first, second, or third, so students at those centers always are grouped heterogeneously. The children understand that a maximum of five children may be at a center at one time. Raelene breaks up her learning centers with a 15-minute recess break between groups 2 and 3. She teaches the ZPD groups, and aide Nichole Bertagnole and the parent volunteers typically supervise the other centers.

    Stacy Butler, another preschool teacher, provides for whole-class activities between each learning center rotation. Her student population is very active, and she finds that they are much more focused in learning centers when she alternates every 7–12 minutes between small-group and whole-class activities, recess, and snack time. She also enhances her transition times with learning sound bites such as "Anyone with two parts or syllables in their name may line up for recess," or "Anyone whose name ends in *n* may go to the snack table."

• Figure 30 •
**Aide Nichole Bertagnole Facilitates a Fine Motor Center
in Which Students Match Letters to an Alphabet Template**

Another preschool teacher who has very unpredictable parent volunteer help has managed to accumulate four student computers in her preschool. The computer programs cross a variety of disciplines, and, therefore, may be used almost every day. This computer learning center rarely requires an adult monitor, freeing the available adults to work with the other groups. The teacher also has a listening center with headphones that accommodates five students. The teacher follows her theme by providing relevant stories that she has recorded for her students. Creating her own tapes has allowed her to model and incorporate fun listening gimmicks such as "Turn the page, and point to the tiger hidden behind the rock as I read about what he does next."

It takes time, planning, and a lot of practice to create and conduct productive, fun, playful, and motivating learning centers. We recommend that teachers begin early in September with only two centers a day for five minutes each. In October, teachers can move to four centers a day for seven or eight minutes, and by November the children should be familiar enough with the routine to extend the time by one minute each week. Teachers can solicit adult and student helpers every day until the children are comfortable with the structure. Teachers should be observant, encourage groupings that work well together, and be flexible: If a center is not going well, the teacher should change it. It is important always to have an alternative plan in mind. Several suggestions for learning centers can be viewed in Appendixes A and D, pages 203–233 and 270, respectively.

We believe that ZPD groups are valuable and ensure that every child receives literacy instruction at the upper end of his or her ZPD every day. Teachers must observe children closely and document where each child is in his or her literacy acquisition to capitalize on this small-group learning time. Knowing where a child is and what he or she needs to learn next is critical to teaching and learning. There is no one program or script that continually can identify each student's ZPD and provide the appropriate scaffolding and teaching. Only an expert, knowledgeable teacher can do that.

Buddy Reading and Independent Reading

Buddy reading, or paired reading as it is sometimes called, is two children or an adult and a child sharing a book together. Independent reading is an autonomous activity that facilitates independence and self-regulation in young children. It is an opportunity for children to self-select their reading materials and direct their own exploration of texts that are of particular interest to them. We encourage teachers to let their preschool children choose whether they want to read alone or with a buddy at this time, and for that reason, we do not separate buddy and independent reading.

> Independent reading is an autonomous activity that facilitates independence and self-regulation in young children.

To facilitate these activities, teachers provide preschoolers with several different book boxes from which they may choose books. One is the child's personal book box, usually named for the child, as in "Joshua's Book Box." This box or basket typically houses a student's favorite books, along with familiar texts that he or she has already read in shared reading, ZPD groups, or both. In January, "Joshua's Book Box" contained two teacher-made books: an alphabet book and *One Potato, Two Potato*; three board books: *Brown Bear, Brown Bear, What Do You See?* (Martin, 1983), *Good Night, Moon* (Brown, 1991), and *Five Little Ducks* (Raffi, 1999); two songbooks: *Down by the Bay* (Raffi, 1990), and *Five Little Monkeys Jumping on the Bed* (Christelow, 1998); and his favorite book: *Chicka Chicka Boom Boom* (Martin & Archambault, 1989a). Every day, Joshua's teacher encourages him to revisit one or two of his favorites from this personalized box. Some books are included all year, and several of the books change each week. The rereading of familiar texts is an age-old pastime of young children. When children know the context of a story well, it becomes easier for them to attend to the finer details of the print when they are ready to move into formal reading instruction.

Other book boxes frequently found in preschools contain trade books corresponding to the presiding class theme. In Raelene's classroom one week, the thematic book boxes were filled with texts that reflect her number book theme: *One Fish, Two Fish, Red Fish, Blue Fish* (Seuss, 1960b); *Ten Black Dots* (Crews, 1986); *This Old Man* (Adams, 1995); *Look Whooo's Counting* (MacDonald, 2000); *Make Way for Ducklings* (McCloskey, 1941); *Five Little Ducks* (Raffi, 1999); and the teacher-made text *I Caught a Hare Alive*. She also has the thematic book box from a previous thematic unit about colors. In addition to the book boxes, there is a class library from which the children are free to choose any book of special interest to them. Trade books and class-made books are displayed on open-faced bookshelves and counters to catch the attention of eager readers.

Independent and buddy reading may occur any time during the day. However, Raelene likes to begin her day in this informal manner so parents dropping off their children will feel comfortable lingering long enough to share a story with them. Reading prompt cards (see Appendix C, page 257, for an example) that provide specific language to encourage positive book interactions are available for parents to refer to as they discuss stories with their children. Independent and buddy reading also allows Raelene time to connect with one or two children individually as they transition from home to school. Finally, independent and buddy reading time models the importance and value that Raelene places on literacy in her life and in the lives of her students.

Assessment

Student growth in early reading behaviors may be assessed in a variety of ways. Literacy checklists (see Preschool Literacy Checklist in Appendix B, page 249) and anecdotal records (see chapter 3) are particularly effective for ongoing observation, evaluation, and lesson planning and for communicating children's progress to their parents and families. More formal assessments that may be used to document literacy development in young children include the Emerging Literacy Screening (Paulson et al., 2001); the letter identification, concepts about print, and writing vocabulary components from Clay's (1996) *An Observation Survey of Early Literacy Achievement*; the Brigance Preschool Screen; and Floyd and Yates's (2001) phonological screening. A student portfolio for each child may encompass one or more of these assessments to document and evaluate his or her progress over time. As mentioned in chapter 3, teachers may consider methodically and consistently adding to a portfolio student samples from a variety of projects and settings that reflect growth in print awareness, book-handling skills, phonological awareness, oral language development, directional behavior, and comprehension. As discussed in chapter 2, it is imperative that teachers (a) carefully observe and assess student performance in literacy acquisition, (b) identify each student's ZPD, (c) refer to literacy developmental compendiums to determine each child's next step for new learning, and (d) plan appropriate instruction to scaffold new learning.

Conclusion

In summary, our preschool framework incorporates a variety of reading experiences that support and ensure the literacy development of all children. Read-alouds provide for an exemplary model of the reading process in which children interact with high-quality children's literature. During read-alouds, new and interesting vocabulary and a medley of language structures are presented in an enjoyable and nonthreatening context. Shared reading in the preschool setting promotes stimulating and thought-provoking conversations, much like those that parents enjoy with their own children at home. ZPD groups, however, may be considered the cornerstone of this literacy framework. These sessions provide a unique time when each child receives the guaranteed specific guidance, nurturing, and adult-child social interaction that he or she deserves every day. Finally, independent and buddy reading set the stage for young children as they rehearse their roles as capable readers. Children have an opportunity at this time to emulate and practice the pragmatics of books that have been modeled for them throughout the other modes of reading. The multiple modes of reading approach allows children daily opportunities to interact with literature in a variety of settings including adult-directed, adult-child interactive, and child-directed situations. Each of these settings is fun, engaging, and playful for all participants.

The multiple modes of reading discussed in this chapter parallel the multiple modes of writing, and this critical reciprocity is addressed in the next chapter. Because these two processes are so intertwined, we regret the necessity for addressing them in separate chapters. We want readers to understand that reading and writing in preschool are mutually inclusive processes, and classroom instruction should mirror this fundamental understanding. The use of thematic units offers children many opportunities to explore reading and writing simultaneously through authentic activities. Chapter 7 discusses how the modes of writing further complement and facilitate literacy acquisition for young children.

Preschoolers as Writers

• • •

Four-year-old Kaitlin used the family computer to write a story and gave it to her mother to read. Her mother saw that the story was a jumble of random letters and numbers and asked Kaitlin to read the story to her. Kaitlin responded with her hands on her hips, "Mom, you know I don't know how to read!! You have to read the story to me!"

Even at a young age, Kaitlin has some essential understandings of the writing process. She knows that when people write they convey meaning to others and that letters and numbers are important in communicating the message. She knows that readers extract meaning from written language and assumes that because her mother is a reader, her mother must know what the story says. Kaitlin is highly motivated to write because she sees constant modeling of writing within her home, preschool, and other environments. She realizes that writing is a useful and purposeful skill, and it is one that she is very interested in exploring, even independently. What she does not understand yet is the important concept that the writer is the one who conveys the message through print to the reader.

Kaitlin's natural exploration of writing is replicated in homes and preschools throughout the world. Although children are not necessarily trying to "write," making symbols and pictures on paper, walls, and any other available surface is a natural progression in a young child's development. The child enjoys the very act of creating a graphic representation on paper that he or she can see and show to others. The body movements, colors, and shapes involved with this creation are aesthetically pleasing as well as pleasurable to make. The symbols also carry the total meaning of any "story" or message a child may want to convey. A very young child has no need of any comprehensible text; his or her meaning is self-evident in pictures and symbols.

Until a child has had more exposure to print and writing, he or she does not realize that creating certain specific symbols can carry the same message as their markings (see Figure 31). As Morrow (as cited in Temple, Nathan, Burris, & Temple, 1992) notes, "Children learn about writing through directions from parents, by observing others more skilled than themselves, and by participating with others in literacy events" (p. 283). This participation with others in literacy events that Morrow writes about is the essential foundation of our preschool writing curriculum. We believe that early reading and writing behaviors develop simultaneously; therefore, children who are exploring early reading concepts very naturally explore early writing concepts, too. Some

• Figure 31 •
A Student Example of Letter Strings

early childhood educators are opposed to writing in preschool, but because we believe that reading and writing are integral parts of the same meaning-making process, we respectfully disagree. Morrow (2001) states,

> Research in early childhood writing has changed these attitudes, which has resulted in dramatic changes in classroom practice. Encouraging writing in preschool and kindergarten and praising children's first attempts to write have become standard practices in early childhood classrooms. (p. 12)

In our view, it is essential that young children have opportunities to explore literature through both reading and writing activities. Therefore, we use writing as a very natural and necessary part of most of our preschools' daily activities. Children experience writing as they sign in each day, draw and write in their journals, make grocery lists at the store play center, create book innovations, record plant growth in the science center, label posters that depict the parts of a plant, and write invitations to the class play. The children are at a variety of ability levels, and each child is accepted and affirmed for what he or she can do, while being helped to stretch a bit more and discover new things that he or she can learn to do next.

Recognition of the reciprocity of reading and writing has been a fairly recent occurrence (Clay, 1991, 2001; Morrow, 2001). For many years, beginning writing was taught in the elementary school only after children learned to read, which was toward the middle of first grade. Educators believed that children could not be expected to use letters, words, and sentences until they had learned how to read (decode). The essential component of expressing thoughts and ideas was not addressed. Once children could read fairly easily at a primer level, formal writing instruction began.

Fortunately, this belief changed during the 1980s and 1990s when whole-language advocates and others began to examine and reconstruct early reading and writing behaviors and teaching methodology (Clay, 1991; Morrow, 2001). The term *emergent reading and writing* signaled a new way of looking at the capabilities of young children as they started to take on literacy skills. Educators began to encourage kindergartners and first graders to write their thoughts or ideas by using invented or temporary spelling. Some children wrote letters, while others drew symbols, made strings of letters, or scribbled lines. Teachers and researchers soon found that by experimenting with the writing process—by trying to encode with letters and symbols—children became more able to decode as well as write. Thus, the reciprocity of reading and writing behaviors in young readers was recognized as an essential component of early literacy instruction. Educators noted that children could learn beginning literacy concepts, such as directionality, spacing, one-to-one correspondence, and that print carries a message, during both reading and writing activities. Exploring print in one area seemed to strengthen knowledge in the other area. As Clay (2001) states, "Writing can contribute to building almost every kind of inner control of literacy learning that is needed by the successful reader and yet there may be no predictable sequence in which the shifts in control occur" (p. 12).

This is not to say that writing is an easy task. In fact, it is quite complex, especially for young children. A young writer must take control of many factors in order to construct a message. First and foremost is the meaning component: The child uses oral language skills to express ideas or thoughts that he or she wants to communicate to others. Second, the child must have phonemic awareness and phonics knowledge to produce a speech sound and attach a symbol or letter to that sound. Third, writing sequences of sentences, phrases, words, and phonemes requires fine motor skills as the child tries to make a written record of his or her thoughts and the sounds that are linked to them. Finally, the child also must use visual skills to decide where to write his or her message and to reread or "retrieve" it.

> "Writing can contribute to building almost every kind of inner control of literacy learning that is needed by the successful reader and yet there may be no predictable sequence in which the shifts in control occur" (Clay, 2001, p. 12).

Writing mirrors the reading process. It takes the reading process apart, slows it down, and turns it around. When writing, a child looks at print from the viewpoint of the creator at the beginning of the process rather than as the receiver of what the print conveys at the end of the process. Despite its complexity or perhaps because of that very factor, writing is becoming an essential component of preschool curricula. When explored in concert with each other, early reading and writing behaviors increase the impact of what young children can learn about text. As Clay (2001) states,

> To notice a preschool child's changing responses to print is valuable, but to believe that writing is going to emerge without the influence of knowledgeable tutors or models is to deny the child access to the arbitrary rules of the writing process.... There has to be opportunity, interaction, and assistance...to gain control over the writing system. (p. 35)

We concur with Clay's views about the importance of preschool children's interactions with more expert writers, and we believe that preschool teachers must individually interact with each child at his or her ZPD level in both reading and writing. We present the following list of writing competencies (similar to ones given in chapter 6 for oral language, phonological awareness, reading, and letter identification), which will help teachers to target what each child is ready to learn, given his or her ZPD for writing. This list is not exhaustive, nor is it necessarily sequential because individual children will differ in what tasks they master before others. The list includes a wide range of competencies because children within one classroom will present their teacher with a similarly wide range of capabilities:

- Scribbles
- Draws simple shapes
- Understands that drawing and writing are different (see Figure 32)
- Uses marks as letters
- Assigns a message to own symbols
- Imitates writing (see Figure 33)
- Uses one hand regularly
- Uses a correct pencil grip
- Uses left to right directionality
- Strings letters to spell words
- Uses return sweep (tracking print from left to right and returning to left again)
- Writes with spaces between words
- Writes uppercase and lowercase letters
- Writes own name
- Writes some correct letter-sound correlations
- Writes some known words (see Figure 34)
- Writes with some punctuation

• Figure 32 •
A Student Example of Understanding That Drawing and Writing Are Different

• Figure 33 •
A Student Example of Imitating Writing

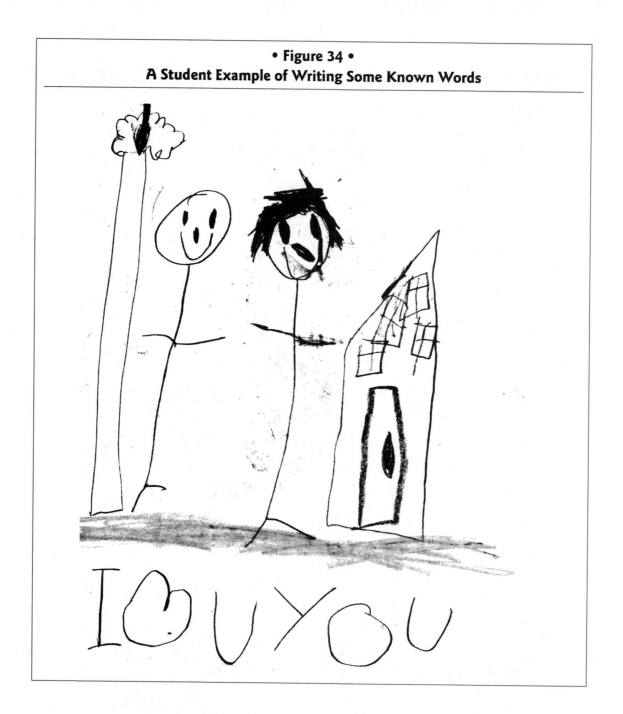

• Figure 34 •
A Student Example of Writing Some Known Words

Modes of Writing

We believe that several types of writing are important modes in a preschool curriculum—language experience, shared, interactive, scaffolded, ZPD, and independent writing. These modes of writing offer a variety of teacher support and child participation. Each has its own purpose in helping children move forward on a writing and literacy continuum, and all support and reinforce early reading behaviors. The structure of these components also allows for a variety of student groupings—the whole class, small groups, and buddies—or for students to work independently.

Children need to be involved in a variety of groupings throughout the day to ensure that they are working as much as possible within their own ZPDs for writing.

When creating lesson plans each week, a preschool teacher should keep these modes in mind and make sure that all students participate in all modes at least once during a given week. Certain modes will be used more frequently as the needs of the children dictate; however, writing in one of the modes is an essential daily activity. The following chart shows the modes of writing and the level of support given by the teacher to preschoolers in each mode.

Writing Mode	Level of Support
Language Experience	Highest Support
Shared Writing	High Support
Interactive Writing	Medium Support
Scaffolded Writing	Low Support
ZPD Writing	Low Support
Independent Writing	Lowest Support

Language Experience

Language experience activities have long been a tried-and-true staple for teachers of young children. In this type of activity, the child creates a message, and the teacher records the child's thoughts on paper. Often, the teacher will act as scribe for the entire class as each child states a reaction to a common experience that the class has had such as a field trip, a read-aloud, or a science experiment. By doing so, the teacher creates a chart that records the children's ideas and thoughts. Then, the class reads the chart chorally as the teacher points to the words.

The purposes for creating language experience opportunities include demonstrating that print conveys a message, showing that writing involves recording what one says and thinks, and letting children see and hear a teacher writing down what they just said. Language experience also affords children opportunities to manipulate and construct language with the help of someone more proficient in both speaking and writing. Later, rereading can emphasize early reading or writing behaviors such as directionality, spacing, return sweep, and making sense, in addition to focusing on important concepts to be learned in other curricular areas such as social studies and science.

Personal experience has taught us to structure these charts carefully. The messages that the children create need to be very predictable in structure so rereading the message will be easy every time. Careful thinking and planning of an appropriate, meaningful sentence starter or topic are vital in constructing a chart that will be read easily by children, always honoring children's own language. Figure 35 shows what four children in one preschool dictated when asked what they liked best after a field trip to the local pumpkin patch. A simple sketch at the top of the chart could serve as a visual reminder of the topic.

• Figure 35 •
Sample of a Language Experience Chart

Our Trip to the Pumpkin Patch
Jonathan liked the scarecrows.
Sarah liked the apple cider.
Shaq liked the tractor.
David liked the pumpkins.

The purpose of each language experience chart is essential to consider. These charts take valuable time to construct and give students powerful opportunities for oral language development and concept building in all curricular areas. Student interest in the charts is usually very high because children know that their names are displayed on the chart, along with their thoughts. If the charts are hung in correlated play and learning center areas after their first readings, children will quickly choose to try to find their own names and "reread" what they and some of their friends said. In our experience, teachers typically make these charts about once or twice a month. Good topics for language experience charts include field trips, guest speakers, read-alouds, vacations, assemblies, science experiment results, scientific observations, innovations on texts, different endings to stories, favorite parts of stories, sequencing events, retellings, lists, and recipes.

Language experience stories also may be constructed when the teacher or a parent works one-on-one with individual children. The individual scripting with a teacher or a parent volunteer keeps the child more attentive to the task and makes the writing more personal. The child has the full attention of the adult and, therefore, is more able to focus on the tasks of creating the message and watching the adult write it down. "Tell me your story, and I will write it down for you" is a prompt often heard in our preschools.

There are many ways to help generate children's stories or messages. Play and learning centers, especially art centers for painting, collage making, and drawing, are wonderful springboards for short stories. After finishing an artistic creation, each child can dictate a sentence about his or her creation, and an adult can write the sentence under the artwork. In addition, innovations from books read to the class (see Figure 36 for a list of texts that promote book innovations) and the creation of new Big Books for shared reading can start with children's art and ideas. Language experience activities are designed to model appropriate writing strategies for children, so these activities always should be meaningful and motivating to children and embedded within the class's current theme.

Shared Writing

The purpose of shared writing is to model how to create and write down ideas and thoughts in a specific way. The teacher and children work together to create a specific type of text with which

---

• Figure 36 •
Recommended Texts for Promoting Book Innovations

Brown, M.W. (1994). *Red light, green light*. New York: Scholastic.

Christelow, E. (1998). *Five little monkeys jumping on the bed*. Boston: Houghton Mifflin.

Gelman, R.G. (2003). *More spaghetti, I say*. Ill. M. Gerberg. New York: Scholastic.

Guarino, D. (1997). *Is your mama a llama?* Ill. S. Kellogg. New York: Scholastic.

Martin, B., Jr. (1983). *Brown bear, brown bear, what do you see?* [Board book]. Ill. E. Carle. New York: Henry Holt.

Peek, M. (Ill.). (1988). *Mary wore her red dress, and Henry wore his green sneakers*. New York: Clarion.

Raffi. (1990). *Down by the bay*. Ill. M.B. Westcott. New York: Crown.

Rosen, M. (1989). *We're going on a bear hunt*. Ill. H. Oxenbury. New York: Margaret K. McElderry.

Seuss, Dr. (1960). *One fish, two fish, red fish, blue fish*. New York: Random House.

Shaw, N.E. (1997). *Sheep in a jeep* [Board book]. Ill. M. Apple. Boston: Houghton Mifflin.

Williams, S. (1991). *I went walking*. Ill. J. Vivas. San Diego: Harcourt.

---

the children can experiment on their own. The teacher acts as the scribe and takes a pivotal role in shaping the language and appearance of the text, while sharing its creation with the children. The teacher models writing strategies through a think-aloud technique that demonstrates to the children what she is thinking about as she writes. Shared writing can be done with the whole preschool class or with a small group.

Shared writing also has a more specific goal than modeling how to write down one's ideas. It can be a powerful tool for modeling the different types of writing that children will encounter within their environments. Before entering preschool, all children have been exposed to a wide variety of print that surrounds them in everyday life. Some of the print they understand, and some they do not. Participation in shared writing activities can implant in children new knowledge about the unique structures incorporated in various writing genres such as letters, recipes, lists, and reminder notes. Our preschool teachers often use whole-class shared writing in the children's free-play centers to demonstrate how different types of writing look. For example, Raelene Shreve modeled a "Do Not Touch" sign after constructing a tall building at the block center. Her students readily followed her example when playing at that center. Another shared writing activity is creating menus that will be used in the restaurant center to help children understand the purpose of menus and how they are created. Demonstrating how to take orders at snack time can be another shared writing experience. In this activity, the students help the teacher decide what to record for each order and how to record it. As a result of shared writing activities, students will feel more comfortable participating in dramatic play that incorporates writing. In addition, children will build background experiences and information that connect to the real world and help to increase their conceptual knowledge of the world around them.

Shared writing can be linked to reading by helping students create the different genres to which they have been exposed within the preschool. The whole class or small groups can create their own simple patterned stories, alphabet books, color books, number books, and poetry. Using a read-aloud as a starting point, children can create together a new text with a structure similar to the text that has been read to them. This activity not only gives the children opportunities to understand the structure of a variety of texts but also offers them a chance to express themselves in a new and different manner if they choose. An example of a frequent shared writing experience in our preschool is an innovation of *Mary Wore Her Red Dress, and Henry Wore His Green Sneakers* (Peek, 1985). Basing her activity on this book, Raelene wrote with the help of the class, "Mrs. Shreve wore her round earrings." Then, she drew a picture of herself wearing the round earrings. Next, each child received a large piece of construction paper on which was written "_____ wore a _____." The children drew a picture of themselves on the paper and, with the help of the adults present at the time, wrote their names and what they wore. After all the children finished, Raelene spiral bound the book and added it to the class's library center.

The next week, Raelene reread *Mary Wore Her Red Dress, and Henry Wore His Green Sneakers* and then asked each child to interview a school staff member and draw what that person wore. For example, Robbie interviewed the principal, Mrs. Frude, and drew her wearing her "cross-checked coat." Mrs. Frude helped Robbie fill in the sentence stem with her name and the words *cross-checked coat*. This activity engaged numerous adults, allowed for a lot of one-on-one instruction, and ultimately resulted in a fun book for the class.

Shared writing can be connected to any of the developmental domains or areas of the preschool curriculum. Writing never should be an end in and of itself, so linking shared writing activities to other areas makes sense. The linking of writing with content area studies allows for the integration of concepts across the curriculum and also is time effective. Therefore, why not provide information and experiences within several developmental domains at one time? More suggestions and ideas for reading and writing activities are given in chapters 9, 10, and 11.

Interactive Writing

In interactive writing, children begin to take a more active part in the writing of a text. Teacher and children "share the pen" to create a text (see Figure 37). The goal of the activity is to model for children how written language works while engaging them in the actual writing process. Interactive writing provides many opportunities for early literacy teaching. See Table 1 for a few of these teaching points.

Interactive writing allows children to get into the writing process, while still being supported by an adult or more capable writer. The child writes what he or she can, and an adult fills in the unknown parts. Kindergarten and first-grade children may write a variety of interactive texts, but we find in our preschools that interactive writing is best used for labeling. Creating a label is perfect for short writing activities that keep the children's interest long enough to accomplish the task. We create labels for classroom objects, such as chairs and tables, and structural items, such as windows, doors, and hallways. Children also may put labels on a chart or poster to mark the different parts of trees, plants, or the human body. In another interactive

• Figure 37 •
Teacher Raelene Shreve and Bradley Write Interactively

• Table I •
Teaching Points for Interactive Writing

Phonological Awareness	Oral Language Development
Rhyming	Idea and sentence development
Alliteration	Vocabulary building
Segmenting	Language structures
Blending	Book language
Concepts of Print	
One-to-one correspondence	Directionality
Print carries a message	Return sweep
Word and letter boundaries	Spacing
Alphabet	**Reciprocity**
Letter identification	Early reading behaviors
Letter formation	Early writing behaviors
Connecting a sound to a letter	Curriculum connections
Upper- and lowercase letters	

writing activity, children can create very short texts such as lists; timelines; holiday or thematic vocabulary charts; patterned phrases from songs, poems, and stories; and student name charts.

When first doing interactive writing with either large or small groups of children, it is best to start with one or two 1-syllable words to write. Clearly explain the task to the group, and model behavior expectations. Give the students a clear purpose such as to label a chart or different items in the room. Slowly say the word that you will write, and then have the children say it slowly with you. Use your hands to imitate stretching a rubber band as you ask the children to stretch out the word. Make sure that each phoneme transitions into the next sound, instead of isolating each sound as you do when segmenting a word. Ask the children what sounds they hear, and have them record the sounds on the label or chart. Initially, many children may be able to hear only the first or last sound in a word, or they may hear none at all. However, modeling how to say words slowly and record the matching symbol is a powerful activity for young children to observe if it is brief and meaningful.

If the children are able to hear the individual phonemes in words and suggest the letter that they hear at the end of the word, praise their responses and tell them that the letter is at the end of the word and they can write that letter when you come to it. Try to overenunciate the word's first sound, and then select a child to come up and write the letter with a dark marker in the appropriate spot on the chart. Provide the child with a model of the letter by writing it on a small chalkboard or dry-erase board, and then show it to the child and the rest of the group before the child writes it. The model will ensure the writer's success and will give the others in the group an example to follow as they write invisibly in the air or on the floor with their fingers while the other child is writing the letter on the chart. Until the entire word is written, continue the process of saying the word slowly, helping children hear the sounds, and selecting children to write the needed letters on the chart. You will need to write the phonetically irregular parts of the words or any other unknown letters. After finishing the writing, make a quick teaching point that is appropriate for the ZPD of the children in the group. For example, the entire class can benefit from the teacher repeating that it helps to say words slowly and verbally stretch them out when writing. In small groups, appropriate teaching points might be writing the letters from left to right or learning how to use the class name chart (a chart of students' names written in large print) as a resource when writing.

Knowledge of each child's ZPD for letter formation and fine motor control is essential for the success of any interactive writing lesson. A preschool teacher needs to know which children can connect a given sound to a given letter, which children can form letters independently, and which children need some support in the actual formation of the letter on the chart. In order for children to learn from the activity, they need to feel successful in any task they are asked to do. This may mean that the teacher will need to guide a child's hand in forming a letter as he or she writes on a chart. For other children, it may mean that a model on the dry-erase board will sufficiently scaffold their writing. The following tips will help to ensure the success of interactive writing lessons:

- Most important, keep the activity brief, meaningful, and motivating. One word per session is enough for most preschoolers.

- Whenever possible, write about play and learning center activities.

- Have a chart of all student names nearby as a reference for letter-sound associations. Pictures of the children before their names will help students connect the written names to the pictures. Use the chart to connect a given sound to a letter such as "*Apple* starts like *Allison*."

- Keep all the children actively involved. While one is writing on the chart or a label, the others can write in the air, on the floor, or if they are capable of it, on a grease board.

- Use 1-inch-wide correction tape to fix errors. The displayed text should always be correct.

- Use dark markers and charts without lines.

- All children in a large group do not have to have a turn to write, but try to involve as many as possible.

- Direct children to resources to help with linking sounds to letters, such as an alphabet chart or other easily seen writing.

The following example illustrates what an interactive writing lesson might sound like. A class is finding out about plants and trees, and the teacher wants the class to help label a poster of a plant. They already have examined real plants and discussed the different parts. The poster is taped to a large easel at a height at which the children can easily write on it. The teacher explains that the purpose of labeling the poster is to help remember the parts of a plant. She decides to write the word *roots* that day and explains to the students that they will start with that part of a plant because it is the first part to grow. She stretches out the word *r-r-o-o-o-t-t-s-s*, and the children say it with her. The teacher points to the class name chart and asks whose name starts with the same sound as *roots*. Someone suggests *Robbie*, and the teacher says, "That's right! *Robbie* starts like *roots*, so we will write an *r* first." She selects a student to write the *r* on the poster and uses a grease board to show how to make the *r*. The rest of the group writes the *r* in the air and on the floor while the teacher helps the child write it correctly on the chart. The teacher has the children slowly say *roots* again and says, "The next two letters say *oo* like the last part of *zoo*." She pauses for a minute to see if anyone offers some letters, and then she writes the two *os* on the poster herself. The teacher and the children say *roots* again, and a child volunteers the letter *s*. The teacher responds that *s* is indeed at the end of the word, but first they must write a letter that comes before that. Emphasizing the *t* sound a bit more, the teacher asks for someone's name that starts with *t*. Tom says, "Mine does," and the teacher responds, "*Tom* starts with *t*, and that is the letter and sound we need just before the *s*." Tom writes the *t* after being shown the lowercase model, and the others write *t* on the floor with their fingers. Then, another child adds the *s* at the end of the word while the others write it in the air.

Interactive writing is a wonderful literacy technique that can fit into any curricular area of preschool. Children will discover more about their world while becoming more capable writers and readers. Creative teachers will discover and design many different opportunities to use interactive writing within their preschool classrooms. One clever preschool teacher, Marti Derringer from a preschool in Rock River, Wyoming, uses interactive writing on the very first day of school to create a personal alphabet chart for her preschoolers. One year, the children wrote the word *apple* for the *Aa* on the first day of school and wrote *bears* for the *Bb* on the second day. In this activity, the older students—helpers from the fourth and fifth grades—typically draw the outline of the apple and bears, and the younger students add color to the pictures. Marti continues having her children interactively write the rest of the alphabet in the following days (see Figure 38). She uses the same technique for the number cards that she posts in the room. Students trace dot-to-dot circles to make a large numeral and interactively write the number word at the bottom of the card. The class members also interactively write their names for a name chart that hangs in the room. Marti knows the power of having children create their own classroom environment and understands that integrating these activities into literacy learning increases the impact of the teaching and learning that happen in her classroom.

Interactive writing activities in preschool should reflect the needs and attention spans of the particular group of students. Our experience suggests that 5–10 minutes is appropriate for this activity.

• Figure 38 •
The Interactive Alphabet Chart

Scaffolded Writing

Scaffolded writing is a technique created by Bodrova and Leong (see Bodrova et al., 2001) to provide temporary support for young children as they begin to write. These authors suggest that a beginning point for preschoolers is making scribble, or play, plans before going to play centers. During this structured time, children individually choose a play center and use a sentence stem, such as "I am going to the _____ center," to say aloud. After doing this for a week or so, the children begin to make symbols or pictures for their play plans. Each child makes a picture as a reminder of what center he or she will go to. Using a colored marker that matches the color of the chosen center, the child makes a picture and adds his or her name to the play plan. As time goes on, the children will become better at drawing pictures and even making letter-like marks to record their plans. For example, some 3- and 4-year-olds may be able to draw pictures and make letter-like marks, while some 3- and 4-year-olds may scribble. The teacher will record their words on the back of their papers. Once the children add more details to their pictures, they may be ready to try scaffolded writing, which we describe in the following summary. The summary presents how scaffolded writing has been used in our preschool classrooms. Any deviations and differences are ours, and we suggest that you refer to Bodrova and colleagues for more complete information about scaffolded writing.

Model for Students. In order for this activity to be successful, a teacher must model scaffolded writing for students daily before they can be expected to try it independently. The teacher explains to students that he or she wants to plan a message so she will not forget it and that making a line for each word will help her to remember the message. An excellent time for this activity is during the morning message at the start of each school day. The teacher can write a predictable message each day so students will find it easy to remember. The steps involved in this activity are as follows:

1. Say a message such as, "Today we will go to music class."
2. Draw a line with a highlighter on a piece of paper for each word in the message.
3. Make each line correspond to the length of the word—a long line for long words and a short line for short words.
4. Say the message while pointing to each line.
5. Have students repeat the message with you as you point to each line.
6. Write the message with a marker on the lines, using correct spelling and punctuation.
7. Reread the message with the children.

After demonstrating this process several times so the children understand it, use it as a teaching opportunity for early literacy print concepts such as directionality, one-to-one correspondence, punctuation, and letter-sound correspondence. Help individual children or a small group get started with writing on their own by modeling the process for them. Have them draw a picture of a recent field trip, classroom activity, or shared-reading book. Then, ask them to write a message about the picture. Follow these steps for writing the message:

1. Have the child or group dictate a message.

2. Make a line for each word with a highlighter, matching each line length to the length of the corresponding word.

3. Repeat the message with the child or group as you point to the lines.

4. Write the message on the lines. The child or group may tell you what to write if the child or children can.

5. Reread the message with the child or group, and have the child or children try to point to the corresponding words.

Teacher-Scaffolded Writing. After having the process modeled for them, children can begin to take a more active part in planning their messages. Working with a group of 4–6 children of mixed abilities will be helpful because the more capable children can help the other students. Again, begin with a child's drawing or, if the child is able to, have him or her create a message independently. Follow these steps for teacher-scaffolded writing:

1. The child dictates a message, and the teacher makes a line for each word.

2. The child points to the lines as he or she reads the message (with help if necessary).

3. The child attempts to write something on each line to help remember the message.

4. The child rereads the message, pointing to each line.

Children will record different things on the lines depending on their literacy capabilities. Some children will scribble write, while others will record a variety of letters, and still others may be able to write one or two correct consonants. Accept whatever the child can do. If it will be difficult at a later time to read the message, record it on the bottom or back of the page.

Student-Scaffolded Writing. Once children become more successful with writing on the lines that the teacher has made, they may be ready to start making their own lines (see Figure 39 for an example). Children show that they are ready for this by accurately reading their messages or spontaneously making their own lines. The child will follow these steps:

1. Think of a message and make a highlighted line for each word.

2. Say the message and point to each line while saying it.

3. Write, scribble, or make symbols on each line.

4. Reread the message.

Tips for Scaffolded Writing. The following tips will help preschoolers to be more successful with scaffolded writing:

• Keep the messages predictable at first so children will find them easy to read.

• Model the process daily, and have students write their own messages two or three times a week.

• Figure 39 •

Ashlynn Uses Scaffolded Writing at a Free-Play Center

- Use alphabet charts with picture clues to help children record a needed letter when they are ready for that stage.

- Use punctuation from the start.

- Help children record only what they hear. They do not need to write a complete word. Suggest that they write what will help them remember their messages.

- Give less support as children become more independent.

Our experience using this scaffolded writing process has been very successful in helping children recall the remainder of their stories when they begin focusing on letter-sound associations. We have found that in teaching students to use scaffolded lines, it helps to begin by making the connection between oral and written language very clear. For example, we conducted a "mystery box" scaffolded writing lesson in which the children felt the object in the mystery box, guessed what it was, named it, and then decided how long the word might be. The scaffolded line that we produced was an approximation of the length of the word. The first child guessed that the mystery object was a horse, the second child guessed that it was a tree, and the third child guessed that it was a reindeer. Together, we all approximated the length of each word. The children knew that *reindeer* was a longer word than the others because it had two parts. As a follow-up activity, the children were partnered and made a list of all the holiday words they knew. They approximated the length of each word, and, in many cases, they wrote the first and/or last letters they heard. Then, we all guessed one another's words. As this and the previous examples show, scaffolded writing is a wonderful tool to support children's thinking and learning as they begin to self-regulate their writing.

ZPD Writing

In the ZPD writing component of our preschool framework, children are even more independent in their writing. The teacher offers support by teaching a minilesson at the beginning of ZPD group time. Children that have similar ZPDs for a given task are brought together in a small group, and they observe the teacher modeling a writing task. Then, the children write independently, trying to use that task in their writing. With this activity, the teacher is trying to widen the capabilities of the writers in a given group by modeling something that he or she feels the children need to know and do next in their writing. This instruction time is geared toward specific children and their needs. We call it *ZPD writing* because it is targeted toward the ZPD for each child.

ZPD writing is a prime instruction time, and it also is a management tool that allows teachers to instruct children with similar needs while other children are engaged in different activities. ZPD writing is typically incorporated in the ZPD groups (discussed in chapter 6) or one-on-one during journal-writing time. During these sessions, each group of students has a target area: One group may be learning how to write more of the letters in their names, a second group may be focusing on writing initial letter sounds, and a third group may be doing some graphic practice (see discussion of graphic practice later in this chapter) such as drawing circles and lines.

ZPD writing also is connected to the other developmental domains in the curriculum and the themes being used in a preschool classroom at any given time. Children can be working in a ZPD group as they label a poster about the habitat of a bat, create a classroom helpers chart (e.g., listing line leader, messenger, teacher helper, and snack server), or make a counting book for the library center. Integration of the developmental domains and curricular areas is an essential element of the preschool daily calendar, and the overlap of areas is part of careful planning and instruction.

Independent Writing

In this mode of the preschool framework, children are the most independent in their writing. They control and manage their writing independent of the teacher and other adults in the preschool. They use their own ideas and language to record stories, reactions, and opinions about their experiences and their world. Independent writing may happen in a journal-writing activity that occurs as the children come into the classroom at the beginning of the day or after outdoor play or movement and music activities. While the class waits for everyone to arrive after another activity, children can write in their journals whatever they are thinking about, recording these feelings and ideas with pictures, marks, and symbols.

In their independent writing, children use their current understandings about reading and writing. Therefore, some parts of this process proceed quickly as children automatically use literacy information that is well within their control, and other parts are more difficult as they try to apply new learning in their writing. What children write independently gives observant teachers a clear picture of what children control in the reading and writing processes, and this picture focuses the teacher's attention on what each child is ready to learn next. As the children write, the teacher circulates around the class and listens to each child tell about what he or she has written. A way to keep children motivated and interested in daily writing is to change the writing instrument and medium on which they write. For example, one day the children draw or write with markers on construction paper, another day they use sidewalk chalk outside, and on a third day they may use dry-erase markers on grease boards.

Writing at play or learning centers is another independent writing activity. We believe that it is essential to provide real-life reading and writing opportunities within each center so children experience firsthand how literacy is interwoven into their daily activities and life in general. It is often necessary to model some appropriate reading and writing activities at a play or learning center when the focus of the center's activities changes. We previously mentioned the examples of using menus and pretending to place orders at the restaurant center. At the block center, children might draw pictures of what they will build and the parts of the house they are making, make lists of the tools that they might need to use, or do both. The writing center itself is well stocked with a variety of writing tools such as different types, sizes, and colors of unlined paper; notepads; order forms; lap-sized chalkboards; grease boards; sticky notes; pencils, pens, markers, chalk, crayons, gel pens, and ink pads and stampers; envelopes; rulers; date stamps; magazines; catalogs; and alphabet charts.

> It is essential to provide real-life reading and writing opportunities within each center so children experience firsthand how literacy is interwoven into their daily activities and life in general.

Independent writing also gives children an opportunity to engage in writing warm-ups, during which they write or record all the letters or words that they know how to write. Clay (1975) calls this the inventory principle—children spontaneously and systematically taking stock of their own learning. We encourage writing warm-ups daily in a transitioning activity in which the children write or make marks with different writing tools each day. This encourages the children to be flexible with using different tools and more cognizant of what they know about symbols, letters, and words. For approximately one minute, the children write all the letters that they know. Some children may be able to write a few words, but the vast majority of children will write only letters. Then, the teacher records the total number of letters and which letters each child writes each week. A copy of each child's writing is added to his or her portfolio every month to track progress and demonstrate growth. A successful way to start writing warm-ups is to model writing *os* and *ls*. To date, all the children with whom we have worked have been able to form these two letters. For several weeks, many emergent writers have warm-up pages with only *os* and *ls*, but soon *ts* and *xs* begin to appear.

Fine Motor Skills

Writing or recording symbols requires the use of fine motor skills in coordination with the eyes, hands, and brain. This capability begins at birth and becomes increasingly refined by the time a child enters preschool. Children who have been given markers, pencils, or crayons have begun to experiment with the marks that they can make on a variety of surfaces, perhaps to the dismay of their parents. Yet this early exploration is a much-needed milestone in learning to control a variety of essential hand "tools." We want to continue and extend this exploration in preschool, so many activities and materials are presented to young children so they will strengthen not only their fine motor control but also their hand-eye coordination.

> **Many activities and materials are presented to young children so they will strengthen not only their fine motor control but also their hand-eye coordination.**

These fine motor activities have long been a staple of preschool curriculum. Clay, pipe cleaners, beads and string, blocks of various sizes, puzzles, scissors and paper, paints and brushes, chalk, crayons, and markers are but a few of the many materials that children will manipulate and use to make their own creations while also strengthening the muscles in their hands. As in other areas, we try to help children expand their abilities and build on what they already can do. For example, with children who have not used scissors before, we have them start by making just one cut in a piece of paper, perhaps creating a fringe border for a picture. Then, as their skill increases, they make more than one cut and learn to cut on a straight line before progressing to curved lines and so on. Many areas of the preschool and its equipment lend themselves to providing opportunities for the children to increase their coordination and muscle strength.

When children use pencils, markers, or crayons to make letter formations, we help them to grasp their tools correctly. This means helping each child have a three-point grasp on the writing instrument so the tool is held between the thumb and forefinger and rests on the middle finger. If the child grips the pencil with all four fingers, a simple way to change this behavior is to provide very short pencils or chalk, and a three-point grasp will naturally evolve. While writing, the child should rest his or her hand on the table, although many young children will turn their writing hands so they hover above the table. This hovering is very tiring and difficult to maintain. We help the child hold the writing instrument by the bottom one third of the tool and place dots or lines on it, if necessary, to help the child see where to grasp it. In addition, if a teacher observes children curving their hands into a hook position, it is advisable to provide inclined or vertical surfaces, such as chalkboards, for each child to write on. The incline will naturally bring the child's wrist down into its proper position.

There are many activities that preschoolers enjoy doing that will strengthen their pencil grasps and increase their fine motor control. Tracings, dot-to-dots, mazes, and coloring books are tried-and-true preschool activities for that very reason. Manipulating a computer mouse is also a task that can develop fine motor and hand-eye coordination competencies. These activities can be offered at a variety of play centers on a daily basis so all students will have many opportunities to explore them. Because children's independent exploration is strengthened when an adult gives some expert guidance—for example, on how to better hold or control a writing instrument—adults should circulate among the centers, observing the children as they explore and play.

Graphic practice is the term that Bodrova and colleagues (2001) use to describe various activities for children that involve making marks or shapes on paper. This practice is another technique that will help children be more precise and controlled in their markings, and it is used in ZPD groups made up of other students at a similar developmental level. Bodrova and colleagues suggest a hierarchy of markings and shapes that children can make on greaseboards or chalkboards. In ascending order, they are dots, lines, circles, squares, and triangles. There is also a hierarchy of how these markings are made. In order from easiest to most difficult, they are that the markings are not touching, touching, big, little, and a mix of big and little. These markings are made within the context of a story or real-life situation, so there is an authentic context for the children to be marking the boards. Classroom themes and inquiries, read-alouds, Big Books, and mathematics explorations can be the springboards for these activities. For example, a class that has been studying plants can make round apples on their boards. Then, they can make tiny dots for the seeds and lines for the branches. Linking graphic practice to authentic experiences is a fun, yet necessary, practice for future writing skills.

Once children are beginning to form letters, we find that it is helpful to use oral cues to aid them in forming letters in an appropriate and easy manner. The oral cues are not targeted at perfect letter formation or handwriting but at providing a scaffold for students to remember what the letters look like. For some of the children in our preschools, these links are essential for triggering from their memories an easier retrieval of a given letter's form. A verbal cue for the letter *b* might be "down, up, and around," and for the letter *h* it might be "down, up, over, and down." Given these prompts, a child can start to say aloud how to make the letter that he or she needs to write. Verbalization of the hand movement is an example of one of Vygotsky's principles, which is that language plays a central role in mental development (Bodrova & Leong, 1996). In this activity, the teacher provides the directional language necessary to scaffold the child's letter-formation skills development. The child echoes the teacher's prompts, eventually internalizing the language and making it his or her own. The child's self-regulation of letter formation is the ultimate goal of this ongoing process.

Another fun and educational way to help children with fine motor control is to have them use toy race cars to trace the outlines of letters. We have made templates of all the letters with arrows drawn on the templates to show where to start the race cars to trace the outlines. We call this activity Race Car Letters, and the children love to do this at a play center. Using the formation prompts with some children also helps them to imprint the letters' forms in their memories.

Assessment

A variety of informal assessments presented in chapter 3 will be helpful in providing an accurate picture of a child's writing capabilities across a variety of tasks. We encourage teachers to collect several writing artifacts or use observations from different activities across the domains to depict each child's writing development. These assessments include anecdotal records, checklists, portions of Clay's (1996) observation survey, the Early Reading and Writing Test Scores and Results Form and the Early Writing Survey in Appendix B, pages 253 and 254, respectively, and portfolios. Anecdotal records will contain a record of what teachers observe children doing within a given time or activity. For writing assessment, anecdotal records might include observations of a child writing in the dramatic play center, writing during journal time, performing graphic practice during ZPD group time, and drawing on the playground with sidewalk chalk. The teacher scripts a child's actions, language, and interactions with others during a set period of time, and the script should be as complete as possible. For example, it is important to note how a child grasps the writing tool, if he or she slowly says the words aloud that he or she is trying to write, and if he or she looks for help from an alphabet chart or poster when copying a letter.

Checklists provide a systematic and organized method for monitoring student progress along the writing compendium. There is a writing portion in both the Preschool Outcomes Checklist (see Appendix B, page 241) and the Preschool Literacy Checklist (see Appendix B, page 249). However, teachers often make their own checklists to record specific information that they want to monitor and evaluate. We encourage teachers to create checklists that are easy to use and meaningful to them as they plan instruction and communicate progress to their students' parents and other family members. Checklists are particularly effective in showing children's progress in acquiring some of the early writing competencies given at the beginning of this chapter. For this reason, it is especially important to share them with families. We like to record a date on each item of the checklist as children show competency in that area within a variety of settings.

Another assessment, the Writing Vocabulary subtest of Clay's (1996) observation survey, asks children to write words that they know how to write. This subtest can be adapted for preschoolers by simply asking a child if he or she can write some words or letters on a piece of unlined paper. The teacher should affirm and encourage the child's attempts. Through this assessment, the teacher is given another insight into what a child understands about words and letters and how to write them.

In addition to the anecdotal records, checklists, and any other assessments, portfolios should contain a wide variety of examples of a child's writing in different settings. Periodically, samples of children's writing should be collected or photocopied and included in their portfolios in order to show how a child has progressed over time. These samples should be taken from all areas in which writing has occurred (e.g., a child's science journal, the labeling of a picture, or a grocery list made at the restaurant center).

Assessment is valuable only if it is evaluated and then used to direct future instruction. Preschool teachers need to take time to look carefully at each student's writing every month to note the differences and similarities that are visible among the pieces of writing. Then, teachers can design teaching opportunities based on these observations that will help each child understand more about the writing process.

Conclusion

Burns and colleagues (1999) report, "High quality preschool programs can boost language and literacy skills and, ultimately, reading achievement. But quality is essential and many preschools fall short in promoting language and literacy" (p. 44). In order to achieve this high-quality instruction, Burns and colleagues suggest that these programs include writing experiences that encourage children to learn about language and print awareness. The daily writing that is an essential component in our preschool framework ensures that each preschooler will have many rich and varied opportunities to create meaning through print in a variety of settings. These activities are augmented by instruction aimed at each child's level of development in writing, thus ensuring that every child not only will increase his or her knowledge of writing but also will expand his or her understanding of language, reading, and a literate environment. Therefore, we believe that our preschool framework contains the "opportunity, interaction, and assistance" that Clay (2001, p. 35) feels are necessary to provide children as they begin learning to write.

Beginning writers seem to become gradually more conscious of the print that surrounds them in their classrooms, homes, and communities. We think that there is a reciprocal effect between writing and print awareness: The more children notice about print, the more that awareness and new knowledge will show up in their writing. In chapter 8, we look at the many types of functional print that help children notice the different types of symbols around them. Then, we present activities that help children look at letters carefully and systematically. This organized and sequential way of viewing print is a new and challenging task, but one that is essential in literacy acquisition.

Preschoolers Learning About Print

• • •

One morning early in the school year, preschool teacher Raelene Shreve was encouraging her children to warm up for writing. She started this activity by saying, "You all know how to write *o*s and *l*s. Let's write some together." Then, she modeled writing the first letter while prompting, "An *o* goes like this... around!" The children imitated her motion in the air, and then each one wrote an *o* in his or her journal. Forrest spoke out and said, "Look, Mrs. Shreve. You're wearing *o*s!" It took Raelene a moment to realize that she was wearing large hoop earrings that formed an *o*. Being an instinctive teacher, she followed Forrest's lead and encouraged the children to search the room for other environmental *o*s.

Forrest's spontaneous observation demonstrates that he is beginning to link conventional print to his three-dimensional world. Raelene interceded at his ZPD by acknowledging his insight and then scaffolding his understanding to the next level by encouraging Forrest and the class to observe environmental print around the classroom and record it on paper. This activity provided Forrest with the opportunity to transform a three-dimensional object into a two-dimensional representation. It is essential that preschool teachers recognize and understand that "a child's sensitivity to print is the first major step toward reading" (Burns et al., 1999, p. 27). In this brief anecdote, Forrest demonstrates that he can discriminate between shapes, understands that *o*s are round, knows that letters have names, and recognizes that letters can be found everywhere in the world around him.

Perhaps most notable in this example is the importance of capitalizing on the teachable moments that children in preschool constantly provide. This does not mean that teachers should watch and wait for these magical moments to occur before they instruct. On the contrary, it demonstrates how careful, thoughtful planning within a stimulating classroom environment can facilitate cognitive growth and learning in young children. This chapter discusses the intentional planning and teaching of print awareness and letter knowledge.

Print Awareness

Owocki (1999) provides an excellent summary of the four functions of print, which are environmental, occupational, informational, and recreational. Environmental print refers to print that is evident throughout one's surroundings such as billboards and store signs. Occupational print means print that is necessary to a specific occupation such as a teacher's class list, an architect's blueprints, and an auto mechanic's work orders. Informational print can organize, store, and retrieve the information that helps in everyday life; examples are calendars and clocks. Finally, recreational print involves printed material that is associated with relaxation and leisure pursuits such as reading for pleasure, surfing the Internet, and playing computer games.

Some print will be classified under only one category, but other print may be multifunctional and included in several categories. A variety of these print types should be provided within the preschool classroom so children can become aware of how print is a functional part of their daily lives. Through this exposure to print types, children also begin to distinguish print from pictures and recognize types of signs. The different types of print should be integrated into play and learning centers so print becomes an integral part of children's play.

Displaying different types of print in the classroom and using different print artifacts in specific activities will encourage children to look at print in different ways than they did previously. For example, having the teacher explicitly model how to use menus and take food orders before children start to play at a new restaurant center will help them understand how and why menus look different than picture books. They will begin to understand that the function of the print is closely linked to its configuration. After many experiences with different types of print, children will analyze print layout and form more automatically. For example, several children were playing at the housekeeping center, and Mike could not find the grocery list that he had made just a few minutes before. Kierra looked around and picked up several pieces of paper that had scribbles on them. She showed them to Mike and asked if the list were one of them. He picked out one and said, "This one has to be it because I made it long and skinny."

Another activity involving print awareness is "writing the room" (see Figure 40). The sole purpose of this activity is for children to distinguish print from pictures in their classroom. Each child takes a pencil and a journal or blank piece of paper on a clipboard and walks around the room, looking for print to copy on his or her paper. The students do this activity for about 5–10 minutes, and then they come together to share their writing. The first steps in sharing are for each child to find a buddy and tell the buddy both what print he or she found and where it is located in the room. This procedure allows for every child to talk and be on task. Then, there is a brief whole-class sharing session in which a few volunteers tell what print they found and where. This whole-class sharing allows children to practice their speaking and listening skills in addition to directing their attention to print in the room that some children would had not have noticed yet. We want to reiterate that the purpose of this activity is not to copy letters or practice letter formations but to build children's capabilities in discerning print in their environment.

Teachers may want to extend this activity into the larger environments of their students' homes and communities in order to demonstrate the enormous amount of print that pervades

• Figure 40 •
Katarina and Rylie "Write the Room"

the students' environments. Children can "write the school," "write their home," and even locate print on a field trip, directing an adult volunteer to take a picture of the pertinent print. This practice will underscore again how different print is displayed and used in the real world.

Preschool teacher Bridget Loftus created an environmental print book to send home with each student to "read" to his or her family. She collected food wrappers and containers from fast-food restaurants and popular snack-food items and pasted each artifact in the middle of a piece of paper. Then, she laminated all the sheets and spiral bound them into a book that each child could easily read. This activity is a wonderful way to help children understand how something taken from their three-dimensional world can be represented in the two-dimensional world of books.

An essential element in expanding children's attention to print is the ability to look at print in a structured manner. This ability is a new and challenging task to preschoolers, who typically have been viewing their world in a random fashion. They have not had to look at the left side of an object first or scan a picture from top to bottom. The conventions of written language, such as left to right, top to bottom, and first and last, have had little place in their daily lives. The world of print, however, demands an organized, sequential approach. Therefore, teachers need to help preschoolers look at print systematically. Clay (1998) suggests that teachers should notice "what a child is attending to and in what order" (p. 120) to understand how any given child approaches text. She terms the ways in which children begin to look at print as "orienting" behaviors (p. 121). This term seems to be effective in signaling teachers that they must take a vital role in helping children establish strategic ways of seeing print in addition to locating familiar features in it.

When children begin to write, they reveal what they already notice and understand about print because those items are evident in their writing, whether the writing is in scribble form or letters. They also gain more control of and build their visual perceptual skills in looking at print as they construct their own messages. Clay (1991) states that "the first explorations of print in the preschool years may occur in writing rather than in reading" (p. 108). Therefore, effective preschool teachers offer children many opportunities to write on a daily basis in addition to providing plentiful graphic-practice activities (see chapter 7) to help strengthen their ability to attend to print features. After children practice making tunnels for cars to drive through and drawing hooks to catch fish with, they may be able to notice more easily the "tunnels" and "hooks" in letter forms.

The hierarchical concepts of a letter, a word, and the first and last parts of a word are also important for children beginning to understand how print works. A child's early experiences typically do not demand discrimination between letters, monosyllabic words, and polysyllabic words. Therefore, one-to-one correspondence, even with simple texts, is a difficult task for novice readers. A meaningful beginning point for preschoolers is to use their names to demonstrate the difference between letters and words. For example, standing next to a large name chart, the teacher writes a large *M* in the middle of the chalkboard and says, "Here is Michael's name. This says *Michael*, right?" The children look at the name chart and respond, "No. That's not his name! You need more!" The teacher says, "You're right. We need more letters." The teacher proceeds to show the children that the *M* by itself is just a letter, but when the appropriate letters are added, it does become Michael's name, which is a word. The teacher and children count the number of letters in the word, and the process is repeated with one or two more names before the end of the lesson. This lesson can be repeated over the following days until all the students' names have been used. The additional skills of locating the first and last letters of a word also must be carefully scaffolded. Identifying the names of the letters is not the lesson's focus. Instead, the teacher asks for a child to point to the first or last letter of a word, as desired. Other related activities might include spreading magnetic letters far apart and then pushing them together to show how letters almost touch when they form a word. Or children's first and last names could be erroneously combined into one long word and then correctly separated into two words.

Shared reading and ZPD groups are ideal times during which preschoolers can learn and practice letter and word boundaries. During shared reading, children can use pipe cleaners to circle words and use highlighter tape to denote individual letters. The letters or words are then counted and tallied by the children and their teacher. Long and short words also can be located to enhance print awareness. Once again, knowledge of the specific letters in the word is not important for this task. The focus is the ability to distinguish letters from words. In ZPD groups, children in one group might count the letters in their first and last names, and another group might count the number of words on a page of a simple, predictable story. Then, the second group may count the number of letters in each word to find the longest and shortest words on the page. A third group may complete the sentence stem "I see a _____" by writing in an animal or object. Then, the third group's task would be to count the number of words and letters in the sentence and find the longest and shortest words. Other parts of the school day lend themselves to similar activities such as using a dry-erase marker to circle words, letters, and the first and last letters in the daily message.

Letter Knowledge

Young children who have a lot of experience with print at home or in preschool usually understand that every letter has its own unique features. For example, they know that letters have names and sounds, the alphabet lists all the letters in sequence, and specific directional movements are necessary to form letters. According to Snow and colleagues (1998), "Among the readiness skills that are traditionally evaluated, the one that appears to be the strongest predictor on its own is letter identification" (p. 113). Experts (Adams, 1990; Bradley & Bryant, 1985) further suggest that knowing letter names is not as important as knowing letter sounds, but they also note that the task of learning letter-sound relationships is often facilitated by knowledge of letter names.

> "Among the readiness skills that are traditionally evaluated, the one that appears to be the strongest predictor on its own is letter identification" (Snow et al., 1998, p. 113).

In our experience, letter learning strategies may be as unique and individual as the children we teach. We have found that children learn letters in many different ways and settings. For the purpose of this book, we encourage teachers to consider and recognize the value of each of the five strategies for how children learn and know letters: in context, by labels, by formation, by name, or by sound. We define and discuss each of these strategies in the following sections.

Knowing Letters in Context

When we refer to a child knowing a letter in context, we mean that the letter or letters that the child recognizes are usually in a familiar word, sign, or logo. A child's name often provides the definitive context in which he or she learns letters. Early childhood teachers have learned over time that presenting new letters in isolation, in an approach such as the letter of the week, is not meaningful for children. Conversely, initiating letter learning through children's names, classmates' names, and environmental print is both motivating and purposeful. We have been awed by the creative methods with which teachers have implemented these letter learning strategies. For example, teacher Raelene Shreve built a learning center with a pocket chart that held photos of all her students and displayed it at their eye level. Then, she provided name cards in a pocket chart for the children to match to the pictures (see Figures 41 and 42). As the year progressed, she changed the fonts used on the name cards to increase the complexity of the activity.

• Figure 41 •
Teacher Raelene Shreve's Pocket Chart With Name Cards Attached

Another approach that provides a meaningful context as children begin to notice and use print in their daily activities is a word wall. Words walls in preschool typically display all the children's names, environmental print, or both. Word walls may be displayed in a variety of locations, including on a bulletin board or chalkboard, underneath windows, or on chalk trays. Some teachers even put them on projection screens, in pocket charts, or on portable room dividers. Perhaps the most effective are interactive word walls located at a preschooler's eye level and backed with magnetic rope on a magnetic surface. This design empowers preschoolers as they manipulate the words on the word wall during literacy activities. During journal writing, for example, children may retrieve a desired word from the word wall to facilitate their own writing and then return it when they are finished. This setup allows children to physically transfer known words from one location to another, helping them eventually to understand that they can identify a known word in a variety of contexts.

Pictures also may accompany names or words on the word wall for immediate recognition. Environmental print word walls may be particularly motivating. Teachers can collect artifacts from local retailers, restaurants, businesses, grocery stores, and the highway department. These artifacts may be enlarged, laminated, and posted in the classroom to encourage students' awareness of environmental print. One preschool teacher displays signs from local grocery and hardware stores and fast food restaurants for this purpose. Then, she provides students with smaller, black-and-white copies of the signs to scaffold their print awareness from the three-dimensional world to the two-dimensional print world. In our highly technological world, with innumerable fonts, children must become flexible in the way they look at print. Preschool teachers may begin this understanding early as they help children to link the *S* in *Stop* to the *S* in *School*.

ZPD group sessions are the perfect time to provide letter learning opportunities within each child's ZPD. One activity may involve children matching magnetic letters to a personalized name template. Preparing magnetic-letter name bags, a template of each student's name, and magnetic boards for each child expedites this activity. The teacher may ask the first ZPD group to put the magnetic letters directly onto the letters of the template, the second group to match the magnetic letters under or over the template, the third group to assemble the letters in their names without a template, and the fourth group to assemble classmates' names. Using the same materials, teachers may provide just the right amount of support during this activity to scaffold new learning for each child. Careful observation by the teacher ensures that the difficulty level of the activity is challenging for students but not frustrating.

In another name game, Raelene draws on the chalkboard the number of lines equivalent to how many letters are in one child's name. Then, she asks the class, "Whose name do you think this is?" The children count the lines and respond, "That can't be my name! It has too many letters!" or "That's not my name! It doesn't have enough letters." Next, Raelene adds the last letter in the name: _ _ _ _ n. Five children—Brooklyn, Logan, Jordan, Ethan, and Shawn—proclaim, "That's my name!" Raelene has each of these children come to the board, touch each line, and orally spell his or her own name. After this exercise, three possible names are left—Logan, Ethan, and Shawn. Next, she adds an *a* so the board shows " _ _ _ a n." The remaining children once again check the spelling of their own names by touching each line and saying the next letter in their names. They discover that the answer has to be either *Logan* or *Ethan*. Finally, Raelene adds the letter *E* on the first line, and the entire class excitedly exclaims, "It's Ethan's name!" This activity is a wonderful way to motivate children to look at and think about the letters in their names. (See Figure 43 for preschoolers playing a name-guessing game.) An extension of this activity may use environmental print names rather than children's names.

Name puzzles are another fun way to involve children in looking at and manipulating the letters in their names. Raelene or the children, if they are able, write their names on narrow strips of paper. Raelene has some children in her class cut their names apart into the separate letters—E - t - h - a - n—and then reassemble them. With other children, she cuts apart only the first letter—L-ogan—, and with still other children, she cuts apart both their first and last names—J - o - r - d - a - n J - e - n - n - i - n - g - s. This game is easily adapted to meet the individual needs of each student by increasing or decreasing the number of letters or parts being manipulated.

Although most preschool-age children have had some experience with their own names, some have not. For example, Ricky entered preschool without knowing how his name looked in

• Figure 43 •
Preschoolers Play a Guessing Game With Names

print or how to write it, but he could write *TONKA*. To use what Ricky already knew in order to scaffold his new learning, Raelene used the letters in *TONKA* to make connections to Ricky's name. When she initially helped Ricky write his name, she wrote *Ric* and then said, "You know the next letter. It is a *K* like in *TONKA*. You write it!" She gradually made other connections for Ricky until he could write his entire name.

Knowing Letters by Labels

Children frequently recognize a letter in the context of a familiar logo, label, or sign—such as knowing the *M* in *McDonald's* because it is big and yellow and refers to food. However, when they see *M* in the word *Mom*, they fail to make the connection. Teachers can support this transfer of letter knowledge. First, the teacher provides other environmental print models that display an *m*, such as labels on milk cartons or signs with the word *market*. Second, the teacher provides opportunities to manipulate and sort three-dimensional magnetic letters, asking the children to look for humps (e.g., in the letter group *m, l, x*) and then to sort for letters with no humps. Third, the teacher provides an opportunity for each child to find the letter *m* in the context of a shared reading of *If You Give a Mouse a Cookie* (Numeroff, 2000).

One preschool teacher created an environmental print alphabet chart that highlighted labels with letters—*Aa* for Albertson's grocery stores, *Tt* for Target discount stores, and *Ww* for Wal-Mart discount stores. In another preschool, the teacher and children took a field trip around the building looking for labels. Then, they interactively created labels for those places that needed them, such as the gym, cafeteria, and office. Encouraging children to label their play centers also motivates them to make connections between letters and their own world. Clay (1993) encourages teachers to "allow children to label letters in any appropriate way—by name, sound or word beginning" (p. 25).

Knowing Letters by Formation

Many children first know a letter by its formation, which we describe as the verbal directions that guide a child's hand movements to record or retrieve a letter. For example, during journal writing, we may hear a child ask, "Teacher, how do you make a 'tuh'? Oh, I remember—down and across!" or "I know *a* is around, up, and down!" In our experience, this letter formation strategy is seldom recognized or valued as a legitimate way of knowing a letter, but it is very helpful to children. We promote the use of standard letter formation prompt sheets to provide consistent verbal directions while children are learning letters and to facilitate this powerful letter learning strategy. Rather than provide a generic prompt sheet that describes specific directional movements for each letter, we encourage preschool teachers to ask local kindergarten teachers what they currently use as letter formation prompts. This process provides a common language for children from preschool through the primary grades. A fun activity that incorporates these prompts is Guess the Letter. The teacher gives directional clues, and the children attempt to record the correct letter. For example, the teacher might say, "Guess this letter: down, up, over, and down!" The children would record the strokes and respond by saying, "It's an *n*!" or "It's an *h*!"

Letter sorts are another powerful way to reinforce letter formations and help children as they begin to discriminate between the finer features of similar letters. The following list offers some characteristics by which children can sort magnetic letters:

- tunnels or holes (*n* and *o*)
- short or long sticks (*n* and *h*)
- open or closed curves (*c* and *b*)
- one or two humps (*n* and *m*)
- tails or hooks (*p* and *j*)
- one or two valleys (*v* and *w*)
- capital or lowercase (*M* and *m*)
- can or cannot hold water (*u* and *n*)
- short or tall (*t* and *c*)

- sticks, curves, or both (*t*, *c*, and *b*)
- slanted or straight lines (*w* and *l*)

Knowing Letters by Name

Most early childhood experts advise that knowing 10 letters is a reasonable expectation for preschool-age children (Burns et al., 1999). However, attaching a name to an abstract symbol without any other associations or props may be the most difficult way for a child to learn a letter. We discourage our teachers from teaching letters in isolation or in a letter-of-week format because it lacks the meaningful contexts that more often facilitate and motivate letter learning. Over the years, many children have been introduced to and have learned letter names with the repetitive singing of the Alphabet Song. This simple song is perhaps the most commonly used instructional tool to teach the English alphabet. We promote the use of individual student alphabet charts as children sing the Alphabet Song with their classmates (see Figure 44). This daily activity enables children to follow along, matching each name to its corresponding symbol as they sing. This activity offers the repetitive practice that many children enjoy and require to take on new learning.

• **Figure 44** •
Preschoolers Sing the Alphabet Song While Using Alphabet Charts to Practice One-to-One Correspondence and Directionality

Knowing Letters by Sound

When children are able to link letters with their corresponding sounds, they have learned what experts refer to as the alphabetic principle. According to Burns and colleagues (1999),

> Although younger preschoolers rarely pay attention to the smallest meaningful segments (phonemes) of words, gaining an awareness of these phonemes is a more advanced aspect of phonological awareness that becomes increasingly important as school approaches, because these segments are what letters usually stand for. (p. 21)

Typically, children hear and isolate letters with continuant, or sustainable, sounds first. The sounds articulated in the letters *a, e, i, o, u, f, l, m, n, r, s, v,* and *z* are easier to sustain than the stop sounds articulated in the letters *b, c, d, g, h, j, k, p, q, t,* and *x*. (The sounds articulated in the letters *w* and *y* are considered glide sounds [Paulson et al., 2001], so they are not included in the two previous lists.) Therefore, it is easier for children to hear the continuant sounds in the word *mom* than the stop sounds in the word *bat*.

In preschool, we typically observe the skill of segmenting words into individual phonemes emerge when children are attempting to encode words in their writing journals. We encourage children to say words slowly as they listen for the individual sounds in words and record them. Many teachers provide phonics phones made from an elbow of PVC pipe to facilitate this process (see Figure 45). The children hold the phonics phones to their ears and slowly mouth and say the words that they want to record. The phone usually makes the sounds easier for children to hear.

• Figure 45 •
Ricky and Stetson Use Phonics Phones to Hear Themselves More Clearly as They Read and Sing *Five Little Ducks* (Raffi, 1999)

• Figure 46 •
Recommended Alphabet Books

Bayer, J. (1992). *A my name is Alice*. Ill. S Kellogg. New York: Dutton.

Catalanotto, P. (2002). *Matthew A.B.C.* New York: Atheneum.

Ehlert, L. (1989). *Eating the alphabet: Fruits and vegetables from A–Z*. San Diego: Harcourt.

Feelings, M.L. (1992). *Jambo means hello: Swahili alphabet book*. Ill. T. Feelings. New York: Dial.

Hague, K. (1999). *Alphabears: An ABC book*. Ill. M. Hague. New York: Henry Holt.

Isadora, R. (1987). *City seen from A to Z*. New York: William Morrow.

MacDonald, S. (Ill.). (1992). *Alphabatics*. New York: Simon & Schuster.

Martin, B., Jr., & Archambault, J. (1989). *Chicka chicka boom boom*. Ill. L. Ehlert. New York: Simon & Schuster.

Marzollo, J. (2000). *I spy little letters*. New York: Scholastic.

Marzollo, J., & Wick, W. (1998). *I spy little animals*. New York: Scholastic.

Mayer, M. (1978). *Mercer Mayer's little monsters alphabet book*. New York: Goldencraft.

Shirley, G.B. (1991). *A is for Animals*. Guilford, CT: Falcon.

ZPD groups provide a supportive setting for teaching the alphabetic principle to children who are ready. Hearing the individual sounds in words is not a standard expectation for 3- or 4-year-olds; however, a few preschool children usually are ready to begin learning this process.

In order to give children more opportunities to interact with print, we recommend that preschool teachers display a variety of alphabet books in their classrooms. Innumerable alphabet texts are available today in a variety of genres, formats, and topics that teachers may read aloud and that children will enjoy exploring independently. The list in Figure 46 offers a few suggestions.

Assessment

A preschooler's print awareness may be evaluated with the assessments mentioned in chapter 3: the Concepts About Print, Letter Identification, and Writing Vocabulary subtests from Clay's *An Observation Survey of Early Literacy Achievement* (1996); the Emerging Literacy Screening by Paulson and colleagues (2001); and the Preschool Literacy Checklist (in Appendix B, page 249). All these assessments are helpful in establishing a child's ZPD in print awareness competencies. A Preschool Outcomes Checklist is provided in Appendix B, page 241, to record and track the writing progress of each student.

Conclusion

Snow and colleagues (1998) state,

> Children who are particularly likely to have difficulty learning to read in the primary grades are those who begin school with less prior knowledge and skill in certain domains, most notably letter

knowledge, phonological sensitivity, familiarity with the basic purposes and mechanisms of reading, and language ability. (p. 137)

To ensure that all students have the experiences necessary to be successful, we recommend that preschool teachers implement the following activities in their classrooms:

- writing daily
- playing name games
- labeling play centers
- doing environmental print work
- using alphabet books
- conducting letter sorts
- creating a class alphabet chart that is meaningful to students
- displaying student names
- building a word wall

Print awareness and letter knowledge work in concert with oral language, phonological awareness, and early reading and writing behaviors to help children become strategic readers and writers. In addition, print awareness permeates all the content areas of study including social studies, science, mathematics, creative arts, music, and movement. The following chapters address each of these subjects and make links to the important literacy competencies that they require.

CHAPTER 9

Preschoolers as Problem Solvers

• • •

While observing in one of our preschool classrooms in Casper, Wyoming, we observed the opening calendar activity. It was the 11th day of February, so the children were counting all the previous days in the month. When they reached the blank square indicating the 11th day, Joseph called out, "It's eleventeenth!" The teacher responded, "You sure know a lot about numbers, Joseph. Eleven is the next number on the calendar, so we say it is February 11." Although 3-year-old Joseph is not precise, he already understands that the language of numbers typically changes with every 10 numbers.

Joseph and his classmates were exploring numbers as part of a natural daily event within the classroom. The teacher was not teaching an isolated mathematics lesson, but Joseph and the other students were being given opportunities to learn and practice new concepts in mathematics within an integrated experience. When children look at their world and explore their surroundings, they do not encounter mathematics, social studies, or science as discrete areas. Instead, they experience their environment as a whole and begin to question and explore the parts in it that interest them or that they need to know more about in order to accomplish a desired task. The school environment is the only place in which these content areas are isolated from one another. In real life, adults encounter many disciplines integrated together in their personal and professional lives, thus concepts should be connected in the everyday activities of preschoolers. Therefore, the content areas that we discuss in this chapter are linked together. We begin with a general overview of the essential components that facilitate quality teaching and learning experiences in thematic units. Later in the chapter, we discuss in greater depth the disciplines of mathematics, social studies, and science.

Choosing Thematic Studies

We use the themes of curiosity and relevance as the underpinnings for our classroom activities. First, we look to the children for guidance when determining their interests. Because Josh, Jane, and Emmanuel are always talking about trucks and all-terrain vehicles, exploring the variety of vehicles used in occupations and recreational activities would help satisfy their curiosity. Susan, Nick, and Quran have pets at home, and although Mary and Asia do not have any pets, they constantly talk about wanting pets and ask about different animals. Therefore, investigating how to take care of pets, finding out which animals make the best pets, and then adopting a classroom pet would be of great interest to them. Both thematic units are directly related to the interests of the children and how these interests apply in the children's everyday lives. Similarly, we think about what is relevant for our students. What do they encounter daily? What do they wonder about? What do they need to learn more about? For example, it is relevant for young children in San Diego, California, USA, to explore different sea life and animals and for children in Casper, Wyoming, to learn more about the mountain animals and plant life that are part of their immediate surroundings.

Student interest alone, however, cannot drive a balanced preschool curriculum. Educators need to be aware of basic concepts and skills that children need to know and understand in the areas of mathematics, social studies, and science. To create multilayered activities that involve learning in many areas across the curriculum, the skillful preschool teacher takes into consideration the children's interests, the relevance of certain topics to the children's lives, and knowledge about fundamental concepts across the developmental domains. Many U.S. states now have early childhood standards that must be met by licensed preschools; therefore, early childhood educators need to find out about their local and state requirements. In addition, discovery and exploration cannot be the only method in which children learn more about their world. Educators actually need to teach young children important early concepts through careful lesson planning, along with asking key questions and helping children clarify their thinking as it changes through participation in classroom activities.

> Educators need to be aware of basic concepts and skills that children need to know and understand in the areas of mathematics, social studies, and science.

Integrating Literacy Into Content Area Studies

In our preschool framework, the interests of the children, the relevance of information to their lives, and knowledge about basic cross-curricular concepts are integrated with good literature. We provide no separate mathematics, social studies, or science time. Investigations into the content areas are woven into reading and writing explorations as children experiment with and manipulate a variety of materials. We select literature because of its emotional impact, its reflection of how the content areas are part of everyday life, and its ability to deliver concept knowledge in a pleasurable and motivating manner. Student learning across the developmental domains occurs when teachers plan lessons based on important concepts, using a variety of teacher- and student-directed activities. Children learn in different ways, so it is essential to present the same concepts in different teaching and learning styles while providing more time for guided practice for children who need it. In any given lesson or inquiry, many opportunities exist for a variety of learning experiences across the developmental domains. Children can improve their capabilities in receptive and expressive language; early reading and writing behaviors; mathematical language and concepts; reasoning and problem solving; scientific thinking such as hypothesizing, observing, predicting, and drawing conclusions; collaborative grouping and social interaction; and confidence and self-esteem building.

Integration of early reading and writing concepts is especially critical in our preschool framework. Therefore, when a classroom is studying how seeds grow, the reading and writing components delineated in chapters 6 and 7 are used as vehicles to explore the basic concepts of life science, such as that living things need food, water, and air. For example, the teacher may use the *The Tiny Seed* (Carle, 1987) as a read-aloud early in the school day;

> **Integration of early reading and writing concepts is especially critical in our preschool framework.**

read a nonfiction Big Book about the life cycle of plants as a shared reading activity; interactively write labels of different seed types on a poster; and have children use multiple copies of *Life Cycle of a Bean* (Royston, 1998) during ZPD group time for guided practice of early print concepts such as one-to-one correspondence, locating known letters, or demonstrating appropriate directionality. Children in this preschool classroom are learning basic reading and writing concepts in tandem with other cognitive areas because the teacher has planned specific activities that incorporate language and literacy acquisition throughout the day. We cannot stress enough the necessity for thoughtful and careful lesson planning in order to maximize every opportunity for interweaving reading, writing, and language concepts into every preschool classroom activity.

Once a preschool teacher chooses appropriate themes, his or her effective preschool lessons need to include the following elements: teacher- and student-initiated activities; active child involvement; opportunities for social interaction and discussion; debriefing, processing, and clarifying activities; and the assessment and evaluation of student learning.

Teacher-Initiated, Student-Initiated, and Open-Ended Activities

Teacher-initiated activities and some explicit instruction are necessary so children learn basic concepts that will become a foundation for learning as they grow. The teacher understands what basic concepts can be learned through investigations and activities in certain areas. The teacher must decide what it is he or she wants the children to learn from a given unit or theme. The theme is most powerful when it is expressed as a generalization or "big idea" (Erickson, 1995, p. 85). For example, when children are investigating plants, the big idea can be that all plants need food, air, sun, and water to grow. Key concepts support the big idea, and key facts support the concepts. Thus, children learn more than just facts, which are certainly important but not as important as how the facts lead to children's deeper understandings about the world around them. The teacher plans the activities in which the children will investigate and learn the important facts and key concepts so that by the end of the study, the children will arrive at an understanding of the big idea.

Many opportunities exist for student choices within these lessons as children explore at the mathematics, social studies, and science centers and during group activities. Student-initiated and open-ended activities are essential for ensuring student motivation and engagement. Children should have opportunities for the free exploration of materials to create their own designs or structures, such as interlocking cubes, pattern blocks, shape beads, and geoboards (small, pronged boards to which children can attach rubber bands in different shapes). Dramatic play opportunities to emulate scientists, doctors, teachers, astronauts, and so on also are student initiated. Exploring and manipulating objects within the science or other centers encourage children to investigate independently and hypothesize about what they see and encounter in their physical world. Such investigations might include exploring objects that sink or float at the water table; using multiple containers, measuring cups, or both at the sand table; and exploring objects that have different textures. All these activities provide preschoolers with opportunities to self-regulate their exploration of materials that the teacher has provided.

Active Child Involvement

Active child involvement is an essential component that involves choosing themes and inquiries that connect with students' interests and then planning activities that engage children in a variety of materials and situations to explore, manipulate, and discover. A good place to start is with "being-there" experiences in which the class has guest speakers, field trips, and other experiences that trigger all the senses. Traditionally, these activities have taken place as the closure for a given unit of study, which reflects a very linear method of learning and instruction. We feel that it is important to immerse children in the whole experience first and then branch out into a variety of different inquiries and activities. Therefore, we begin theme units with field trips and guest speakers. Immersion in thematic units takes more than a few isolated lessons, and inquiries should last for several weeks so one lesson builds on the previous days' investigations and learning. In this forward-moving manner, the daily review of previously learned concepts builds a strong base for the concepts and learning yet to come.

Active child engagement also means having the children use materials and manipulatives; conduct experiments; make hypotheses; record with drawings or writing in their science journals; and explore the mathematics, social studies, or science centers. Young children in particular need to be actively participating in tasks, rather than passively watching and listening to others. Hands-on interactions with concrete objects engage children's interest and enthusiasm and ensure their attention to the task within an individually appropriate setting. Further, these activities enhance children's abilities to use all their senses to begin to observe, question, and make predictions about what they see and experience.

Social Interaction and Discussion

Child involvement also includes the natural social interaction and discussions that take place when children work side by side and in groups as they make their explorations. Their conversations and reactions are vital parts of the total learning experience as each child's learning builds on the knowledge and reactions of the children and the adults around him or her. The teacher is an important element in the social dynamic of learning as he or she facilitates and guides discussions in directions that will help children understand and learn the key facts and concepts that are at the basis of the experience.

Debriefing, Processing, and Clarifying Activities

Teachers are an especially important part of debriefing, processing, and clarifying discussions. Although the children in a preschool classroom may have seen and recorded quite a few phenomena in their studies, the teacher must help them pull these reactions together into a cohesive understanding. The teacher may have to help clarify students' remaining questions or misunderstandings and bring closure to the study by helping the children verbalize how the key facts and concepts lead to a greater understanding of the big idea.

Teachers can help with the debriefing, processing, and clarifying discussions best by helping children keep track of their thinking. Starting a thematic study with a chart of what children already know about a topic helps to base their inquiries in concepts with which they are familiar. It also allows teachers to correct any of the children's misconceptions. The recording of information as the study progresses—both by the children in their science journals (drawings and some writing attempts) and by the teacher on large charts and graphs—helps children see and understand their thinking more clearly. This process is part of the formal scientific method that they will encounter in later schooling. Labeling picture parts and posters with appropriate thematic vocabulary strengthens children's learning in all areas, particularly vocabulary development, and immerses them in the topic at hand. Key facts and concepts can be written on charts and then be referred to as a review preceding new learning. When walking into a preschool classroom, one should be able to tell immediately what thematic unit the children are investigating by the variety of print and visual information on the walls and throughout the classroom. Interactively created thematic charts, posters, and pictures may support children's independent writing and reading attempts. For example, during Raelene Shreve's plant study, the children interactively labeled the parts of a flower on a large butcher-paper diagram. The words *roots*, *stem*, *leaf*, *petal*, and *flower* could be detected daily in the children's language, artwork, classroom chores (watering their flowers), journal writing, and dramatic play.

> When walking into a preschool classroom, one should be able to tell immediately what thematic unit the children are investigating by the variety of print and visual information on the walls and throughout the classroom.

As we assert in our discussions in other chapters, we believe that providing opportunities to explore and discover mathematics, social studies, and science concepts is an important and essential component in developmentally appropriate and best-practice preschool teaching methods. However, we also feel that teachers need to be very skilled at intervening gently in children's play, discussions, experiments, and inquiries to help children probe for clarification and understanding, make connections between old and new learning, and deepen their questioning and thinking. These interventions need to relate to the conceptual underpinnings of each content area so children make mathematical connections when appropriate and scientific or aesthetic links at other key times. This does not mean that the teacher takes over the activity or play. Instead, he or she gently becomes part of the social interaction in order to help new learning and understandings occur.

Assessment and Evaluation of Student Learning

The assessment of thematic units is mainly conducted informally via ongoing observations and annotations. Anecdotal records are very important because they provide actual records of what a child said and did during a given activity. Teachers need to record both the actions and language of the child as much as possible to best capture his or her thinking. Students' science journals and their other drawing and writing in a learning log give teachers another picture of how children are thinking in different media. Artifacts such as paintings, structures, models, and projects can be photographed, and the photograph can be kept in the child's portfolio. Talking with children and gently probing for what new information they understand when the unit is over offer still more information as children use their expressive vocabularies to show their new learning. Developmental checklists, such as the Preschool Outcomes Checklist in Appendix B, page 241, provide a guide for teachers as they note student accomplishments and determine what to teach next. All the assessments discussed here are collected over time and evaluated by the teacher to find out what concepts each child understands and has control over and in what areas the child may still have questions or misunderstandings. All this information helps determine future instruction.

Literature Across the Curriculum

At the beginning of a theme unit, literature that supports children's existing understandings and that will help extend their thinking should be evident in the preschool classroom. Many commercially prepared Big Books written about mathematics, social studies, and science themes are available. After the class's introductory field trip or immersion experience, the teacher may read a related fiction or nonfiction Big Book to the children, and this first exposure to the book should focus on enjoying the text, understanding the story elements, and recognizing how the book is related to the present theme. Then, the next reading of the book should provide opportunities to find and discuss the content and concepts that relate to the theme. The teacher should direct students to locate and cover important vocabulary with highlighter tape. Finally, teachers and students can interactively write critical vocabulary words to label a large picture poster.

Many quality fiction and nonfiction texts that are appropriate to use with young children are now available, so several texts that correlate to the unit of study may be read aloud each day in the preschool classroom. Some nonfiction books are too long for preschool children, but others have pages with large pictures, appropriate language structures and vocabulary, and important concepts that can be read and discussed. Additional books can be placed in centers, especially the library center, for children's independent exploration, and each day the teacher can rotate which books are read aloud. Sometimes, the teacher might read aloud a small portion of a text as an introduction or conclusion to an experiment. As the thematic unit draws to a close, the teacher can continue to support the children as they review what they have learned and arrive at the big idea using questions such as the following:

- What did you observe?
- What did you notice about that?
- Why do you think that happened?
- How might that affect _____?
- What are you thinking now?
- What surprised you?
- What have you learned?
- What do you now know about _____?

This closure also needs to be illustrated and documented through a semantic map, photographs, drawings, murals, or charts and celebrated as children realize how their thinking changed and new understanding grew throughout their study. Then, the class's illustrations are available to compare and contrast with graphics from other studies so children can create even larger generalizations based on what they learned over the course of several months.

Essential Elements of Cross-Curricular Integration

We believe that the following basic elements are necessary in order to have successful thematic units in preschool:

- selection of a theme based on student interest; relevance to real life; and students' cognitive, social, emotional, and physical needs
- careful planning of a key generalization with supporting concepts and facts
- active child engagement with manipulatives, experiments, and investigations
- immersion activities such as field trips, guest speakers, and real-life situations
- careful planning and integration of literacy acquisition activities
- social interaction and discussion opportunities
- records on large charts of student thinking, questions, and knowledge
- children's observations drawn or written in a journal
- creation of charts, posters, pictures, graphs, and labels with thematic vocabulary
- use of correct terms and vocabulary
- immersion of the classroom in thematic print, texts, pictures, and artifacts
- teacher facilitation of discussions to process and clarify information and to encourage divergent thinking
- ongoing student assessment and evaluation that informs instruction

Elements of the Preschool Day

Opening and Calendar Time

Traditionally, the first whole-class activity in preschools is an opening during which everyone is greeted and procedures such as taking attendance, doing the milk count, saying the pledge of allegiance to the U.S. flag, and making announcements are begun. When combined with calendar activities, there are many opportunities during this time for teachers to reinforce mathematics, social studies, and science concepts that also are being taught at other times during the day. This period can be fun and lively if each activity transitions fairly quickly into the next one. There is a definite routine that children learn as they take turns being the one who helps the teacher with manipulating some of the materials. Because children do these routines every day, the activities help them with memorizing by rote the days of the week and the months and seasons of the year; learning how to count by ones; recognizing numbers; describing and monitoring the weather; remembering birthdays; understanding the concepts of yesterday, today, and tomorrow; learning a variety of songs and chants; and manipulating materials. Effective teachers make wise use of this time by using each activity to teach several things. For example, children can select the next date that goes on the calendar by pointing to the previous dates, counting them aloud, and finally saying the new date. When the children find the correct date, the teacher can have the class look at the patterns and colors on the number date cards (e.g., day 1 is red and 2 is blue), and then the children move on to the next activity.

Many activities can be included in the opening session each day, so it is smart to vary the activities a little so the children do not become bored and attend better to the few small changes that occur. For example, the weather does not have to be discussed at length, but when there is a significant change in it, that is a time to focus the children's attention on it. Also, the whole calendar activity does not need to be completed in one sitting. Some items, such as noting the weather or saying the days of the week or months of the year, may be done as children line up for outdoor play or while some children are finishing their cleanup at centers or tables.

Circle Time and Community Building

In circle time, children get to know one another better by sharing information about themselves and their families, and they begin to build a sense of trust and of belonging to a group. During this time, the teacher can share the day's agenda so the children will know exactly what will be happening that day. The teacher can highlight current class themes through movement activities and relevant songs, which are imperative for keeping children engaged and on task at this time of the day. In addition, the teacher and the children can discuss and resolve any problems and conflicts. A sense of community needs to be built among the members of any group, and preschoolers will benefit from the sense of security, safety, and power that being an active group member brings. These circle times are necessarily short to hold the interest and attention of the children, but they should be a daily occurrence.

Mathematics

Mathematics in preschool involves giving children opportunities to manipulate and explore concrete objects that will help them understand basic mathematical operations and concepts (see Figure 47 for a mathematics manipulative center). While building their knowledge and understanding with three-dimensional objects, children learn during these explorations to think in mathematical terms, reason and solve problems, recognize the patterns and relationships inherent in mathematics, and construct a knowledge base for further thinking and learning. We provide these explorations as listed in the Preschool Curriculum Framework and as they appear in the Preschool Outcomes Checklist (in Appendix B, pages 235 and 241, respectively) under the following headings: Exploration; Matching, Sorting, and Patterns; Number and Numeration; Mathematical Language; Time; Measurement; Shapes; and Colors. We briefly discuss each area in the remainder of the chapter, in addition to discussing mathematics centers and linking computers and literacy.

Exploration. Exploration is a fine starting point for all of these mathematical concepts. Children are natural investigators and questioners, and they love to manipulate a variety of materials. The preschool classroom should be stocked with a variety of colorful and sturdy materials that will entice children to explore and use them in many different ways. Some beginning materials include pattern and shape blocks, chain links or interlinking cubes, beads, counters, puzzles, and building blocks. Families also can contribute everyday items that are great for exploration as well

• Figure 47 •
Ricky, Shawn, and Jordan Make "Real" Graphs With Conversation Hearts

as sorting and classifying. These items might include jar lids, buttons, keys, 1-inch tiles in different colors, poker chips, game pieces, measuring items, and clothespins. However, children need to explore more than materials. They need to explore the mathematical concepts themselves, and that happens through the provision of quality materials and learning opportunities. Exploration also means reasoning through a mathematics situation and beginning to develop some problem-solving skills by using mathematical strategies such as pointing to each object while counting and putting similar items together in a group.

Matching, Sorting, and Patterning. In these activities, children use visual skills as they match and sort objects by their physical appearance. More complex thinking takes place when children begin to classify objects by categories other than for what purpose they are used. Ordering is a basic skill in which children put objects in a certain sequence based on physical characteristics such as size or color. For example, a child may arrange cars in a line from the smallest to the largest. In patterning, there is a hierarchy for the difficulties in patterning activities. From easiest to most difficult, the activities are as follows: locating a pattern, finding the same pattern, copying a pattern, extending a pattern, and creating a pattern. Children do not necessarily go through all these stages in order as they become more skilled. However, it is important for preschool teachers to know the typical sequence of skills so they can tailor instruction to individual student needs.

Number and Numeration. There are many important concepts to be explored and learned in numeration as children learn to count, learn what number means, make groups of items that match a given number, demonstrate one-to-one correspondence and conservation of number, and attach the correct numerals to groups of objects. These complex skills will take children quite some time and many concrete experiences to master.

Mathematical Language. Mathematical language involves understanding and using correctly terms such as *more, most, less, least, big, little, short, tall, beside, above, below,* and *between*. Teachers need to use this language with preschool children as they explore materials across all curricular areas. With careful teacher questioning and prompting, children will understand these terms and be more capable of using them independently. Mathematical language also will help students understand more mathematical concepts.

Time and Measurement. Time and measurement go hand in hand as children begin to think about the sequence of days and nights and understand basic calendar and seasonal timetables. Understanding time is a way of measuring and sequencing it. Order and sequence are essential in any type of measurement, which preschoolers begin to realize as they explore a variety of measuring experiences that include size, length, width, weight, and volume. Children become comfortable with using standard measuring tools such as rulers, measuring cups, and spoons after many explorations using nonstandard measuring tools such as hands, feet, and pencils. They can successfully make their first attempts at estimating length, weight, and volume by starting with small amounts or quantities.

Using charts, graphs, and simple maps helps children learn measurement concepts through collecting and charting data and then correctly interpreting them. Graphs or charts made from real objects are excellent to start with because three-dimensional items make understanding the graphs easier for children. For example, one preschool teacher created an authentic graph with the children's shoes. She had each child remove a shoe and place it in the appropriate section of a large strip of butcher paper. The children sorted their shoes by sneakers, slip-ons, boots, tie shoes, and shoes with buckles or Velcro. After discussing which column had the most, least, or same number of shoes, the children drew their own graphs. There is no limit to the number of relevant graphs preschoolers can create. They can graph desserts that they like, favorite colors, favorite games and sports, pets, number of siblings, family vehicles, people who wear glasses or not, types of hats, favorite snacks, and so on. After many experiences with real graphs, children will become familiar with representational graphs. Reading charts and graphs gives children opportunities to count, compare, problem solve, and use mathematical language that connects to real-life situations.

Shapes and Colors. Shapes are an important part of beginning investigations into geometry and visual-spatial relationships and forms. Children need experience in sorting and classifying three-dimensional shapes and then replicating them on paper with crayons, markers, or other materials such as yarn, macaroni, or toothpicks. Creating with different media their own forms or shapes with curves, straight and slanted lines, and corners gives children the opportunity to learn while placing items on a page and spatially arranging materials. Many preschoolers explore shapes with tangrams (multishaped wooden or plastic blocks) and geoboards. This competency also may be connected to literacy learning because in both activities children must attend to the intricate features of varied shapes, symbols, and forms. Asking children to sort letters with sticks, circles, or triangles is a simple way to integrate these areas.

Preschoolers can explore and learn colors in numerous settings. Read-alouds and shared readings of books such as *Mary Wore Her Red Dress, and Henry Wore His Green Sneakers* (Peek, 1985) or *Brown Bear, Brown Bear, What Do You See?* (Martin, 1983) allow children to view multiple colors in texts. Learning centers can incorporate activities such as sorting objects by color, creating patterns with colors, blending and creating new colors with paints, sharing colors during small-group show and tell, and connecting foods to colors. Color has a great impact on a child's world, so this concept can be integrated easily into the preschool day.

Mathematics Centers. A well-equipped mathematics center is necessary for ensuring fun and informative mathematics exploration, play, and learning for preschoolers. Although mathematics is integrated into all curricular areas, there needs to be one place to hold and organize mathematics materials. Organization is key so children can easily use the materials and just as easily clean up, returning materials to their containers. The mathematics center should be located where it is easily accessed but not in the middle of a key traffic pattern in the room. Posters, print, and pictures should be displayed as should graphs, charts, and a number line from 1 to 100. Small number lines from 1 to 20 need to be available for children to have in front of them if necessary. Teachers should make it easy for children to sit at a table or work at a counter but still be able to use floor space to spread out materials when necessary. Counting, shape, and color books, and paper, markers, pencils, and crayons need to be part of the center because children may want to record their work or use the materials as part of their manipulations.

Mathematics centers can be designed to provide both free-exploration opportunities and specific activities to focus student learning on a particular outcome. A mathematics center in Raelene's preschool integrated insect study and the concept of addition. The children each had ladybug templates on which they added manipulative spots. The children put a certain number of spots on one side of the ladybug's thorax and a different number on the other side. Then, they added the numbers together. As we observed, the children were manipulating and counting aloud the ladybug spots. It was a fun and engaging activity for the children.

Computers. Computers provide another modality for reinforcing mathematics, social studies, and science skills in addition to reading and writing concepts. Computer skills and competencies are essential in modern society. Preschoolers can and should have opportunities to learn and explore the basics of computer technology (see Figure 48). Kid Pix Studio Deluxe from Riverdeep (www.riverdeep.net) is the program of choice in many of our preschool centers. There are so many different activities on this one program that many of our classrooms use it extensively.

• **Figure 48** •
Ben and Christian Use Computers to Create Abstract Designs

Children not only explore multiple content areas, but they also internalize computer terms such as *monitor, mouse, keyboard, disk,* and *printer.*

Mathematics and Literature. Selecting appropriate texts for whole-class read-alouds that accompany or enhance mathematics investigations is not a haphazard task; preschool teachers need to consider carefully the selection of key learning points for early literacy and math concepts. Skilled teachers go beyond choosing books that have numbers and opportunities for counting in them. Instead, they look for books that highlight mathematical situations and thinking or that explain or demonstrate concepts in a clear and understandable fashion. Simple counting books can be placed in the mathematics or library centers and read by children individually, so it is easier to use them for reinforcement of counting or learning numerals. These books can be board books and simple concept books, and teachers also should provide color, shape, and number books. The books that highlight mathematical situations can be used during the opening activity to a mathematics lesson or to summarize what has just been learned.

Author Tana Hoban has many wonderful books that are appropriate for preschoolers and that focus on mathematical concepts in all developmental areas. We also have discovered MathStart books written by Stuart Murphy for three age levels. The ones for preschoolers are categorized as Level 1 and are geared for children ages 3 and up. Each story incorporates a mathematics concept and additional activities, and recommended book titles are given at the end. The concepts covered in Murphy's books include patterns, size and amount comparisons, shapes, odd and even numbers, matching sets, ordinals, and sequencing. Some of the books are somewhat difficult, so teachers should choose the ones best suited to their own students.

See Appendix E, pages 274–277, for an annotated list of mathematics texts to use with young children.

Assessment. Mathematics pervades the preschool classroom and is present in some form or other in almost every activity that occurs. It is easy to integrate mathematics concepts into any activity or lesson that a preschool teacher prepares. Teachers should be thoughtful and creative and make wise use of opportunities to count; predict; find shapes, colors, and patterns; categorize; measure; and use mathematical language at appropriate times (see Figure 49). What is more difficult is knowing where each student's ZPD is in relation to each mathematic concept and building on that knowledge to help a child move on to the next important learning stage. Careful observation and use of checklists for mathematical concepts will help to record student growth. Materials selected from student work in centers, learning logs, and drawings and writing should be copied or kept in a student portfolio to share periodically with families and to study and use for future lesson planning. The Preschool Outcomes Checklist provided in Appendix B, page 241, addresses each mathematical competency discussed in this chapter. For further information, see the Preschool and Kindergarten Mathematics Checklist in Appendix B, page 252. These checklists are only recommendations, however, and we urge educators to inquire about their local or state standards for specific information.

• Figure 49 •
Forrest, Shawn, Ethan, and Logan Sort and Classify

Social Studies

We believe that social studies in the preschool curriculum revolves around the young child and his or her place in the family, preschool, and local community, including the essential understandings of how these units are interrelated. Children learn about families and family relationships and responsibilities, citizenship responsibilities in school and the local community, how local community members' work and play affects the community, and finally how these understandings connect to the lives and relationships of people in other communities. Through thematic units in social studies, children need to learn some basic big ideas that are at the core of units such as friends, jobs, and families. These big ideas focus on the following concepts:

- People are different and alike.
- People need food and shelter.
- Families are made up of people who love and depend on one another.
- Being a good citizen and classmate is important.
- Rules or procedures help everyone in a community.
- The child's town is special.

Children need opportunities to discover the similarities and differences among themselves as classmates. That is why self-discovery units are so prevalent in preschools when the school year begins. This type of observation and comparison is necessary because it leads to the preschoolers' awareness that although each child is unique in many ways, all classmates have many similarities, too. In turn, this awareness builds in each child a sense of trust and belonging. As children understand what it means to be good citizens in the classroom and responsible members of a family unit, making connections to good citizenship and community responsibilities naturally follows. Therefore, the teacher helps the children understand that people have a web of connections within their families and communities. An effective unit of study in this area may have a direct impact on the social and emotional development of each preschool child.

As preschoolers begin to understand that children and people in other places have similar wants and needs, they learn to appreciate the diversity that is evident among peoples and cultures. Finding out more about other peoples and cultures within the local or wider community can be fostered through activities that explore art, music, movement, and literature. Children also need to be able to locate their own homes in relation to familiar landmarks within their community and begin to develop a sense of where that community is within their state. A beginning point for this understanding is to create activities that have children locate items within the classroom by following certain directions such as above, below, near, far, between, and beside. Discussions about places within the community such as what store is nearest to school and how long it takes to drive to Grandma's house help students learn more about their community and locate themselves within it. Teachers should have a globe, a state map, and a community map handy for these activities. The use of these items, in addition to geographical terms such as *near*, *far*, *north*, and *south*, will expand the children's receptive vocabulary and introduce them to the underlying concepts of distance, proximity, and geography.

The essential elements of planning and providing instruction for thematic units in social studies are discussed in the beginning of this chapter. However, we want to reiterate that all these components are important for high-quality teaching and learning in social studies. Field trips and guest speakers are especially key in this area because some children may not have had opportunities to visit many places in the community. Students who have been to the field trip locations previously can deepen their knowledge by experiencing the environment while being guided by an expert teacher. Almost any place in a community can be a destination if it is connected to the key concepts and big ideas that are the focus for class activities. In addition, parents and family members can serve as guest speakers to share information about their occupations and hobbies.

Common social studies themes for preschoolers are self-discovery, community helpers, diversity and commonality, families, friends, nutrition, places in the community, and safety. See Appendix E, pages 277–282, for suggested texts to use with these thematic units.

Science

Children are natural-born scientists. They love to explore, discover, and ask questions about what they see around them. Preschool science activities capitalize on this innate curiosity and inquisitiveness by focusing on real things children will encounter in their daily lives. This means investigating three areas of science: life, earth, and physical science. Preschoolers are interested in topics in each of these areas, and it is vital to plan and carry out inquiries and lessons that use hands-on activities, real-life experiences, and guest speakers. Within these areas of science, children will try to answer some of their own questions; therefore, they will begin to use the scientific method of making a hypothesis and proving or disproving it. Scientific terms and problem-solving strategies will become authentic parts of children's activities and discussions, giving them opportunities to hear and learn scientific language and skills.

Again, the inquiries need to focus on big ideas or generalizations that children will learn through participation in thematic activities. The big ideas need to be well planned, with supporting facts and concepts, and be related to the preschoolers' everyday lives. When investigating these generalizations, children must be able to interact with materials that will allow them to observe, question, describe, record, theorize, and draw conclusions. That is why common preschool science themes include animals; construction, machines, and vehicles; earth, water, and air; the human body and health; plants; weather and the seasons; and the ways that things move (see Appendix E, pages 282–289, for suggested texts to use with these thematic units in science). The big ideas that are conveyed through these themes are important for preschoolers to learn and relevant to their lives. In addition, hands-on explorations are possible within these areas.

Life science involves discovering the characteristics of things that are alive and not alive (see Figure 50), learning about the basic needs of living things, and understanding how these

• Figure 50 •
Preschoolers Study Ladybugs

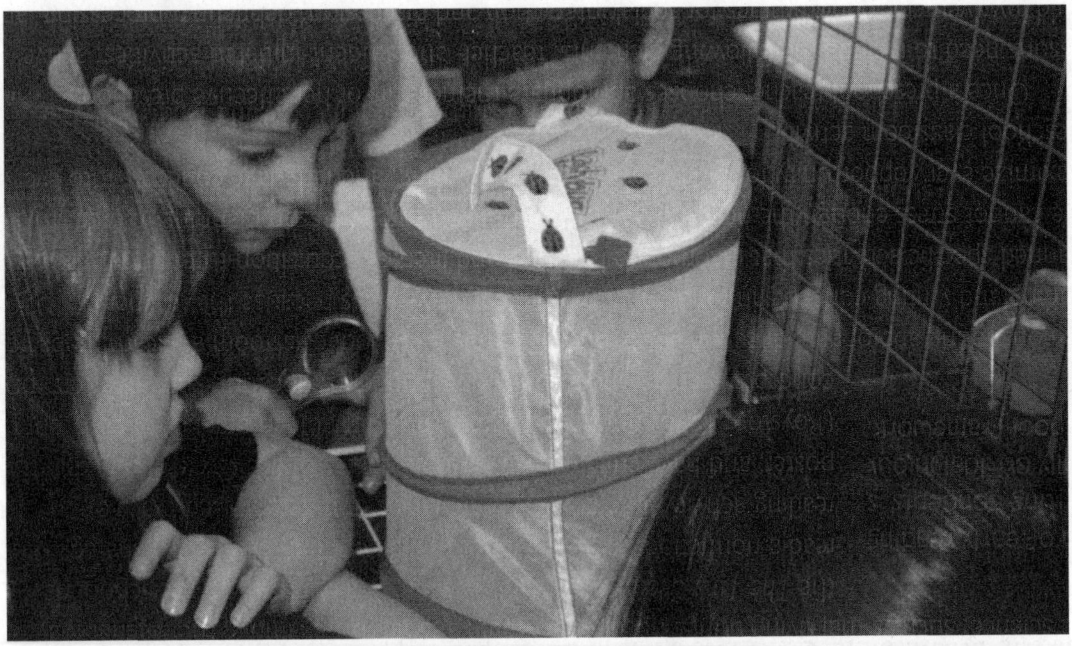

concepts are related. Earth science explores the earth, water, and air to find similarities and differences and weather changes and patterns. Physical science examines the characteristics of objects through sorting and classifying by different attributes. The science center provides many opportunities for children to explore and investigate concepts in these three areas. The science theme at any given time will be reflected in the materials provided, so materials will change as the type of science and theme changes. Basic materials for science areas include blank paper; pencils, crayons, and markers; rulers; measuring cups; droppers; string; paper plates and cups; plastic spoons and forks; recycled and clear plastic containers in various sizes; smocks; magnifying lenses; pitchers; straws; seeds; soil; objects that float and sink; magnets; thermometers; flashlights; and cleaning materials such as a small broom, rags, and paper towels.

Science learning always is enhanced with "being there" experiences. The following list offers a few field trip suggestions that are available in many communities:

Zoo	Petting zoo	Farm
Grocery or supermarket	Hospital	Bank
Garden center	Art museum	Post office
Children's museum	Science museum	Newspaper offices
Police station	Cafeteria	Hardware store
Forest preserve or park	Bakery	Airport
Train station	Port or harbor	Concerts
Library	Dairy farm	Animal shelter
Construction site	Factory	Television station

Assessment

An important first step in assessment is to check your local or state preschool requirements for standards and outcomes. If there are no set standards, find out your local kindergarten outcomes and select themes and topics that will provide introductory activities in the same areas. As in other areas of the preschool, making anecdotal records, creating and using checklists, and collecting and photocopying student work samples and artifacts to include in a portfolio are critical to demonstrating a child's knowledge of basic social studies and science concepts. Once again, the Preschool Outcomes Checklist in Appendix B, page 241, highlights each science expectation noted in this chapter. Teachers may use this checklist to document children's growth and determine competencies yet to be explored.

Conclusion

We do not provide specific lesson plans or units in this chapter because we believe that these activities are best designed by individual teachers who know the prior knowledge, background, interests, relevance, and capabilities of their preschoolers. We hope that the suggestions we have made will provide teachers with a successful framework for creating themes and inquiries that are motivating and effective for children learning fundamental mathematics, social studies, and science concepts. Additionally, these investigations provide numerous authentic opportunities for development and growth across all the developmental domains. However, more specifically, mathematics, social studies, and science themes offer endless possibilities for literacy and content learning. Children are genuinely curious and will eagerly follow the lead of an enthusiastic, inquisitive teacher who will help them to investigate the questions that they have about the world around them. Therefore, effective teachers plan lessons and activities that offer children more knowledge about content areas in addition to literacy and language acquisition.

In this and previous chapters, we focus on teaching and learning in several important cognitive areas. However, growth and development in arts and the physical domain also are critical for the preschool child. We continue our study of the content areas with the arts, music, and movement in chapter 10 and the study of physical development in chapter 11. Development in these areas is essential for children to experience and expand their natural abilities in self-expression and creativity. These content area studies provide additional opportunities for children to explore their own innate talents and their ideas of how these disciplines support their literacy understandings.

CHAPTER 10

Linking Literacy and the Arts

• • •

All the students in one of our western Wyoming preschools speak English as a second language. Claire taught a read-aloud lesson to the class one day with *Little Rabbit Foo Foo* (Rosen, 1990). After introducing the book and setting a purpose for listening, she read the book aloud, and despite the language barrier, her dramatic reading and enthusiasm—coupled with the texts' illustrations—conveyed the meaning of the story. Claire read aloud the book a second time, modeling for the children appropriate hand gestures to help support their comprehension and vocabulary development, in addition to actively engaging them. By the third time through the story, the children were keeping up with the hand gestures and story line. As the final event, Claire added a melody to the story's words and sang the lyrics while the children stood up, moved to the beat, made appropriate hand gestures, and had a great time.

This vignette demonstrates how music, movement, and the creative arts can cross language barriers to engage student interest while communicating the central theme of a text. The use of artistic illustrations and children's movements of their hands and bodies to a catchy melody exhibits how multimodal strategies can enhance early literacy learning. In this chapter, we describe how to integrate music, movement, and the creative arts into the daily preschool curriculum.

Music always seems to have the ability to evoke some type of response or participation from people of all ages and cultures. Therefore, it is not by accident that music, movement, and the creative arts are discussed together in this chapter. They are linked by commonalities of appreciation, enjoyment, free expression, discovery, engagement, and uniqueness. There is little that is right or wrong when children participate in activities in these essential areas. Rather, young children have opportunities to express their own individuality and imagination more fully and take pleasure in the very acts of creation (see Figure 51). In these developmental areas, the end product is not as important as the participation in the creative event. Preschoolers are inhibited only by the depth and breadth of their own imaginations and the knowledge and skill of their preschool teachers in providing opportunities for children's originality to be expressed.

• Figure 51 •
Sammy Creates a Painting of Her Own

Music, movement, and the creative arts also are connected because they provoke strong emotions, especially in young children. When participating in activities in these areas, children activate both the right and left sides of the brain, stimulating and expanding all the brain's cognitive, social, and emotional regions. Therefore, it follows that not only will young children freely enjoy and participate in activities that evoke strong feelings, but they also will remember and learn from these activities. Brain research confirms what teachers of young children have always known: "that our brain may be designed for music and arts, and music and arts education has positive, measureable, and lasting academic and social benefits" (Jensen, 1998, p. 36).

According to Jensen (1998), "A strong art foundation builds creativity, concentration, problem-solving, self-efficacy, coordination, and values attention, and self-discipline" (p. 36). The creative arts have a significant place in a preschool framework for several reasons. First and foremost is the core role that all the arts play in the aesthetic development of every child. The active engagement and enjoyment of children as they participate in any visual and performing art activity is valued in itself, although it also may lead to further appreciation and knowledge of the beauty inherent in the wide spectrum of artistic creations. Children live in the moment of their participation and interpret their reactions and emotions through movement, song, or other artistic responses. Recent discussions in early childhood circles have focused on the necessity for more opportunities for preschoolers to develop an understanding and appreciation of art (Epstein, 2001). Preschoolers are not too young to begin to use appropriate language to describe what they see and do in their own artistic work and observe in the work of others. Modeling specific descriptive language will widen preschoolers' receptive and expressive vocabularies while deepening their understanding of the concepts that are portrayed in the art itself. Educators need to help children develop an appreciation of the arts and the vital role that they play in children's lives and environments. Children should learn how their world is brightened and enriched by the broad diversity of art forms.

Second, music and movement easily lend themselves to transition times during the preschool day. Preschool teachers change activities quickly to hold the attention of their students, and music and chants help to signal that changes will take place. They prepare the children's minds and bodies for new activities and new demands for attention. They also are an important part of routines that provide a safe structure and a nonthreatening environment for young children away from their families. Children feel more comfortable when they begin to recognize a routine and realize that the same thing happens in the same way every day for some parts of the school day. For example, in one preschool, the children know that first thing every morning, they will get their personal book boxes and "pretend read" until they hear the teacher start the welcome song. Then, they put the book boxes away and head for the circle meeting place. These times of routine and structure reassure each child that there is a certain amount of predictability each day. However, these times also enable children to be more confident in taking risks at other times when there is a new activity or a new person in the classroom. For example, preschools with preestablished routines and procedures allow children to feel more comfortable and less threatened when there is a guest or substitute teacher in the classroom.

> • • • • • • • • • • • • • • • • • •
> Music and movement easily lend themselves to transition times during the preschool day.
> • • • • • • • • • • • • • • • • •

There is probably a song for every routine in the preschool day and many versions of each song. Preschool teachers should find ones that they like and that their students find easy to learn and sing. However, learning a new routine song often can be fun and challenging for all. Common routine songs include ones for welcoming or saying "good morning;" naming the days of the week or the months or seasons of the year; and noting the time to clean up, get into a circle, do show and tell, listen, or go home.

Fast music with a strong beat will help children change to an activity that involves moving their body, possibly around the room. Use this type of music before going outside to play, doing gross motor activities, playing organized games, or singing and dancing. Slow music, especially instrumental music, will transition children to slower-paced activities that require more of their active attention and listening skills, such as participating in read-alouds, listening to guest speakers, working in ZPD groups, and going to learning centers. (See Appendix E, pages 289–292, for a list of music and movement resources.)

Finding and selecting good music for transition times is not difficult. There are many teacher-created songs that have original lyrics set to well-known melodies that are conveyed by word of mouth whenever teachers gather together. One example is singing a song about the days of the week to the tune of "Frère Jacques." Children's music artists in the United States and Canada, such as Hap Palmer, Greg and Steve, Raffi, and Red Grammer, have created their own routine songs. The only difficult thing about discovering new songs is finding the time to scan teacher education catalogs or visit retail stores that carry a wide selection of children's music.

Third, all the creative arts have a powerful and effective link to literacy acquisition and learning in other curricular areas. When children are developing their musical capabilities, they also are strengthening their cognitive, social, emotional, and physical domains. The active engagement and interest of the children as they participate in musical activities help to trigger new learning or cement their mastery of other concepts while also being fun and memorable. Jensen (1996) states that

> music activates more than the right brain. It elicits emotional responses, receptive or aggressive states, and stimulates the limbic system. The limbic system and subcortical region are involved in engaging musical and emotional responses. But more importantly, research has documented the limbic part of the brain is responsible for long-term memory. This means that when information is imbued with music there's a greater likelihood that the brain will encode it in long-term memory. (p. 218)

Although we will present music, movement, and the creative arts separately in the following sections, children participate in them as part of an integrated experience.

Music

Singing and listening to songs are two of the most pleasurable experiences for people of all ages but especially for young children. Preschoolers are not self-conscious about their singing voices, and they love to sing along with anyone. Songs combine the ingredients of catchy melodies, strong rhythms, and memorable lyrics in a unique manner to invite even the most reluctant listener to take part in singing. Most children also become adept at creating and singing their own impromptu melodies and lyrics as they engage in dramatic play or wander around the classroom. Simple songs, chants, and finger plays that are set to music are engaging for all preschool students and need to be a natural part of the school day. Using student names in songs is sure to produce giggles, laughs, and a lot of fun. Echo singing can be a fun and effective way to help children remember tricky lyrics or melodies, and it adds a different dimension to singing activities.

The following suggestions will help teachers create musical experiences that children will enjoy while feeling comfortable with expressing themselves in different ways:

- Use music throughout the day and across the curriculum.
- Choose music from a variety of genres—instrumental, big band, folk, rock, country, jazz, and multicultural.
- Listen to lyrics before using new songs to ensure that they are free of stereotypes, biases, and inappropriate language.

- Use music and instruments from the different cultures of your students.
- Select songs that allow children to interpret and direct their own responses.
- Offer opportunities for children to listen quietly to music for short periods.
- Invite guests to demonstrate different musical instruments.
- Provide children with a variety of musical instruments for their use in open-ended activities.
- Share with your students your own childhood and adult experiences with music.
- Attend short musical performances given by older children or at community cultural events that are targeted at young children.
- Model appropriate appreciation of musical performances, and encourage the children to share their favorable reactions.
- Model the fun and enjoyment of singing, and do not worry about a less-than-perfect voice.
- Model and encourage the use of appropriate musical vocabulary such as *fast, slow, loud, soft, rhythm, steady beat, melody, long, short, high,* and *low.*

Movement

Young dancers who will become gifted performing artists later in life are often "born" within the confines of a preschool classroom if provided opportunities to respond to different rhythms and genres of music in spontaneous and individual ways. The beat and rhythm that are inherent in music pull in the young listeners as they hear and "feel" the beat and then move their bodies in time to its cadence (see Figure 52). Even adults find it difficult to sit still when listening to lively music. Children automatically respond to what they hear with their whole bodies. Once again, preschools need to offer a variety of activities that will foster balance, coordination, and an exploration of the variety of ways children can move their body and its parts.

Because children move naturally and automatically in response to music, they do not need to be taught how to move. However, they do need the support of a teacher who values their individual responses and encourages experimentation of expression by saying things such as "How many different ways can we move to this music?" Children often will provide their own spontaneous movement responses during a given day, but there should be planned activities within the preschool week so children are ensured of participating regularly in a variety of movement activities. The following suggestions will help teachers in planning these activities:

- Model appropriate behavior, and set the limits for where children may move within the classroom.
- Model how to create personal space by having children extend their arms from their sides, making sure that they cannot touch anything or anyone. Then, they can move safely within the area designated by their arms.
- Teach children how to freeze when the music stops or the volume lowers.

• Figure 52 •
Logan, Ricky, Chandler, and Jackie Dance

- Children will watch others and may copy their movements, so encourage them to try new ways of moving.
- Use a variety of props such as scarves, streamers, long pieces of yarn, pompoms with handles (not sticks), and ribbon sticks.
- Be aware of safety concerns both in areas of movement and the use of props.
- Select music with a variety of tempos and from various genres for movement activities.
- Keep musical instruments handy so children can use them as part of their movements.
- Create your own musical instruments from everyday items, and encourage children to use them to create their own sounds and movements.
- Balance your selection of movement music so children can explore free expression activities in addition to following the directions of the song lyrics.

- Children will be energized and excited following most movement activities. Help them to wind down by using slower music or turning down the volume to bring closure to the activity.

- Model and encourage the use of appropriate vocabulary connected to movements such as *march, dance, wave, skip, hop, gallop, sway, step-hop, step-touch, side to side, shimmy, shake, twist, over, under, between,* and *around.*

- Find videos of short dance or movement performances for children to watch, and then discuss their responses to the videos. Help children begin to appreciate the beauty in making their bodies move in certain ways and in watching others by modeling your reactions and using appropriate nonjudgmental language.

Creative Arts

The creative arts also are essential in a quality preschool. Children demonstrate free expression and creativity as they explore and manipulate a variety of art media, and, again, they take pleasure in the creative act itself. As children become more experienced with using different art media, their products and how their art looks become more important to them. The teacher, however, should always target the process. Preschoolers love to try new materials and experiment with how they can use their hands or other tools to make the material look different (see Figure 53). They can begin to dabble in the area of art appreciation with gentle guidance and careful language prompts when admiring the work of others, whether it is the illustrations in a picture book or finger paintings created by their classmates.

Art activities should be open-ended for the young child. Art is the expression of one's individuality and unique view of the world, so generic coloring pages and drawings are not recommended. Preschoolers like to experiment with, discover, and use art media in unusual ways, and their curiosity needs to be supported and encouraged. This goal is accomplished by planning activities and providing materials that will give children opportunities for self-expression and exploration. The following tips are helpful for teachers planning art activities:

- Do not show a teacher-made model of a specific art project. A model is not necessary in open-ended art projects.

- When children ask for help in creating something, reassure them that whatever they produce will be acceptable.

- Provide a variety of media for children to use both at the art center and in an exploration in which the class is participating.

- Ask children if you can keep their work to display it or if they prefer to take it home. After all, the art belongs to the child, not the teacher or the class.

- Model procedures for how to use the materials appropriately, such as using one brush for each color of paint at the easel or keeping the Play-Doh on the mat at the clay area. Model cleanup procedures.

• Figure 53 •
Robby and Stetson Make Play-Doh Sculptures While Jackie and Jordan Paint

- Provide smocks or paint shirts to protect children's clothing.

- Comment on the colors or choice of strokes in painting, and encourage the child to tell you about his or her artwork.

- Accept how each child chooses to represent a real-life object, such as a green cow or a blue apple.

- Try to use some materials that are recycled such as coffee and margarine containers or Styrofoam trays.

- Model and encourage the use of art vocabulary such as *line, form, thick, thin, shape, curved, straight, light, dark, bright, vivid, bold, subtle, pale, big, large, little,* and *tiny.*

- Encourage children to find the "art" in everyday objects and surroundings. Have them look for shapes, lines, forms, patterns, and different tones or shades of one color within their preschool or the surrounding neighborhood. Take the children on a walk to look for shapes, forms, and patterns. Take close-up photographs of what the children find and hang the photographs in the classroom. Have children re-create the pictures using a variety of media. This activity helps children see the beauty that surrounds them and helps them become more observant of, reflective on, and appreciative of the world.

- Model and encourage the use of language that describes rather than judges children's own art and the art of others. Ask for their emotional reactions or what they see rather than what they like.
- Remember that art involves the whole child—emotions, social interaction, language, perception, problem-solving skills, gross and fine motor movements, cognitive areas, and representational thinking. Therefore, art can tell us much about individual children.

Basic art concepts that are appropriate for preschoolers to explore include geometric and free-form shapes, line varieties (straight, curved, diagonal, and spiral), colors, patterns, and textures. Children also should explore different art media such as paints, colored pencils, markers, crayons, chalk, glue, paper, clay or Play-doh, and recycled materials. There are a wide variety of each of these items; for example, paints exist in watercolor, tempera, and finger-painting varieties, which provide countless different art experiences for preschoolers.

Numerous books about the arts are available and appropriate for young children. Titles particularly relevant to the creative arts are listed in Appendix E, pages 292–294.

Literacy and Curriculum Links

Good music always will catch and keep the interest of young children. When quality music is linked to cognitive learning, the impact of the musical experience becomes much greater as it expands a child's growth and development into broader arenas. Singing and listening to songs capture in a motivating and enjoyable way the many cognitive, social, emotional, and physical concepts that children must develop in their early years. These concepts expand children's capabilities in the following curricular areas:

Language
- Expressive and receptive vocabulary
- Phonological awareness
- Functions of written language
- Language structures

Mathematics
- Numbers and counting
- Patterns and sorting
- Measurement of time and space

Social and Emotional
- Self-discovery
- Feelings
- Getting along with others
- Self-esteem

Creative Arts
- Dramatic play—visual and performing arts

Reading and Writing
- Enjoyment and appreciation of literature
- Understanding early concepts of print
- Understanding book language
- Book knowledge

Social Studies and Science
- Home, school, and community
- Children's environment
- Thematic units

Physical
- Gross motor movement
- Fine motor movement
- Creative and expressive movement
- Health and safety

• Figure 54 •
Robby and Ryann Sing and Sort Letters Together

Activities that integrate music and movement into the above areas are powerful educational opportunities because they help children link familiar concepts to new learning with multiple modalities that increase the children's ability to understand and retain their new knowledge (see Figure 54). In our preschool framework, the integration of music, movement, and the arts into literacy and other curricular areas is the impetus for providing meaningful learning opportunities for children. In a short, two-and-a-half-hour day, integration is essential and developmentally appropriate for accomplishing teaching and learning throughout the various domains.

Oral Language and Phonological Awareness

Children learn simple songs and chants quite easily because they are captivated by the rhythm, beat, language structures, and vocabulary that make songs memorable and easy to learn. However, preschool classes must use a variety of song forms and melodies so each song is distinguishable and children can easily relate the song to something in their world. By hearing and singing the same words over and over, children enlarge their expressive and receptive vocabularies and begin to recognize certain characteristics of songs just as they do different types of texts. They can understand the purpose of the song based on the melody and the words; therefore, they are learning about music as well as language. Exploring language, words, and how they fit together increases children's awareness and use of more sophisticated language structures.

Preschool teacher Marti Derringer's students in Rock River, Wyoming, used music, movement, and creative art to perform the teacher-made story *Five Little Speckled Frogs* for their schoolwide arts festival. The children practiced the song with a song chart and acted it out with child-made props. They created the pond with blue butcher paper and painted the fish, frogs, tadpoles, and algae that they had studied throughout their thematic unit on frogs. The frogs' headpieces were made by using sun visors with Styrofoam balls attached for the frog's eyes. Green garbage bags with holes for each child's head and arms became the frog-body costumes. The performance was a wonderful cumulative activity for the class's three-week frog study.

Early Reading and Writing Concepts

A wealth of songs have been transposed into books for children. These books help the words in the songs come alive on the books' pages. Although oral language development and phonological awareness are key to later reading success, using texts made from songs or poems is a very powerful and engaging way to take children even further into their new education about written language. They can see how the words that they heard and sang are recorded on paper, which reveals to them how print carries a message. We use these types of materials with children in several ways.

First, we teach children a simple song, such as "The Wheels on the Bus," by singing it for them and having them sing when they can. With repetitious phrases and stanzas, the echo singing may not last long as the children learn the words fairly quickly and are able to sing along. Then, we either instruct the children in hand or body movements or allow children to individually express themselves in conjunction with the singing. In our preschool classes, we enjoy the experience of singing and then sharing what the song is about, so when children know the song well, we write the stanzas on chart paper and point to the words with a pointer as the children sing along. This activity demonstrates one-to-one correspondence, directionality concepts, and that print carries a message. We also try to involve the children actively by having them eventually come up and point to words in different stanzas with us. Other literacy teaching points with songs might involve the children locating letter or word boundaries, capital letters, periods or question marks, and spaces between words in the song. Then, we might encourage the children to make pictures in their minds about what the bus in the song looks like, who is on the bus, and what they look like. After sharing their descriptions in groups, the children can use art media to display their ideas visually.

Depending on each student's ZPD, during ZPD groups we might model finding long and short words on the chart, finding a letter as opposed to a word, locating the top of the page, and using the pointer to go down the rows. Then, we have the children try these activities. Any of the activities discussed in chapters 5 and 6 may be used with songs that are in chart or text formats if they are correctly linked to the ZPD of each child on a given task. If the song is available in a text format that is small enough for children to handle easily as individuals, we provide them each with the text. We can explore it together by discussing the illustrations, reacting to how they conveyed the song's meaning, comparing them to children's own ideas of what the bus and the people looked like, and then singing the song again as the children hold their own copy of the text. Future activities would be to read the story in a whole-class or large-group setting. The children could explore the texts individually if they were available in the library center and in children's personal book boxes for later singing and pretend reading. A class book could be created, with each child illustrating a page of the song or making innovations and changes to the text. Poems, finger plays, and chant activities follow somewhat the same procedure as songs in that they need to be known well by the group before further literacy exploration takes place. Teachers can make their own Big Books and student books of songs, poems, and chants by creating their own illustrations and formats and then laminating and binding them to preserve them. However, copyright laws prevent teachers from photocopying print or illustrations from existing books.

Another way that we use songs with our preschoolers is by creating interactive charts with sentence strips. Many such charts are commercially available and can be found in catalogs or teacher support stores. When using them, a phrase or stanza from a song is cut apart, and the teacher displays and reads the first part of it. The children use their own ideas to finish the line, usually with a rhyme, while the teacher writes it on a sentence strip. Then, everyone reads the new phrase or stanza. A common example of this activity is patterned after the stanzas in *Down by the Bay* (Raffi, 1990): "Did you ever see a _____, eating a _____?" Children love creating their own silly rhymes. After letting the children enjoy the language play, teachers can teach and reinforce early language and literacy skills with this activity.

Texts and the visuals arts also have a strong connection that can be used in the classroom. Many beautiful picture books are available that show young children the variety of images that can be used to depict thoughts, feelings, or objects in their environment. Books that support a theme, such as farming or vehicles, should be spread throughout the preschool classroom so children can investigate and explore them during the day (see Figure 55). Planned activities also are essential for children so they can talk about what they see and hear and learn new language from one another. Skillful teachers take the time to have children really look at the illustrations in the books and talk about how the illustrations represent the content and/or the ideas and feelings of the characters. Teachers need to discuss the variety of ways that authors and illustrators present written and visual information. This discussion helps children understand the layouts and formats of different texts. When they see captions under pictures, children can predict that the text is not a storybook with a beginning, middle, and an end but is a nonfiction book instead. Young children like to use grown-up language, so teachers should use the real names of things with them instead of teaching them vocabulary that will not translate well into the literacy learning that they will be doing in grade school.

> Planned activities also are essential for children so they can talk about what they see and hear and learn new language from one another.

Teachers also can teach preschool children to compare and contrast the work of different illustrators in books. For example, the children can begin to notice that Tomie dePaola creates pictures that are clearly outlined and rounded in shape and Eric Carle and Ezra Jack Keats most often use collage-style illustrations. Making these comparisons helps children understand artistic

• Figure 55 •
Kiara Reads and Sings "Old Macdonald" in the Play Center

language and concepts because contrast-and-comparison activities develop visual perception, discrimination, and oral language capabilities as the children try to find and describe differences. When children see the differences between how illustrators depict the same events or objects, they may feel more secure when their own creations look remarkably different from others in the class. Another way to teach children about illustrations is to have guest speakers briefly display their artwork or show children appropriate artistic techniques to explore, exposing the preschoolers to real-life examples of people who use art in their daily lives. As a result, some children become motivated to emulate these artists and their artistic techniques.

Preschool teachers should build their own libraries of books that connect songs, music, and the arts to literature. For example, *Water Dance* (Locker, 1997) describes the water cycle in brief, descriptive poems that are accompanied by vivid oil paintings. All the aspects of rich language, movement, music, and visual art are combined in this book. The illustrations are large, and the short poems offer preschoolers hints about a dance that they could create with their bodies. Finding appropriate background music to play while reading the poems to the children would heighten their use of all the senses. Children could move along with the reading of the poems or interpret their reactions to the music after the teacher has read the book to them. Children also could create their own representations of the various aspects of the water cycle—the rain, the mist, and the sea—that Locker uses so effectively. Two other books in this same genre are *Mountain Dance* (Locker, 2001) and *Cloud Dance* (Locker, 2003). *Rain* (Kalan, 1991) has illustrations by Donald Crews in which the word *rain* is printed over the pictures on the pages where it is raining. At the art center, children could explore different ways to use paint, crayons, or markers to depict rain in their own pictures. In *Ten Black Dots* (Crews, 1986), the same illustrator uses black dots to create coat buttons or a snake. In response to this text, teachers can give cutouts of circles, triangles, squares, and rectangles to children during a planned art project time, so the children can create their own real-life pictures, patterns, and designs with the shapes.

Art activities can be initiated in different ways. Teacher-initiated art activities may extend a previous literacy experience by having students explore an illustrator's artistic style, media, or viewpoint. Other teacher-initiated art activities may be linked to the current class theme or integrated into ZPD lessons in other content areas. In our preschools, this activity type typically happens during learning center time. Student-initiated art activities also are essential and occur during free-choice play center time. Both teacher- and student-initiated art activities are important and appropriate within a preschool framework.

To facilitate students' art projects in response to texts, the art center needs to be located so it is convenient to use water for activities and easy cleanup. We recommend that the center have bare floors that can be mopped or that teachers use plastic protective cloths or mats on the floor to avoid staining carpet. Wall space in this area can be used to display rebus pictures for cleanup procedures or creating art with specific directions in a given media. Important materials to have on hand include varieties of paper, finger paints, crayons, markers, watercolors, colored pencils, chalk, glue sticks, cotton balls, cotton swabs, rounded scissors, yarn, and different sizes of paint brushes.

Conclusion

Appendix A, pages 211–215, offers sample lessons that use different songbooks as the basis for shared reading activities and ZPD groups. The lessons include connections to other curricular areas and suggestions for other read-aloud books, and they are meant to be beginning points that creative teachers can adapt, adding their own ideas based on what they know about their students. If the preschool is housed in an elementary school, teachers can expand their lesson plan potential by establishing a strong relationship with the specialists in art and music because these staff members can offer additional resources and information.

Careful observation of children as they explore music and the creative arts will give teachers valuable insights into children's feelings and thoughts about themselves and their places at home and in the preschool community. Children who are hesitant about participating in the arts are revealing different information than those who plunge right into these activities. Some children who are slow to take on literacy concepts may be very expressive and skilled in the creative arts. Teachers can use these strengths to help their students learn literacy concepts by integrating the arts and literacy as much as possible. The Preschool Curriculum Framework and the Preschool Outcomes Checklist (see Appendix B, pages 235 and 241, respectively) each include a section on music, movement, and the creative arts. Preschool teachers should observe children's participation, appreciation, and responses in these areas. As we have already stated, play is the leading learning activity for 3- to 6-year-olds. The musical, movement-based, and artistic play discussed in this chapter will augment a child's learning in all the developmental domains.

CHAPTER 11

Preschoolers on the Move

• • •

While visiting a preschool early in the school year, we watched the children role-playing *We're Going on a Bear Hunt* (Rosen, 1989) while the teacher read the story aloud. Children were "crawling" through the grass, "swimming" across the river, "shlurping" through the mud, "stomping" through the forest, "howling" through the snowstorm, and "tiptoeing" through the cave. Everyone had a wonderful time enjoying the story in a physical way.

The preschoolers in this class used a variety of movements to interpret a story and express their individual ways of imitating the sounds and movements in the text. This integration of free expression with movement and literacy events should be common in quality preschools. Yet the basis for movement instruction in preschool needs to be more than free-expression activities. This chapter discusses the development and growth of preschoolers in the critical areas of gross motor, fine motor, and health and safety skills. These three areas play a significant role in building healthy attitudes, habits, and capabilities in young children and provide an essential foundation for lifelong movement and physical activities. According to Jensen (2000), "The period from two to six years old appears to be particularly critical to a child's motor development as muscle strength, coordination, balance, and spatial skills—which ultimately impact cognition—are initiated at this stage" (p. 60). Preschool teachers need to integrate instruction in movement, balance, tool manipulation, spatial orientation, and coordination into active games and lessons so children have opportunities to practice and improve their skills in these areas. The instruction also must be developmentally appropriate. Sanders (2002) notes, "In terms of creating appropriate movement learning experiences for children...the program must take into account children's ages and individual, instructional, and cultural needs. All elements must be present for a movement activity to be considered developmentally appropriate" (p. 5). Children's capabilities take much time and many experiences to increase and expand. A teacher's careful observation is necessary to determine each child's unique level of development in the different skill areas, and then the teacher must track and record the child's progress in each area. The observations and record keeping ensure that each child will have opportunities to learn and practice skills within his or her own ZPD for a given task. The expectations are that children will progress in increments along a continuum rather than meet arbitrary benchmarks determined by their ages.

Although physical development is the focus of the activities discussed in this chapter, children's education in gross and fine motor movements extends beyond the physical domain. Children strengthen perceptual motor skills as they become more aware of their bodies and their directional and spatial movements. Cognitive learning is reinforced through the teacher's integration of concepts from other developmental domains into movement activities (see Figure 56). Reinforcement activities are the easiest to integrate and include counting while bouncing a ball and naming body parts while standing in place. Children's affective learning also is enhanced when they learn the importance of teamwork, fair play, honesty, self-control, and sportsmanship.

• Figure 56 •
Ashlynn, Zack, and Alex Use Both Their Physical
and Cognitive Abilities to Fish for Letters

The movement activities described in this chapter generally fit under the heading of physical education and gross motor development, and their purpose is to advance children's specific physical growth. Creative movement activities that integrate well with music, literacy, and other creative arts are discussed in chapter 10.

Gross Motor Skills

Gross motor skills involve the use of the child's whole body as he or she moves about the surrounding environment. Gross motor skills that are appropriate for preschoolers to explore are classified under the headings of locomotor, stability, and manipulative movement (Gallahue, 1993), and we focus on these areas within our preschool framework. Locomotor movement refers to the ability to move the body from one point to another within the environment. Stability movement involves both keeping the body in one place while using axial movements, such as twisting or turning, and using balance and coordination skills. Manipulative movement includes using tools in coordination with body movements, such as kicking a ball or swinging a bat. Children benefit from opportunities for instruction and practice in these areas as they become more involved in sports activities. Specific instruction will occur within the elementary curriculum, but it is important for preschool children to begin exploratory activities with movement. Additionally, children's muscular strength and endurance, joint flexibility, and cardiovascular endurance are developed through movement activities and are part of a child's general physical fitness level. Therefore, these components are the building blocks for the physical activities that promote health and well-being as children become active adults. The adoption of a healthy lifestyle is the basis of an effective physical development curriculum in preschool.

Effective preschool movement activities are augmented by additional factors that help children to acquire basic movement skills. For example, a positive and supportive atmosphere is essential for helping children to learn and practice new skills in any area but especially skills in the physical domain. The development of new physical skills takes a lot of practice and effort, and because these skills develop slowly, it is easy for children to become discouraged. Teachers' cheerful encouragement and positive affirmation of children's effort and improvement will bolster children's lagging spirits and support their risk taking and perseverance. The presence of parent volunteers during movement activities increases the amount of support and encouragement individual children will receive. Schoolwide track days are a common example of parent involvement in the support of children's physical development and skills. Parents come to school to watch their children participate in a variety of noncompetitive physical activities such as jumping rope, kicking balls, hopping, and maneuvering through an obstacle course. The focus of physical instruction should be on improving performance rather than mastering a given task; therefore, elimination games should not be used in preschool. Because these games result in some children watching others participate in physical activities when all children should be involved, they are too difficult for children to handle emotionally.

Another key factor in physical education is providing many opportunities for practice. Children need repeated practice of the same skill offered in a variety of activities over a long period. Teachers need to return to previous lessons for review so children who were not ready to move forward at that time will be able to do so when they are ready. Any given preschool classroom will have children who are at many different skill levels; therefore, frequent reviews and repeated activities are necessary. Another way to ensure valuable practice time is to plan activities so each child is actively engaged all the time. The teacher needs to provide enough equipment so each child has a ball, scarf, hula hoop, or whatever other equipment is necessary. Children should not wait in line to practice kicking or throwing. When every child is involved in an activity, more learning and guided practice take place and fewer management and discipline problems occur. Therefore, relay-type games should be used infrequently if at all.

> Children need repeated practice of the same skill offered in a variety of activities over a long period.

The third factor for successful physical education is to provide a variety of equipment. Some preschoolers are more successful at throwing and catching a smaller or larger ball than others. If a variety of ball sizes are offered, each child can choose the size that he or she feels more comfortable with, the differences are not noticeable to the rest of the class. Similarly, even though some children can catch a foam ball more easily than a firm ball, so offering several ball types will help children to be more confident and successful at the same time that it helps them learn within their ZPDs.

The following additional tips will help preschool teachers in providing effective movement activities:

- Begin any movement curriculum by helping each child establish his or her own personal space. Children can put out their arms so they do not touch someone else, or they can stand on a large carpet remnant.

- Define the appropriate boundaries of the play area, especially when outdoors, and model how to stay within them.

- Establish a start and stop signal, which can be a whistle when outside or a phrase such as "One, two, three, look at me!" when inside.

- Organize the equipment so the children can easily get it out and clean it up. Label each container with a picture and a word. Model the procedures that the children should use for finding, using, and cleaning up the equipment.

- Change the pace and the activity to match the attention spans of the children.

- Engage the children's imaginations. For example, young children love to pretend, so two parallel jump ropes easily become a river or a gorge to jump across. No fancy props or equipment are needed, just the children's imaginations.

- Move among the children as they participate in an activity, and give encouragement, support, and verbal cues to each child within his or her ZPD.

- Expect children to be active listeners and follow directions as they do in other preschool activities.

- Build a spirit of teamwork, good sportsmanship, and effort with your enthusiasm, positive feedback, and modeling of these qualities.

- Help children to self-regulate their actions and development appropriately through modeling and scaffolding their abilities to perform appropriate new physical tasks.

Locomotor Movement

Locomotor movement includes walking, marching, galloping, jumping, hopping, running, leaping, sliding, and skipping. Locomotor movements develop in a hierarchical progression, and the skills mentioned here are listed in sequence from easiest to hardest (Sanders, 2002, p. 40). Although there is a general pattern of children progressing from the easiest skill of walking to the most difficult one of skipping, not every child will progress sequentially through all the movements. For novice early childhood educators, there are some important nuances in locomotor movement that need to be defined. It is easy for adults and children to confuse the correct movements in jumping, hopping, leaping, and galloping. Jumping means to move both feet up in the air and return to the ground on both feet at the same time. Hopping is moving up in the air on one foot and returning to the ground on the same foot. Leaping involves moving from one foot to the other in a forward manner. Galloping refers to one foot consistently leading in a forward movement while the other foot pulls up behind it.

These movement skills develop when children are young, so activities that use these skills will enable preschoolers to increase control of their large muscles. As with other areas of the preschool curriculum, some skills from one area will overlap and integrate with other areas. Therefore, activities that promote locomotor movement growth also may provide children with needed practice in stability and manipulative skills. This overlap allows for the frequent review of and transitions between activities that are vital to providing opportunities for the growth of each child's ZPD in all movement areas.

Children love the variety of games and make-believe situations that offer them necessary practice of movement skills. Each locomotor movement can be practiced in myriad ways, such as running on tiptoe, quickly, slowly, forward, backward, or around simple obstacles; hopping four times on one foot, on the other foot, quickly, or in time to music; and leaping like a frog, like a tiny bug, like a giant, quickly, or slowly. Many movement activities can arise from thematic units and may include adaptations from songs and stories. For example, a unit on insects might include the song "The Ants Go Marching One by One" or the book *Amazing Anthony Ant* (Philpot & Philpot, 1994). Children we observed in one preschool enjoyed the opportunity to display their locomotive dexterity by marching around the playground singing, "The ants go marching down to the ground to get out of the rain, boom, boom, boom."

These types of activities also are excellent for connecting to other areas of the curriculum. For example, children can move in ways similar to animals that they investigate in science lessons. Cones with colors, numbers, or letters taped to them can be placed strategically around the area, and the teacher can direct groups of children to jump to a designated color, number, or letter. Icons or pictures in different sizes can be taped to the cones, and children can hop to the large or the tiny cat, for example. Colors, numbers, shapes, or letters can be used for team names, and the children can be given directions such as "The triangles are on this side of the line, and the circles are on the other side." Children can wear tags around their necks that are prepared ahead of time and easy to rotate for a variety of concepts. These tags can be in different shapes—such as triangles, circles, squares, and diamonds—or colors for each team. Animals, letters, and numbers also can be used for the tags, so the teacher might say, "All the red letters need to stand by me." This variety provides for good classroom management as well as reinforcement of content area knowledge. Or children can dramatize or role-play social studies, science, or health and safety situations. Creative teachers will find many ways to integrate physical education activities with other developmental domains.

Stability Movement

Stability movements include bending, twisting, turning, stopping, swaying, and balancing (Gallahue, 1993). Balance may be the most important of these skills because there is an element of balance inherent in all motor activities. Stability movement and practice usually blend well into other movement practice, but the following activities isolate stability movement skills:

- Simon Says games in which children copy the leader in movements such as bending forward or side to side or lifting an arm or leg
- balancing on one foot and then the other while listening to music
- standing in place while listening to slow music, with each child bending or twisting his or her body to interpret the music
- dancing with a hula hoop and making sideways movements
- painting a 4-inch-wide line on the ground outside or using masking tape to create one inside so children can practice walking on this "balance beam"
- touching and moving body parts as the teacher names them and suggests a movement such as "Point your elbows forward, and make a circle with them"
- playing Hokey Pokey, Lubey Loo, and Head, Shoulders, Knees, and Toes, which are popular in the United States, or other circle games that involve moving body parts

Other games that incorporate stability movements are listed in Appendix D, pages 272–273.

Manipulative Movement

Manipulative movements involve the use of tools or equipment such as balls, bats, scarves, bowling pins, and other equipment (see Figure 57 for preschoolers using bubble wands). Children throw, catch, kick, strike, and roll this equipment through the use of their arms, legs, or

• Figure 57 •
Aide Nichole Bertagnole and a Group of Preschoolers Practice Blowing Bubbles

both. Manipulation is the most difficult movement skill for preschoolers because hand-eye and foot-eye coordination are necessary to complete the tasks. Throwing, catching, rolling, and kicking moves are the most basic ones that preschoolers need to explore. A variety of balls or objects are key for effective activities that will help all children to improve their manipulative skills. Different ball sizes, textures, and degrees of firmness are essential to ensuring success for children at all levels of physical ability. Standard ball sizes are often too small for preschoolers, so larger balls should be provided. Beanbags, yarn balls, foam balls, beach balls, whiffle balls, and sock balls add variety and fun to manipulative activities.

When planning activities involving manipulative movement, teachers initially should provide opportunities for children to investigate a variety of ways to manipulate the tools. These activties allow for exploration by the children and give the teacher an opportunity to observe each child's skill level with the tools. As the teacher observes the children, he or she should move among them to suggest ways to change the task depending on the abilities of each child. The teacher should give each child cues that will make the activity easier or more challenging depending on the child's ZPD level (Sanders, 2002).

Specific cues depend on each child's level of control. For example, when throwing a ball, children learn to step forward with one foot and throw the ball with the opposite arm. Also, as children develop skill, their throwing arms reach back before going forward. When kicking a ball, children learn to step up to it with one foot and kick it with the opposite foot, using a backswing motion with their leg before kicking. In order to catch a ball, children will learn to keep their eyes on it and be ready to catch it by turning their thumbs inward to catch a ball above the waist and outward to catch a ball below the waist. When rolling a ball, children use a straddle stance, holding the ball with their palms facing each other and bending at the waist to release the ball on the ground. In general,

> in the preschool movement environment, the teacher designs tasks or learning station activities he or she believes all children can successfully accomplish 80% of the time. The idea is to design the activity in a way that enables children to participate and to be successful. (Sanders, 2002, p. 51)

It would seem that pairing throwing and catching together as activity partners would be ideal. However, preschoolers are just beginning to develop their throwing skills, so it is best to provide a lot of throwing practice first in which each child has a ball, throws it, and then retrieves it him- or herself. This activity can take place in several different ways. Children can throw foam balls outside and retrieve them. They can throw beanbags at an outside wall or large target area. They can play the game Snowball, in which the class divides into two teams with a rope line down the middle of the area, and children on one side throw soft objects, such as newspaper balls, yarn, or foam balls, to the other side of the line. Then, the children on the opposite side pick up the objects and throw them back to the other side as fast as they can. When the teacher signals everyone to stop, the objects on both sides are counted and then the process is repeated. These types of games or activities keep all the children throwing and practicing their technique while the teacher is free to move about, giving suggestions where needed.

Once the majority of children in the class seem proficient at throwing, pairing children to throw and catch can be a fun and effective activity involving manipulative movement. It is best to pair students of similar abilities so more skillful children do not become impatient with those who need more practice. Ball rolling is a good paired activity and one in which children are more successful in controlling the ball than when they are throwing one. Children can roll the ball to one another quickly and slowly, using a large ball at first and then decreasing the ball size and increasing the distance between themselves as they become more skillful. They can aim at inanimate objects, such as plastic bowling pins, containers, or cones, and gradually increase their distance from the objects. During this type of activity, teachers should be using language to enhance each child's physical performance. These verbal cues also may support children in improving their oral language competencies. For example, the physical context provides children with the opportunity to practice using past-tense regular and irregular verbs such as *caught*, *threw*, *fell*, and *rolled*. Teachers who are aware of the connection between physical activity and language can capitalize on the teachable moment.

Games and activities that use basic locomotor, stability, and manipulative skills will develop the fundamental movement concepts and self-confidence that children need to be successful in physical education activities in elementary school and sports and leisure activities as they grow. More activities and games for these areas are given in Appendix D, pages 272–273.

Fine Motor Skills

The development of fine motor skills is essential for children to become independent in daily living and in cognitive and physical tasks. Fine motor skills are necessary for manipulating objects and tools, and they require strength, control, and coordination of the smaller muscles in the fingers and hands with the child's sight. As 3- and 4-year-olds mature, they begin to take responsibility for the many self-care tasks that are necessary in their daily schedules, such as buttoning clothes, using zippers, and brushing their teeth. These daily actions provide some of the practice necessary to gain strength, control, and coordination. Therefore, expecting and supporting children to be independent in these routines will help them to develop that very independence. Likewise, the other tasks that are involved in preschool activities will improve performance in informal ways. These tasks might include opening containers, twisting off bottle caps, tearing paper for an art project, dressing a doll at the dramatic play center, manipulating shape blocks to create a pattern, pouring sand at the sand table, or using Play-doh to make shapes (see Figure 58). These opportunities help children grow in other developmental areas, but they also help to increase their fine motor control. As with the gross motor skills, fine motor skills come with many experiences given in many different ways over a long period.

Teachers also can target fine motor control in more direct and planned methods. However, these activities should be integrated into other areas both for multiple learning outcomes and for enjoyment and pleasure. In chapter 7, we discuss specific activities for pencil grip and graphic practice. Mathematics, science, and social studies inquiries and centers present numerous possibilities for the manipulation of tools and equipment—such as rulers, measuring cups, items found in nature (rocks and leaves), blocks, magnets, and magnifying glasses—and the creation of drawn and written records of learning. Art is another area filled with abundant ways in which to provide fine motor control activities. Using tools such as brushes, scissors, markers, crayons, cookie cutters, clay, glue sticks, and chalk is intrinsic to the art experience. However, art activities also give preschoolers the vital practice needed for controlling, strengthening, and coordinating small muscle groups and improving hand-eye coordination. Within a preschool, materials at all centers—puzzles, blocks, beads and string, cars and other vehicles, and interlocking cubes and links—are used daily for other educational purposes, but fine motor skill improvement is also an important outcome.

Teachers need to observe carefully how children manipulate these tools and give support and suggestions for more effective uses of them. For example, some preschoolers may use scissors with their thumbs to the side rather than on top of the tool. Encouraging these children to have the "hungry hippo eat the paper," rather than to cut with the "lazy lion" who has his head to the side, may give them an easy cue to keep their thumbs on top of the scissors while cutting. Observing what centers children visit most frequently also will help teachers see if some

• Figure 58 •
Zack Enhances His Fine Motor Skills at the Play-Doh Center

children are using the same muscles in the same way. A child needs more variety of fine motor activities than just using brushes and scissors at the art center. Manipulating clay and tearing paper are different motor experiences than easel painting. Choice is essential in center participation, but gentle suggestions from a teacher for children to try new areas can help preschoolers develop small muscles in different manners.

Health and Safety Skills

As previously mentioned, preschool-age children begin to become more responsible for self-regulating and self-care tasks. Teaching children these responsibilities is an essential part of a preschool health curriculum and instills in them crucial hygiene and personal care habits. Dressing, using the toilet, washing and drying hands, and using tissues for noses are routines that need to be established by modeling, providing simple rebus pictures, and giving individual support when necessary. Positive affirmations such as "I like how you all are taking care of washing your hands before snack time" or "Robert, I am so proud of you for trying to zip your coat by yourself before you asked for help!" not only praise children and make them proud of themselves but also restate the appropriate behavior and serve as reminders for those children who need them. Using functional print, such as pictures and simple words posted by the sinks in the bathroom and the art area and other places where necessary, helps children complete expected tasks and underscores the necessity of print in daily life.

Safety is another area in which children need to have some basic knowledge, and it links well to basic personal care tasks. The goal is for preschoolers to learn to keep themselves healthy and safe by taking some common-sense actions, including covering the mouth when sneezing and then wiping the hand on a tissue, using a tissue for a runny nose and throwing it away, and washing the hands before handling snacks. Safety issues in the preschool also include not climbing on shelving, tables, and chairs; walking with scissors or pointed objects wrapped in a fist and pointed downward; using proper procedures on the playground equipment; and knowing what to do during a fire drill.

> The goal is for preschoolers to learn to keep themselves healthy and safe by taking some common-sense actions...

More formal instruction and activities with safety issues might include children learning about strangers, fire safety at home and school, community helpers who keep them safe and healthy, nutritious food, and their bodies. We suggest that teachers treat these topics as social studies and science themes and follow the suggestions given in chapter 9 that incorporate hands-on experiences and literacy activities through which children can explore and learn the concepts. Again, it is necessary to decide what the children need to learn from the theme before constructing activities and lessons. See the suggested books on science in Appendix E, page 286, for a subset of books that focus on the human body and health.

Assessment

As in all the other developmental domains, teachers need to be diligent child observers in order to track and record the growth of each child. Growth in the areas of gross and fine motor skills is no different than in any other early learning domain. Instead of the mastery of specific skills, progress over time in physical growth is the focus for each child. Anecdotal records are appropriate for recording what a child is doing at any given time. In gross motor areas, it is important for the teacher to watch for and record how a child completes a movement to best help him or her move forward with physical skill accomplishments. This would include asking specific questions such as, Does the movement flow smoothly, or is it jerky? Does the child have to stop and think before the movement, or does it appear to be automatic? Can the child look up or forward rather than watching his or her feet? Can the child maintain personal space within a group of children? Can the child complete the movement correctly, such as leading with the opposite foot? Observing children's social and emotional responses within a physical context is also important. Teachers should watch for and document items such as how children take risks in trying new or more challenging tasks, persevere or quit when a task is difficult, and initiate experimentation or exploration with movement and movement materials. Once again, this careful observation is targeted toward planning the next appropriate instructional move for each child.

Observations, checklists, and anecdotal records concerning each child's progress in movement areas should be kept in an individual portfolio. The goal of the portfolio is to house a variety of assessments that give an accurate picture of how each child progresses in his or her gross and fine motor development. Then, teachers communicate the progress to students' families and use the information for planning further instruction. The Preschool Outcomes in Appendix B, page 236, offer indicators in gross motor, fine motor, and health and safety areas, and the Preschool Outcomes Checklist in Appendix B, page 241, also includes these areas. As mentioned in chapter 3, the Brigance Preschool Screen assesses several physical milestones and provides cutoff scores that may alert teachers when further, in-depth physical analysis of a particular child is needed. We encourage teachers who notice any indications of delays in a child's physical development to contact their local child development center, special education services, or both.

Additional information about instruction and assessment in physical education activities can be obtained from national organizations in the United States such as the Council on Physical Education for Children, the National Association for Sport and Physical Education, and the NAEYC. In addition, the book *Active for Life: Developmentally Appropriate Movement Programs for Young Children* (Sanders, 2002) also presents a wealth of information about developmentally appropriate and effective movement programs.

Conclusion

Movement in preschool and throughout the day is critical in helping children to develop in a healthy and well-rounded manner. Unfortunately, obesity is on the rise for people of all ages in the United States but especially for children who eat too many high-calorie snacks and do not get enough exercise. According to the U.S. Centers for Disease Control and Prevention (CDC; n.d.), "young people are, in large measure, inactive, unfit, and increasingly overweight." This is alarming information, yet we all know children who sit in front of television sets or video games while their rough-and-tumble play habits of years past decline as they get older. Preschoolers, however, enjoy being active, and we can help them create and maintain a mindset of enjoying outdoor and active play. Consistent and frequent movement opportunities allow children to release pent-up energy, restore to the brain the oxygen necessary for cognitive learning, learn concepts through multiple modalities, and build skills for participation in physical activity throughout their lives. The CDC (n.d.) encourages parents and teachers to "help all children, from prekindergarten through grade 12, to receive quality, daily physical education." The movement suggestions in this chapter endeavor to provide preschoolers with many and varied ways in which they can strengthen and develop their burgeoning physical skills.

CHAPTER 12

Empowering Parents

• • •

Mr. Smith (a pseudonym) was a single father of a child in our preschool the first year we started. He rode a motorcycle; wore a torn, raggedy shirt; had several tattoos; was missing a front tooth; and in general, did not look like an approachable individual. He and his wife had divorced after he was convicted of a nonviolent crime and incarcerated, but he had been rehabilitated, gotten a job bussing tables at a local restaurant, and regained custody of his two daughters, ages 4 and 7. The older daughter was in our special reading class at that time, so we encouraged Mr. Smith to have his 4-year-old screened for the preschool. The free day care was all the enticement he needed, and he immediately enrolled his younger daughter in the preschool. Mr. Smith was aware of the two hours per week that he was required to serve as a parent volunteer, but within the first month of the school year, it became apparent that he did not intend to fulfill his commitment. The principal called him and said that his participation as a volunteer was mandatory, or his daughter would be dropped from the preschool.

Mr. Smith protested that his work would interfere, so the principal gained his permission to call his employer. Mr. Smith's employer granted a paid, early two-hour lunch on Thursdays, and Mr. Smith began his weekly visits to the preschool. At first, he sat in the corner of the classroom, just watching. His unkempt appearance kept wary parents and staff at bay. The children, however, were not deterred. One precocious child pulled on Mr. Smith's pant leg and said, "Mr. Smith, I need help! I can't cut this!" That unassuming child and his classmates taught us all a wonderful lesson that year. Mr. Smith became a great parent volunteer. His involvement at school enhanced his awareness of the school culture and his daughters' social and cognitive needs. It was an incredible revelation for all of us. On Thursday mornings for the next six school years, we all recognized the familiar sound of Mr. Smith's motorcycle parking in front of the school. His daughters both mainstreamed into regular classroom settings from the special services that they initially had received, and they finished elementary school with their average peers.

Quality preschools provide families with the opportunity to begin their school years together. For many families, early intervention breaks the generational cycle of school failure. Young children involved in preschool often feel more secure starting school with their parents at their sides. This situation enables parents to become an integral part of their children's educations from the first day of school and prepares them for active participation throughout their children's academic careers. In Mr. Smith's case, his weekly interactions with the school culture enhanced his social and academic awareness and enabled his daughters' acclimation to it. At the same time, the school faculty acknowledged and respected his persistence, and a new, mutual partnership emerged. Recent research about the effectiveness of family involvement in public education shows benefits similar to those found in the Smith family's scenario. In fact, years of research have shown that one of the best predictors of children's school achievement is not the family's income or the parents' levels of education but the extent to which the parents are concerned with their children's educations and become involved at school (see Figure 59). Increasing evidence exists that "the values, attitudes, and expectations held by parents and other care givers with respect to literacy are likely to have a lasting effect on a child's attitude about learning to read" (Snow et al., 1998, p. 138). Parents are their children's first teachers and should be acknowledged and respected as such.

• Figure 59 •
The Counts Family Interacts in the Preschool Classroom

Building Lasting Home-School Partnerships

As we proceed with our discussion of the critical and sometimes sensitive topic of parental involvement, we want to assure readers that the vast majority of the parents with whom we have collaborated have been wonderfully positive, supportive, and helpful. However, several of the parent stories cited in this chapter address problematic home-school situations that we have encountered. We present the parent-teacher scenarios to empower and reassure educators as they endeavor to develop and nurture successful home-school relations, and in no way do we wish to imply that the majority of communications with parents are difficult.

The expected role of families in education and even the definition of *family* have changed dramatically over the past several decades. Traditionally, families provided emotional, social, custodial, physical, and financial support for their children at home. In the school setting, children attended class, and their parents participated primarily as the "homework patrol" or by attending special school functions such as holiday parties, plays, concerts, and sports activities. The educators were viewed as the knowledgeable experts, providing all the necessary services and information. The parent involvement of the past included conferences, meetings, tutoring, parent classes, and newsletters. The home and school cultures functioned independently, often leaving the child as the only communication channel. Family-focused, home-school collaboration has developed significantly as educators have recognized the power of partnerships with families. Given the variety of family configurations found in modern society, we will use the label *parent* to describe any adult who is predominantly responsible for the care and nurturing of a child or children.

> Family-focused, home-school collaboration has developed significantly as educators have recognized the power of partnerships with families.

The home-school partnerships that we propose include five essential elements. The first is the establishing of equal partnerships. School personnel can guard against setting up a climate of unequal partnerships by communicating messages with a sense of equality and flexibility and a sharing attitude. Second, the school community should initiate home-school interactions by keeping families informed and educated about school programs and policies. Third, the school community should establish and nurture a rapport with students' parents. Collaborative relationships can be established through active listening, compassionate responding, and mutual problem solving. Fourth, the school community should not stereotype families. Parents should feel a sense of choice, ownership, and empowerment in the education of their children. Finally, ongoing surveys of the home-school partnership model should be implemented and used to measure changes in families' attitudes and interactions.

Equal Home-School Partnerships and Initiating Interactions With Parents

Through the collaboration model, families are viewed as essential and equal partners in their children's educations. They provide invaluable wisdom, knowledge, and insights about their children. The school identifies and accesses families' strengths and special interests as crucial assets in the design and implementation of thoughtful, tailored classroom instruction. The school also values, respects, and celebrates diversity and individual family differences. Family-focused collaboration embraces a positive approach to home-school relationships, as opposed to the deficit approach of the past.

In our preschools, we have noted the additional benefits of family partnerships in preschool have been greater daily attendance by students, improved attendance at Parent Teacher Association (PTA) meetings, increased volunteerism in other classrooms, and a greater participation in schoolwide policymaking. Also, parents who are involved in their children's educations have a better understanding of specific teacher expectations for student performance. As a result, they can support their children more effectively at home. Parents who initially are comfortable within their children's school environment are likely to continue to be involved throughout their children's academic journeys. The following are some basic tips for teachers in initiating and facilitating home-school partnerships:

- Schedule and make a home visit to introduce yourself to the student's family.
- Schedule an informational parent open-house night, and invite the principal to help explain the preschool's policies and procedures.
- Prepare and distribute any parent forms during the open-house night (e.g., immunization, field trip, and permission slips).
- Copy, discuss, and distribute a parent handbook (see Appendix F, pages 296–302, for an example).
- Require parents to volunteer for two hours each week. Explain the parent volunteer sign-up calendar (see the Sign-Up Sheet for Parent Volunteers in Appendix F, page 303), and have parents sign up for visits.
- Schedule parent meetings to discuss necessary items such as curricula, questions, or concerns. Always provide refreshments at the meetings.
- Write and send home a weekly newsletter detailing events and activities.
- Locate a parent workroom close to the preschool where parent volunteers can put their personal belongings. Make the room comfortable, have coffee, and put out magazines targeted to parents.
- Post in the classroom specific ideas for ways in which parents can help.
- Place teacher help baskets where other teachers can submit projects that they would like volunteers to do.
- Plan and prepare instructions and prompt cards for use during parent visits (e.g., how to work with journals and mathematics manipulatives).
- Provide training sessions for parents to learn how to use school equipment such as the photocopier and laminator.
- Celebrate family partnerships with bulletin board displays, newsletters, and attendance awards.
- Be flexible and understanding with parents because a positive demeanor is the key ingredient to a successful parent involvement program.

- Provide baby-sitting for *all* after-school activities or meetings.
- Post a large school calendar outside the classroom door with special school programs or activities marked on it.

Establishing Rapport: Listening and Responding to Parents

Building rapport or a sense of community with children's families creates cooperative, trusting relationships. Getting to know parents as partners, helpers, and collaborators improves the educational process for everyone. When parents feel confident and comfortable communicating with teachers, problem solving is ongoing and collaborative. Teachers with great interpersonal skills develop and nurture these parent partnerships easily. One way that preschool teachers have facilitated this process is by scheduling independent-partner reading in the first part of the school day. This activity allows the teachers the time and flexibility to greet and visit with parents personally. We advise teachers to have their aides monitor the children during this period so the teacher-parent conversations can occur. This part of the day should be a fun, interactive, adult-to-adult time and an opportunity to get to know parents better. These conversations should build trusting relationships that are the foundation for future discussions. Remember to talk often to your students' parents in person, on the phone, by e-mail, or via a combination of all three.

> Building rapport or a sense of community with children's families creates cooperative, trusting relationships.

In chapter 3, we discuss using anecdotal records to observe students informally and to inform further instruction. We would like to suggest that anecdotal records about each student's family might facilitate better home-school partnerships. One of our preschool teachers keeps brief notations of her interactions with parents, and what began as a record of communications about students' progress evolved into a register of parents' talents, hobbies, professions, and interests. She currently uses this register to plan class themes and activities. For example, when she initiated a truck theme, she called one father who had shared with her that he drove a cement truck for the highway department. She asked him to drive the truck to school for the preschoolers to explore. The father felt valued for his experience and expertise, and the children learned new terminology related to the trucking profession such as *18-wheeler*, *engine*, *drum*, *chute*, and *ignition key*. The same teacher also discovered that another student's father was a country music entertainer. His visits became filled with wonderful country songs and square-dancing opportunities. Parent anecdotal records also have enabled the teacher to recall special parent interests and occurrences, allowing her to engage more comfortably in ongoing daily conversations with her students' parents. She comments that these "nonsystematic" observations of her parents have given her a more inclusive view and understanding of the families with whom she interacts.

The following list offers several other rapport-building suggestions that preschool teachers can use with their students' parents:

- Arrange for preschool carpooling to support parents.
- Help organize a day-care cooperative.

- Personally invite each parent to PTA meetings, and give each one a personal reminder.
- Organize an after-school craft activity, such as T-shirt painting, dried-flower arranging, watercolor painting, or pottery making, for parents and school staff.
- Schedule a potluck meal for staff and parents.
- Schedule a family fun lunch, for example, at a local restaurant after class on Fridays.
- Schedule a bingo night, an ice cream social, or other event.
- Acknowledge preschool families and activities in the media.
- Combine some of the previously mentioned activities with computer lab nights, open gym nights, or library storytelling nights.
- Schedule stops by the Book Mobile (a minilibrary housed in a bus or large van) during preschool hours.
- Post community activities that are available for preschool students, such as swim nights, youth sports, museum hours, and community library hours.
- Have a parenting resource section available in the school library.
- Post literature for the General Educational Development (GED) test, adult literacy classes, first-aid and cardiopulmonary resuscitation (CPR) information, immunizations, and well-baby clinics.
- Schedule fitness classes at school, and provide baby-sitting.
- Survey parents to ascertain special interests and areas of expertise to share with the preschoolers.
- Get to know parents and family members.

Setting Clear Goals and Expectations for Preschoolers and Their Families

Setting clear goals and expectations for the preschoolers and their families is very important. Ask parents about their expectations, and then educate them about preschool education, philosophies, and policies to avoid any unnecessary conflicts that may otherwise occur. We suggest that preschool teachers present the philosophy of the preschool framework early in the year to maximize families' understanding of it and divert any misconceptions about educational practices. All of our preschoolers' parents receive a parent handbook that includes a synopsis of our early childhood educational philosophy, the goals and objectives of the preschool program, a preschool parent contract, a discipline policy, and parent guidelines for working within the preschool (see Appendix F, page 296–302).

Family Volunteers: Providing for Ownership and Choice

Parent and family volunteers feel more comfortable volunteering when they are given specific parameters and guidelines to follow so they know where to go and what to do. Teachers and paraprofessionals can support this process by modeling expectations for parent-student interactions, providing frequent explanations, and supplying written directions. Giving parents the time at the beginning of the school year to observe and synthesize classroom procedures before being expected to interact with the students may ease their volunteering responsibility. Providing opportunities for parents to share in lesson design and implementation also personalizes instruction for preschoolers and generates a sense of ownership for their parents. Using parents' special interests and talents when planning lessons provides a unique opportunity for families to bring their backgrounds and traditions into the classroom environment. Teachers who know and value parents' expertise and talents find the parents' weekly presence helpful and invigorating. Parents' help with small-group learning centers and show and tells, free-choice play centers, and snack times is invaluable.

Posting prompt cards will serve as a cue or reminder for teachers, aides, parents, and other classroom visitors about the ways that they can facilitate the children's learning and development in play and learning centers. (See Appendix C, pages 258–269, for reproducible play and learning center prompt cards.) Often, centers are viewed as random and aimless activities, when in actuality they are designed to enhance and promote purposeful learning in a variety of content areas and developmental domains. The center prompt cards enable teachers to underscore the goals and objectives to be stressed in each center. The prompt cards may be printed in color and displayed at or near each center for easy reference. Preschool curricula, such as individual state's early childhood readiness standards, and the *Head Start Program Performance Standards* (U.S. Department of Health and Human Services, 1998) may be helpful resources for teachers as they develop prompt cards to coordinate with their thematic and realistic play centers. We encourage teachers to cite the state standards that they are addressing in each center, but we have not included the standard citations on our prompt card examples because they will vary slightly from state to state.

Surveying and Monitoring Home-School Partnerships

Surveying parents and early childhood educators may be the most helpful and informative way to collect useful data about a preschool program's effectiveness. Asking parents about how the staff can enhance their family's school experience is the easiest way to measure the success of home-school collaboration efforts. We hesitate to present a generic home-school partnership survey because each community has unique preschool opportunities and parent populations and numerous reasons and occasions to survey parents and educators. For example, several early childhood agencies throughout the Casper, Wyoming, community recently came together to discuss networking and collaboration issues. Together, the agency representatives, including our preschool principal, Christine Frude, and Claire, determined that many families were being required to fill out repetitive paperwork when they moved from one early childhood organization to another. As a group, we drafted a universal registration and referral form that could be transferred from one preschool setting to another just as easily as from one public school to another. We also discussed some concerns about overlapping services. To document our hypothesis of duplication of services, we surveyed parents about their preschool and day-care needs. As a result, several of the early childhood agencies have made adjustments to their school and day-care hours to accommodate the needs revealed in the survey.

Understanding that there are innumerable reasons to survey families about their school involvement, we would like to suggest a few questions that ultimately may change the ways that teachers and school personnel think about and interact with parents. We believe that schools need to differentiate or individualize involvement for families as much as they need to differentiate instruction for children. Knowing students' families and their special capabilities, interests, and emotional and physical needs is fundamental to quality home-school partnerships. Perhaps the answers to some of the following questions will enlighten school personnel about the families with whom they work:

- What is unique about your family?
- Do you have a family hobby or a special interest?
- What does your family do for fun?
- What activity, food, and/or event is the most motivating for your child?
- What do you like to read about?
- What is your favorite family movie?
- How would you like to be involved at school—in your child's classroom, the PTA, or committees?
- What are your goals for your child?
- How does our school schedule match with your work schedule?
- What is the best time of the day for you to come to school for a brief visit?

Families Getting to Know School Personnel

Parents, students, and families need to know the school staff, too. As teachers and school personnel, we need to share our feelings and interests. When families walk into a school knowing all the staff members, the school becomes a very welcoming, safe, and comfortable place to be. Too often, home-school relationships are limited to the preschool teacher, the child, and one family member. Broadening that circle to include the office staff; principal; nurse; playground aides; speech or language pathologists; social workers; and art, music, and physical education teachers is empowering for parents. Although all these staff members may be part of a student's daily interactions, parents may have no contact or experience with these people unless an effort is made to introduce them. Several simple ways exist for teachers to familiarize families with extended school staff:

- Display staff photos labeled with names and assignments near the school entrance.
- Encourage staff to wear name tags.
- Encourage staff to stop and introduce themselves to parents and family members they see in the school.
- Invite extended staff to holiday parties, field trips, or special class events.

Parents Volunteering in Preschool

Most of all, parents are and should be viewed as valuable resources by preschool teachers (see Figure 60). Parents' expertise, knowledge, and cultural differences should be acknowledged and used to personalize and support the preschool classroom. As previously noted, in our preschool framework, we recommend that parents be required to volunteer two hours per week at school. One hour must be spent in the preschool, but the second hour may be spent in the preschool or elsewhere in the elementary school in which the preschool is housed. Although the parent participation requirement initially may seem rigid, a collaborative, welcoming preschool environment soon transforms a regulation into a refuge. In our experience with over 20 preschools, 95% of the parents honor their pledge to volunteer, and many exceed their obligation.

We believe that the key to a successful parent involvement program in preschool is an intervention that provides convenient, nonthreatening, personalized involvement for parents and children. Parents and children become acquainted and comfortable with the school's staff, surroundings, environment, and philosophy in a way that, it is hoped, will continue throughout the children's elementary years. They learn the lunch, recess, and assembly routines, and they also become comfortable with teaching staff and school specialists well before the children's

• **Figure 60** •
A Preschool Parent Leads a Small-Group Show and Tell

kindergarten immersion. This intervention offers a seamless transition from home to school and generates new attitudes in parents who often have had negative school experiences themselves.

The observations and interactions afforded to parents, teachers, and preschoolers alike are two of the most beneficial aspects of the preschool-parent partnership. Parents see education professionals teaching and interacting positively with their children in a variety of physical, cognitive, emotional, and social activities. Read-alouds, language development, mathematics activities, social behaviors, and appropriate consequences all are modeled in a manner that is easy for parents to integrate into their own home situations and frequently enhances their relations with their children at home. Therefore, parents are confident in helping their preschoolers with school activities and are likely to continue to be involved as their children grow older.

> The observations and interactions afforded to parents, teachers, and preschoolers alike are two of the most beneficial aspects of the preschool-parent partnership.

The parents with whom we have worked have frequently told us about changes that they have made in their parenting based on experiences in the preschool. For example, one parent told us about verbal methods of disciplining her child that she had learned and subsequently used successfully with her child at home. Another parent in preschool teacher Dusty Haigler's classroom commented that she had learned to say, "That was not a good choice! Now you may pick that up, or you may go to the 'thinking chair'!" Numerous parents also have communicated to us the new knowledge that they have acquired about how children learn to read and write. The most frequent comment we hear is, "I thought reading started with letters and sounds. Now, I know that there are lots of other things my child needs to know, too!"

Parents also have spoken to us about new relationships that they have developed with other adults and staff in the preschool. It is obvious that our preschool parents have become our most active participants in and advocates for school committees, programs, and activities. Many of our preschool parents have acquired clerical skills, such as operating the copy machine and doing basic computer work, and have had school experiences during their volunteer hours that have resulted in employment as school district aides, computer technicians, and secretaries. Others have enjoyed their experience so much that they have gone back to college to become preschool teachers themselves. This development by the parents has been perhaps the most surprising in our preschools' evolution. We expected to grow as educators and expected the children to grow socially, emotionally, physically, and cognitively, and we even expected that parents would grow as parent teachers, but training unemployed adults to become employable has been an unforeseen bonus.

Many preschool teachers find the parent component of our preschool framework the most challenging. Even with the majority of parents fulfilling their hours conscientiously, there are always parents who do not. Teachers frequently voice concerns about the same parents with countless explanations to excuse their delinquent volunteer hours. Teachers lament over the time that they spend sending notes home with students and making phone calls to encourage parents to fulfill their commitment. In our experience, the preschools that have overcome this problem are the ones with strong administrative support and monitoring. The problems are alleviated when parent obligations are made clear from the outset of the program (see the Parent

Handbook in Appendix F, pages 296–302), few or no exceptions are made, and administrators do the initial follow-up and continuous monitoring. The one- to two-hour requirement for parents supplies between 18 and 36 hours of volunteer support in a preschool each week. Given that most preschools meet for three hours a day and five days a week, this model should ensure that a least one parent is volunteering in the preschool classroom every day. Parent involvement in preschool and beyond is critical to complete the home-school connection and to support at-risk children as they embark on their academic journeys.

Visiting Preschoolers' Homes

Early childhood educators should visit each student's home prior to his or her preschool attendance. Home visits provide invaluable insights into each child's background experience. Seeing firsthand a child's existence beyond the classroom empowers teachers as they make critical connections between the school world and a child's real world. We encourage teachers to be very observant during these home visits and to glean and record as much information as possible about family interests and unique hobbies. An opportunity to view the child's room and assess his or her sleeping and playing environments may help to facilitate later collaborative decision making between parents and teachers about how to better meet the child's needs. The teacher's awareness of the types of literature and writing materials available in a home may determine the contents of a daily take-home bag for a particular student. For example, one teacher's home visit revealed an abundance of electronic equipment but no children's books or writing materials, so the teacher made a conscious effort to send home paper, pencils, crayons, markers, and an appropriate children's book each afternoon.

Too often, parents believe that their children are too young to enjoy or use literacy materials. However, as they observe the interest that their children show in reading picture books and writing notes, they often embrace and facilitate the process at home. One preschool parent who we interviewed said,

> I never knew my son could do things. I used to just put him in front of the video. Now after seeing what he can do at the preschool, I have him help me cook Jell-O, do the dishes, and lots of stuff. He even reads to his little brother.

As early childhood educators, we need to acknowledge and use parents' strengths and scaffold their parenting skills through positive interactions and modeling opportunities.

Parent-Child Interactions in the Preschool Classroom

Many parents sit and read with their own and other children when they drop them off for preschool each day. One way in which we have tried to support our parents during these partner reading times is by modeling and offering reading prompts to improve the children's reading experience and enhance parent-child book conversations. We tell parents that we use a prompt card (see the Reading Prompt Card in Appendix C, page 257) to augment the reading experience for young children and suggest that perhaps they might find them to be helpful, too. We have found that after using this card for several weeks, our parents naturally embrace this teacher language as their own and no longer need the cards. This is one way we scaffold new learning for our parents as well as our new teachers.

Parents and other class volunteers also facilitate small-group show and tells, learning centers, and free-choice play centers and prepare class activities; drive on field trips; and do much more. These activities give teachers nonthreatening opportunities to establish new parent language as parents interact with and guide small groups of children in a variety of activities. During small-group show and tells, we encourage teachers and parents to have conversations instead of interrogation sessions with the children in the groups. To facilitate the process, we provide the Show and Tell Prompt Card in Appendix C, page 257, to guide and enhance their discussions.

Teachers can be empowered by the adult helpers and other role models they enlist in preschool. They benefit enormously from the extra support and expertise that parents bring to their classrooms. For example, several of our preschoolers' parents are bilingual and provide invaluable support for our non–English-speaking children. One father, as we previously mentioned, is a country music singer and used his volunteer time to sing and play his guitar with the kids. Parents are empowered and feel valued when their special capabilities are recognized and appreciated, and open and ongoing communication between parents and teachers facilitates this type of interaction.

As positive as we hope parent participation will be, there is always the exception. Teachers need to be cognizant of the occasional parent who may not have the social skills to interact appropriately or even safely with young children. For their own protection and the protection of the children in the preschool, parents should never be left alone with students. If any parent presents a danger to his or her own children or other children, the appropriate authorities should be contacted immediately. When involving adults in a preschool classroom, always follow school district policies and guidelines to ensure everyone's security. Some undesirable adult behaviors, however, may be mediated without excluding the parent entirely.

The most recent example from our experience is a mother whose only apparent discipline strategy was raising her voice at the children. The teacher would intervene thoughtfully, explaining that we do not yell at school, and she would model an appropriate intervention. However, the undesirable yelling was so ingrained in this mother's social schema that her behavior persisted. To intervene and change these inappropriate interactions, we did two things. First, we developed and posted a classroom discipline template on a large chart with the desired adult prompt (see the Stop and Think Behavior Chart in chapter 4 on page 58). The classroom aide and teacher referenced and modeled its usage daily. Soon, all the parents were using the suggested discipline prompts, and the mother who used to raise her voice slowly began to change her language. Another parent commented, "I don't have to yell at my son anymore at home. I just tell him, 'You can make the choice of the "thinking chair" or what I said to do.' It really works, too." Second, to further support the mother's appropriate use of discipline, we solicited the support of our local Early Head Start program. One-on-one adult modeling and support was provided in her home to encourage appropriate parenting skills and interactions with her baby and toddler, and she was allowed to serve her required volunteer hours with the Early Head Start mentor. Together, the preschool teacher and the mentor modeled and taught this mother the social pragmatics that will benefit her and her children in the years to come.

Home-school partnerships enhance and facilitate the education of young children. Teachers who value and incorporate the curriculum of the home into the classroom will find that their students assimilate more smoothly into the school culture. To serve as an effective channel between home and school, preschool should reflect the environments of both settings. Couches, beanbag chairs, and pillows; convenient restroom facilities; and kitchen amenities, carpets, plants, and homey window dressings create a home-like atmosphere within the preschool classroom. Familiar and comfortable routines also ease the transition from home to school for young children. Read-alouds with familiar stories from home or shared readings with relevant themes, such as having friends, getting along with others, and helping at home, also may support this process. The books in Figure 61 reflect some of these familiar and relevant themes.

Establishing equal partnerships, initiating home-school interactions, nurturing and establishing rapport, and creating a sense of ownership and empowerment for parents in a school environment are the essential elements for successful home-school collaboration. To accomplish these goals, schools must provide an open, two-way communication link with families. Educators and parents need to work at getting to know one another as associates and partners in the nurturing and development of all children. The parent involvement model of the past neglected the partnership-building component that we advocate. We truly believe that quality

---

• Figure 61 •
Recommended Books for Home-School Connections

Barton, B. (1991). *The three bears*. New York: HarperCollins.

Bogart, J.E., & Freire, F. (1989). *Ten for dinner*. New York: Scholastic.

Boynton, S. (1995). *Blue hat, green hat*. New York: Simon & Schuster.

Carlstrom, N. (1996). *Jesse Bear, what will you wear?* New York: Simon & Schuster.

Hill, E. (1984). *Spot goes to school*. New York: Putnam.

Kraus, R. (1994). *Leo the late bloomer*. Ill. J. Aruego. New York: HarperCollins.

Martin, B., Jr. (1983). *Brown bear, brown bear, what do you see?* [Board book]. Ill. E. Carle. New York: Henry Holt.

Martin, B., Jr., & Archambault, J. (1989). *Chicka chicka boom boom*. Ill. L. Ehlert. New York: Simon & Schuster.

Mueller, V. (1997). *Monster goes to school*. Ill. L. Munsinger. Morton Grove, IL: Whitman.

Munsch, R. (1988). *Love you forever*. Ill. S. McGraw. Willowdale, ON: Firefly Books.

Perkins, A., & Gurney, E. (1969). *Hand, hand, fingers, thumb*. New York: Random House.

home-school partnerships in preschools can change a child's educational prognosis and ultimately change a life.

Assessment

Parent involvement successes and concerns may be assessed in a variety of ways. As we mention in this chapter. anecdotal records targeting family interests, talents, and special situations will empower home-school relations and facilitate a collaborative educational approach for each child in the preschool. A record of the parent volunteer hours served also provides valuable information about program effectiveness (see the parent volunteer sign-up form in Appendix F, page 303). Parent surveys on an array of topics and issues also help teachers to address the needs of their students' families continually. Finally, the childrens' annual assessments may corroborate the parent participation data.

Conclusion

The parent involvement model that we suggest does not permit parents to abdicate their essential responsibilities or influence their children's education fundamentals. Goldenberg (2002) reveals that too often, "parent involvement efforts are open only to those parents who can or will go to training sessions, [and] we inevitably exclude substantial numbers of families, those perhaps with the greatest need" (p. 224). The required parent volunteering that we recommend in preschool classrooms allows parents the flexibility to begin their home-school experience with a significant amount of flexibility within the fixed two-hour-a-week obligation. The parents to whom Goldenberg refers in his statement are those we frequently see sitting in the corner of the preschool room observing for the first few weeks. They are encouraged, but not forced, to engage within the ensuing activities. Rather than imposing our beliefs and attitudes on these parents in a "stand and deliver" training session, parents may choose the activities and events in which they feel most comfortable engaging. Over time, teacher modeling and student enticements draw in even the most reluctant parents. Parent involvement is critical to support children in reaching their social, emotional, physical, and cognitive potentials. Expert teachers may initiate and encourage supportive connections between the school and home cultures, but we believe that it is the parent's response that solidifies the partnership.

One of our ultimate goals in developing this parental component of the preschool framework is to model for parents the power of adult-child social interactions in the growth and development of children. Parents need to understand and recognize how their thoughtful and sensitive conversations can influence and have an impact on not only their children's social and emotional stability but also their cognitive ability. According to Hart and Risley (1999),

> The data lead to a simple message for parents. When you talk with your children a lot about things that are not important, you automatically give them experiences that are important to their cognitive and emotional learning. While your children are little, your conversation matters.

Children get better at what they practice, and having more language tools, more nuances, more fluency, more steps in the social dances of life is likely to contribute at least as much to your children's future success as their heredity and their choice of friends. (p. xiii)

We believe that the continuous, positive adult-child interactions in which a child engages early in life ultimately have an impact on his or her academic, social, and emotional success in the future. Parents and teachers working together can provide the critical underpinnings that support and nurture children's interpersonal skills and enable their school success. However, children are not the only beneficiaries of the home-school partnership: Parents and teachers are empowered, too, as they learn and grow together in the educational process.

Looking Back and Looking Ahead

...

Reflection and vision seem very "individually appropriate" at this particular juncture of our early childhood practice and studies. Certainly in our minds, the reciprocal processes of reflection and vision support one another in the spiraling of our new thinking. As we reflect over the past 10 years since the inception of our preschool journey, we are staggered by the infusion of new brain research, early language and literacy data, school readiness standards, new reading comprehension strategies, differentiated instruction, new English as a second language learning models, early intervention programs, assessment and accountability, and universal preschool mandates, just to mention a few topics prevalent in educational arenas. Amazingly enough, our Vygotskian-based roots ring true through it all. After 50 cumulative years of experience in the field of education, we remain convinced that purposeful, sensitive teaching and social interaction within a child's ZPD is still the most powerful educational intervention available to children. This philosophical conviction may be the one educational perspective that will be unchanging in the years to come.

Reflecting on the various topics presented in this text, we would like to underscore the fundamental themes and beliefs that we consider central to the development of a quality preschool environment. These themes include social interaction and learning, language and literacy instruction, individually appropriate practice, education embedded in playful and realistic experiences, parent involvement, and self-regulation. We believe that through social interactions with others, children's learning and cognition are directly influenced. We believe that explicit instruction in literacy and language during a child's early years is beneficial and enables later school success. We believe that learning opportunities rooted in realistic and playful activities promote student motivation, curiosity, attention, and independent problem solving. We believe that children flourish when parents are actively involved in their learning. Finally, we believe that the development of self-regulation skills is primary to the learning process.

As Berk and Winsler (1995) state, "According to Vygotsky's...sociocultural theory, cognition is a profoundly social phenomenon. Social experience shapes the ways of thinking and interpreting the world available to individuals" (p. 12). This hypothesis is fundamental to the beliefs that we hold about how children learn and acquire new knowledge. Thus, the teaching and learning model that we advocate in this book embraces the importance of purposeful daily social interactions between children and adults and between student peers in a variety of stimulating settings and social groupings. These socially stimulating settings and groupings occur in many ways within a quality preschool environment—via whole-class read-alouds, small

ZPD groups, buddy reading, free-choice play centers, class field trips, and many other options. Unlimited opportunities for socially mediated interactions between preschoolers and others ultimately empower children as they synthesize and construct their own cognition.

The channel that connects a child's social interactions to his or her internal thinking is language. According to Berk and Winsler (1995), "Vygotsky regarded language as a critical bridge between the sociocultural world and individual mental functioning; he viewed the acquisition of language as the most significant milestone in children's cognitive development" (p. 12). In turn, oral language development, vocabulary development, social pragmatics, and phonological awareness all serve as critical precursors to reading and writing development. This complex process typically begins long before children enter elementary school. Tragically, many children do not come to school with these critical language and literacy competencies, and thus they seldom catch up to their better-prepared peers. Language and literacy instruction in preschool can and does make a difference for young children.

As stated by the IRA and NAEYC joint position statement on developmentally appropriate practices for young children (2000), "The ability to read and write does not develop naturally, without careful planning and instruction" (p. 6). Thus, Schickedanz (as cited in Roskos, Christie, & Richgels, 2003) notes that "early literacy instruction must often be explicit and direct, which is not to say that it must be script like, prescriptive, and rigid" (p. 57). We firmly believe that literacy and language instruction can and should be delivered in a playful and individually appropriate manner, where the child is the only script. To achieve this skilled level of instruction in a preschool environment, teachers must know and understand each individual child across the developmental domains, preschool curricula and appropriate developmental compendiums, and how to provide both explicit and implicit instruction. This system of intentional and thoughtful instruction supports and empowers early readers as they begin to synthesize what they know about language, pictures, and print and begin to decipher, comprehend, and compose texts.

Integrating learning, particularly language and literacy learning, into playful, real-life experiences provides a relevant context in which young children can understand and internalize new concepts more easily. Connecting new learning to familiar routines, recognizable surroundings, prior experiences, previous understandings, and special interests scaffolds preschoolers in the learning process. Implementing meaningful and appropriate thematic units also integrates the content areas and makes learning more interesting and germane. The class's thematic unit should be evident immediately to all who enter the preschool classroom. Free-choice play centers, learning centers, and read-alouds should reflect the general theme of study. Embedding explicit language and literacy instruction into playful, realistic, and meaningful contexts provides children with tangible and concrete scaffolds to support their new learning.

Children's learning is most effectively enhanced when parents and teachers work together to forge the home-school connection. Preschool teachers can offer parents valuable information about early language and literacy learning, social and emotional development, individually appropriate instruction, and much more. In turn, parents can provide valuable insights into their children's social and emotional needs, special talents, and interests, in addition to sharing their own. As parents and grandparents ourselves, we feel strongly that family members are the first and primary teachers in children's lives and should be respected as such. Positive parent-teacher partnerships provide the critical support necessary to nurture children's confidence and success in school.

Children's levels of confidence are readily apparent in their abilities to plan, choose, and monitor their own actions and behavior. This ability, commonly referred to as self-regulation, is perhaps the most significant and overriding capability that young children develop. Bodrova and colleagues (2001) state, "Before a child is able to regulate his or her own behavior, the child has to have experience being regulated by other people and regulating other people's actions" (p. 20). As self-regulation competencies develop, they can be seen in such situations as a child's pragmatics during social interactions, sharing during play centers, word choice and syntax usage in conversations, and picture and print usage in literacy acquisition. Dramatic play provides a wonderful framework in which adults can observe young children practicing self-regulation. While pretending to be nurses or firefighters, children self-regulate or adjust their actions to reflect the characteristics that they associate with the professional they are emulating. Ultimately, this ability to govern their role-play behaviors based on known information translates into the vital ability to self-regulate their learning in academic situations.

Having summarized what we believe to be appropriate and stimulating educational environments for preschool children, we would like to conclude with what we perceive to be the staff development essentials of our teacher colleagues and future early childhood educators. In our opinion, expert teachers are the cornerstones for any successful educational framework. Training expert teachers who can deliver individually appropriate instruction for every child in their classrooms is perhaps one of the greatest challenges before U.S. colleges, universities, and policymakers today.

Our vision for effective teacher training programs includes quality preservice and inservice opportunities that prepare educators to face the unique educational challenges of the 21st century. Teachers have been isolated in their self-contained classrooms for too many years with little or no site-embedded support or guidance. Similar to our students, teachers need daily educational interactions and conversations with peers that challenge and extend their thinking to new levels of understanding and knowledge. The current structure of our standard public school classrooms, Head Start centers, and child development centers typically provides only for teacher-to-teacher collaboration outside the classroom doors during staff meetings, workshops, classes, or special education meetings about individualized education programs (IEPs). We believe a more inspiring and dynamic teaching atmosphere may evolve when two or more expert teachers collaborate to observe, plan, and teach the same children within the preschool setting.

As we look ahead, we hope that policymakers will have the wisdom to understand that prescriptive programs cannot and will not ever meet the individual needs of every child in a classroom of 20 or more students. We need teachers who control and manage educational programs, not educational programs that control and manage teachers. In our opinion, experienced, knowledgeable, and motivated educators working in collaborative teams are a valuable ingredient that may significantly increase the quality of classroom instruction in the future years. Knowledgeable teachers connect what they know about their students as learners to what they know about curricula, developmental compendiums, and teaching strategies to facilitate and enhance their daily instruction.

Since the beginning of this early childhood endeavor, we have held tight to our fundamental belief that constructive, deliberate adult-child interactions can have an impact on and accelerate learning for all children. To achieve this worthy goal, teachers with expertise in early childhood growth and development, developmental compendiums, implicit and explicit instruction, and—most important—in child observation are imperative. To accomplish and maintain this level of expertise, we propose the following 10 interventions for stakeholders to contemplate:

1. Offer site-embedded staff development for teachers to observe new instructional techniques and strategies in their own classrooms with their own students. Trainings that are site embedded more often are tailored to address specific student populations and their needs rather than more generalized projects and procedures. Monthly visits to classrooms at the teacher's own grade level, as well as grade levels above and below, will provide invaluable knowledge and information. This inservice strategy benefits teachers of all grade levels; however, we believe that it would be particularly beneficial for preschool educators. Too often, preschools are set off campus, and early childhood educators have little or no opportunities to collaborate with primary-grade teachers. Early childhood teachers must be intimately aware of kindergarten and first- and second-grade developmental compendiums and content standards. Knowing what students are going to be expected to do in succeeding years is critical to provide smooth transitions and a common language between grade levels and schools.

2. Offer ongoing mentoring opportunities by a variety of specialists. For example, in most school settings speech or language pathologists provide pull-out services for identified children twice a week for approximately 20 minutes at a time. In our opinion, this model would be greatly enhanced if these services were brought to the classroom, where the speech or language pathologist could share his or her specialized training with the classroom teacher. Then, this collaboration would not have an impact on one student but on numerous students as the teacher becomes more and more skilled in the oral language and articulation instructional strategies. Other specialists, such as reading teachers, special education teachers, audiologists, technology technicians, and physical education and art teachers, also may offer unique insights and embedded trainings for classroom teachers. Ultimately, these collaborative opportunities empower both the classroom teacher and the specialist and consequently, the students they share.

3. Offer new ways to empower young prospective educators with experience in differentiated instruction, explicit and implicit instruction, and early intervention strategies. One option may be to require all preservice teachers, particularly early childhood educators, to take several core classes in special education in conjunction with their regular education degrees. This approach would accomplish two things: (1) early childhood teachers would receive a background in early detection, observational strategies, interventions, teaching strategies, assessments, and alternative services that may thwart later special education services, and (2) early childhood teachers would receive more training in planning and implementing IEPs for children. This ability may provide the teachers with many of the tools that they need to differentiate instruction and may prevent erroneous behaviors from being entrenched without intercession. The special education training also provides teachers with vital knowledge about federal legislation and gives them insights into educational alternatives for young children with special needs.

4. Create professional development schools (PDSs) to provide a unique model for delivery of preservice education. In PDSs, junior- and senior-level college students attend all their classes within an existing preschool or elementary school. Integrating prospective educators daily into actual classroom settings promotes the blending of teaching's theoretical and practical aspects. Novice educators have an early opportunity to rehearse new instructional strategies under the tutelage of a seasoned professional while continuing to study and converse with their professors. This model allows college students to participate in the essential conversations with more knowledgeable others, which Vygotsky advocates to extend their thinking (Bodrova & Leong, 1996).

5. Provide student-teaching opportunities, which some colleges incorporate now, that allow undergraduates destined for preschool classrooms to teach for 6–8 weeks in primary-grade classrooms, 6–8 weeks in special education classrooms, and 12–16 weeks in a quality preschool. This part of the preservice program may facilitate new and more global insights into the expectations that preservice teachers have for their own teaching. Placing our preservice teachers with the most knowledgeable preschool educators available is a must to develop the desired level of expertise.

6. Encourage state accreditation boards to consider the recertification requirement of three graduate credits in special education courses every five years. This mandate will ensure that educators continue to hone and enhance their skills in differentiating instruction. In addition, teachers will be kept current with new and innovative interventions and federal mandates for at-risk and special education children.

7. Offer team-teaching opportunities with two certified teachers in each preschool. This situation would provide for the ongoing collaborative conversations about children's growth and development that exploit and promote deliberate instruction. As we discuss in this book, most preschool programs provide one certified teacher and a paraprofessional. This setup is a positive step toward a team-teaching model; however, two certified teachers would be the ultimate goal to achieve the highest level of teacher instruction and collaboration deserved by all children. Two teachers with comparably high levels of training and expertise may not only serve the children in their care more competently, but their conversations also will very likely reflect their collegial status.

8. Provide peer coaching that allows for ongoing professional conversations. Once again, opportunities to talk with coworkers and peers, plan for instruction, reflect after instruction, and discuss students' strengths and needs all help to improve and differentiate instruction. Peer coaching may be used effectively at grade level, across grade levels, and across the community and state.

9. Organize book studies and cohort groups to provide occasions for teachers to have professional conversations about the challenges facing them in their classrooms. Book studies and cohort groups may focus on any number of topics, including educational trends, the latest research, classroom organization, children's literature, behavior management, oral language development, play activities and centers, and, most important, implications for the classroom.

10. Give teachers opportunities to attend regional and national conferences such as the IRA Annual Convention or the NAEYC Annual Conference. These conferences provide teachers with the occasion to communicate with other teachers from around the world, to hear a variety of presentations on any number of educational topics, and to view innovative materials and programs for young children. These conferences offer ideal settings to extend and broaden early childhood educators' learning and thinking as they converse with recognized professionals in their field.

A Final Note

Writing this book has been a daunting task for both of us as we continue to teach full time at schools 1,000 miles apart. However, it has given us a remarkable opportunity to think in depth about our teaching practices in early childhood education and our beliefs regarding what is possible and necessary for our young students. We hope this book elicits a similar examination by our readers as they question, reflect on, and refine their teaching practices and belief systems in regard to young children. Teaching and learning in preschool should be a daily, reciprocal process that occurs between thoughtful and effective teachers and their students.

Lesson Planning Forms and Thematic Literacy Lesson Plans

• • •

This appendix includes the Preschool Lesson Plan Template, the ZPD Groups Lesson Plan Template, a generic lesson plan format, and 16 thematic literacy lesson plans. We provide these items as suggestions for busy preschool teachers, who may choose to use and adapt them to the needs of their individual students.

The Preschool Lesson Plan Template helps the teacher and aide plan and record weekly classroom activities. This concise overview can be given to parent volunteers so they will better understand what has happened prior to their arrival. Most areas on the chart are self-explanatory. The center portion offers sections for recording planned lessons for ZPD groups.

The ZPD Groups Lesson Plan Template offers teachers another way to record their lesson plans for ZPD group time. This chart gives teachers more room and includes a place for writing activities.

The generic lesson plan format gives teachers a suggested framework as they implement a learner-centered preschool. We have not included times for each activity because each school population has its own unique time frames.

The thematic literacy lesson plans offer 16 different ways to include in your school day ideas for shared reading, learning centers, read-alouds, and interactive or scaffolded writing. We have included some very general suggestions for ZPD groups because specifics would depend on the learning needs of the students in each group. A variety of content area themes also would be appropriate to use within this lesson plan design. We have not provided any here because, once again, those themes would depend on each preschool population. These thematic lesson plans are targeted for part of the preschool day. Other daily events, such as the opening and recess, would happen before and after these activities, as indicated in the generic lesson plan format.

PRESCHOOL LESSON PLAN TEMPLATE

Week of_____

Teacher_____   Theme_____

Time	Monday	Tuesday	Wednesday	Thursday	Friday
Independent and/or Buddy Reading					
Opening and Calendar Activities					
Shared Reading					
Learning Centers					
ZPD Groups					
Group 1	LID PA/O CAP	LID PA/O CAP	LID PA/O CAP	LID PA/O CAP	LID PA/O CAP
Group 2	LID PA/O CAP	LID PA/O CAP	LID PA/O CAP	LID PA/O CAP	LID PA/O CAP
Group 3	LID PA/O CAP	LID PA/O CAP	LID PA/O CAP	LID PA/O CAP	LID PA/O CAP
Group 4	LID PA/O CAP	LID PA/O CAP	LID PA/O CAP	LID PA/O CAP	LID PA/O CAP
Read-Aloud (Book)					
Interactive and Scaffolded Writing					
Free-Choice and Dramatic Play Centers					
Small-Group Show and Tell					
Closing Activities					

LID = letter identification (what letter work will be done)
PA/O = phonological awareness and/or oral language activities
CAP = concepts about print and print awareness activities

ZPD GROUPS LESSON PLAN TEMPLATE

ZPD Groups	Monday	Tuesday	Wednesday	Thursday	Friday
	LS/LID: PA/O: CAP: Wtg:	LS/LID: PA/O: CAP: Wtg:	LS/LID: PA/O: CAP: Wtg:	LS/LID: PA/O: CAP: Wtg:	LS/LID: PA/O: CAP: Wtg:
	LS/LID: PA/O: CAP: Wtg:	LS/LID: PA/O: CAP: Wtg:	LS/LID: PA/O: CAP: Wtg:	LS/LID: PA/O: CAP: Wtg:	LS/LID: PA/O: CAP: Wtg:
	LS/LID: PA/O: CAP: Wtg:	LS/LID: PA/O: CAP: Wtg:	LS/LID: PA/O: CAP: Wtg:	LS/LID: PA/O: CAP: Wtg:	LS/LID: PA/O: CAP: Wtg:
	LS/LID: PA/O: CAP: Wtg:	LS/LID: PA/O: CAP: Wtg:	LS/LID: PA/O: CAP: Wtg:	LS/LID: PA/O: CAP: Wtg:	LS/LID: PA/O: CAP: Wtg:

Designed by Dusty Haigler, National County School District, Casper, Wyoming.

LS/LID = letter sounds or letter identification

PA/O = phonological awareness and/or oral language activities

CAP = concepts about print and print awareness activities

Wtg = writing

Teaching and Learning in Preschool: Using Individually Appropriate Practices in Early Childhood Literacy Instruction by Elizabeth Claire Venn and Monica Dacy Jahn. © 2004. Newark, DE: International Reading Association. May be copied for classroom use.

GENERIC LESSON PLAN FORMAT

Welcome and Attendance

Independent and/or Buddy Reading
Students individually or with a partner read their own student books.

Opening and Calendar Activities
At the opening of the school day, the teacher begins with a community-building activity and then may preview class themes and special events and discuss them with students. The teacher can use the morning message as a literacy learning opportunity. Calendar activities may incorporate social studies and science skills into conversations about numbers, patterning, and appropriate clothing for the weather conditions.

Shared Reading
The teacher and students read a Big Book based on a class theme. The shared reading incorporates links to students' prior knowledge of the topic, models reading comprehension strategies, and highlights concepts about print such as directionality, one-to-one correspondence, and attending to print.

Learning Centers
During this part of the day, ZPD groups meet while other students engage in independent writing or themed, content area activity centers. This is a teacher-initiated activity time.

Recess and Snack

Read-Aloud
The teacher reads to and discusses with students a book related to the class theme and incorporates information about oral language structures and phonological awareness such as rhyming, syllable segmenting and blending, phoneme discrimination, letter-sound association, and isolation of a word's initial and final consonant sounds.

Interactive and Scaffolded Writing
The teacher models the reading-writing connection and engages students in the writing process.

Free-Choice and Dramatic Play Centers
Students engage in centers supplied with computers, art materials, math manipulatives, science information, blocks, writing materials, dramatic role-play props, and so on. This is a student-initiated activity time.

Small-Group Show and Tell

Closing Activities

This schedule varies based on the individual needs of children, daily special classes—such as music, computer, library, or physical education classes—and field trips or school events. All developmental domains and content areas are interwoven throughout daily instruction and playful activities.

Teaching and Learning in Preschool: Using Individually Appropriate Practices in Early Childhood Literacy Instruction by Elizabeth Claire Venn and Monica Dacy Jahn © 2004. Newark, DE: International Reading Association. May be copied for classroom use.

THEMATIC LITERACY LESSON PLANS

In this section, we develop the shared reading, learning centers, read-aloud, and interactive and scaffolded writing portions of the school day into specific activities.

FAIRY TALE LESSON 1

Shared Reading of *Goldilocks and the Three Bears* (Cauley, 1992)

Materials

- a copy of the text
- student- or teacher-created transparencies of scenes from the story
- an overhead projector
- character masks made from construction paper

Procedure
This activity focuses on teaching language structures and "talking like a book."

1. Before reading, introduce the fairy tale by saying, "This book is a fairy tale, and fairy tales are pretend stories written about long-ago times. Fairy tales frequently begin with the phrase *once upon a time*. Let's say the phrase together now, and listen for it in the story."

2. During reading, focus on "story" language structures—such as "This porridge is too hot!" or "This bed is too big!"—reading with a lot of intonation and expression.

3. After reading, model acting out the fairy tale with an aide and parent helpers. Use student- or teacher-created transparencies that illustrate the story's important scenes, such as the house in the woods, three bowls of porridge, the three chairs, and the three beds. Use construction paper masks of the three bears and Goldilocks.

Learning Centers

Materials

- student copies of *Goldilocks and the Three Bears*
- student- or teacher-created transparencies of scenes from the story
- an overhead projector
- character masks made from construction paper
- journals
- pencils and crayons
- watercolors
- paintbrushes

- large sheets of art paper
- nonfiction books about bears
- graham cracker bears
- a construction paper number template shaped like a bear

ZPD Groups

This activity focuses on language structures and talking like a book. Each small ZPD group acts out *Goldilocks and the Three Bears*, using the transparencies, overhead projector, and character masks. Provide all students with explicit instruction in phonological awareness, letter identification, writing, and concepts about print based on the ZPD of each group's members. Be sure to embed these brief prompts into instruction in a meaningful way.

Journal Writing Center

In journals, have students create their own bear stories or rewrite *Goldilocks and the Three Bears* with their own words, pictures, or both in pencil or crayon. An adult helper also may serve as a scribe for a student wishing to dictate a story.

Social Studies and Science Center

Have students paint pictures of the three bears with watercolors on large sheets of art paper. Have nonfiction books about bears available for students to use as references.

Mathematics Center

Have students count graham cracker bears and match them to a bear template with numerals on it. For example, if the template shows the number *4* in one spot, the students should place four graham cracker bears in that spot. Some templates also may provide an outline of the required number of bears, requiring the students to match one bear to each outline.

Read-Aloud of *Jesse Bear, What Will You Wear?* (Carlstrom, 1996)

Materials

- a copy of the text

Procedure

Have the students chant the repetitive lines in this story as you read from the text.

Interactive and Scaffolded Writing

Materials

- a large dry-erase board or chalkboard for the teacher
- small dry-erase boards or chalkboards, or white paper on clipboards for students
- chalk or dry-erase markers for the teacher
- dry-erase markers, chalk, pencils, markers, or colored pencils for students

Procedure

1. Tell students, "Let's brainstorm a list of the clothes that Jesse Bear is wearing in the story." Model writing a brief list of clothing items on the large dry-erase board or chalkboard.

2. Then, find out what word your students would like to write—such as *hat*—and have them write it on their own dry-erase boards, chalkboards, or sheets of white paper while you write it on your large dry-erase board or chalkboard.

FAIRY TALE LESSON 2

Shared Reading of *Each Peach Pear Plum* (Ahlberg & Ahlberg, 1999)

Materials

• a Big Book copy of the text

• a Big Book stand

Procedure

This activity focuses on looking for picture clues and completing rhymes.

1. Before reading, explain to students that you will be reading a rhyming book about familiar fairy tale characters. Tell them that if they look closely, they will see the characters hiding in the pictures. Look through all the book's pictures first, searching for the hidden characters.

2. During reading, have students complete each rhyme as you read. For example, say, "Each, peach, pear, plum. I spy Tom _____."

3. After reading, play I Spy with the students. For example, say, "I spy someone in our class whose name begins with *S*" or "I spy someone in our class who is wearing the color purple."

Learning Centers

Materials

• student copies of *Each Peach Pear Plum*

• journals

• colored markers

• a teacher-created audiotape of *Little Red Riding Hood* (Ransom, 2001)

• student copies of *Little Red Riding Hood*

• a tape recorder

• headphones

ZPD Groups

This activity focuses on rhyming. The level of instruction may be varied to teach at the ZPD of each group's members. Each small ZPD group interacts with student copies of *Each Peach Pear*

Plum for rhyme recognition ("Do *plum* and *thumb* sound the same or different?"), rhyme completion ("Each, peach, pear, plum. I spy Tom _____."), and rhyme production ("Who can tell me a word that rhymes with *hood*?"). Provide all students with explicit instruction in phonological awareness, letter identification, writing, and concepts about print based on the ZPD of each group's members. Be sure to embed these brief prompts into instruction in a meaningful way.

Journal Writing Center
Have students use colored markers to write in their journals all the letters that they know, practice writing their own names, or both. Some students may attempt to draw the fairy tale characters' names with accompanying illustrations.

Social Studies and Science Center
Have students play I Spy with the aide. Students may initiate the "I spy" clues. Explain to students that they will need to look carefully around the room to discover the desired object, similar to how scientists need to make close observations.

Listening Center
Have students listen to a fairy tale, such as *Little Red Riding Hood*, on a teacher-created audiotape and follow along in their own copies of the book.

Read-Aloud of *The Little Red Hen* (McQueen, 1987)

Materials

• a copy of the text

Procedure
Have the students orally repeat the repetitive lines from the story (e.g., "'I won't,' said the duck!").

Interactive and Scaffolded Writing

Materials

• a large dry-erase board or chalkboard for the teacher
• small dry-erase boards or chalkboards, or white paper on clipboards for students
• chalk or dry-erase markers for the teacher
• dry-erase markers, chalk, pencils, markers, or colored pencils for students

Procedure
Using your large dry-erase board or chalkboard and with students using their smaller boards or sheets of white paper, interactively write rhyming words such as *hen* and *pen* or *red* and *bed*.

NURSERY RHYME LESSON I

Shared Reading of *Jack and Jill: And Other Nursery Rhymes* (Cousins, 1996)

Materials

- a Big Book copy of the text
- a Big Book stand
- a pointer

Procedure

This activity focuses on looking for picture clues and completing rhymes.

1. Before reading, introduce students to the concept of a nursery rhyme, explaining that it is generally a poem or short story that rhymes. Cite other nursery rhymes that you previously have shared with the class, and ask students to name other nursery rhymes that they know.

2. During reading, have students act out the nursery rhyme, pretending to walk up and fall down the hill. Note how the pictures in the text support the storyline.

3. After reading, briefly discuss the word *crown* and its meaning in the context of this nursery rhyme.

4. Do a second reading of the text, engaging students in rhyme completion, such as "Jack and Jill went up the _____?"

Learning Centers

Materials

- student copies of *Jack and Jill*
- teacher-created name strips of students' names
- journals
- glue
- crayons
- tongue depressors
- a teacher-created audiotape of nursery rhymes from *Tomie dePaola's Mother Goose* (dePaola, 1985c)
- student copies of *Tomie dePaola's Mother Goose*
- a tape recorder
- headphones

ZPD Groups

Each small ZPD group interacts with *Jack and Jill* student books for rhyme recognition ("Do *Jill* and *hill* sound the same or different?"), rhyme completion ("Jack and Jill went up the _____?"), and rhyme production ("Who can tell me a word from the story that rhymes with *mail?*"). Provide all students with explicit instruction in phonological awareness, letter identification, writing, and concepts about print based on the ZPD of each group's members. Be sure to embed these brief prompts into instruction in a meaningful way.

Journal Writing Center

Have each student cut up his or her own name from a teacher-created name strip and make a name puzzle. Have students practice reassembling their own names several times and then glue the letters in proper order in their journals. Have students copy or trace their names if there is time.

Art and Drama Center

Have each student color his or her own hill, Jack, and Jill puppets and glue them onto tongue depressors. Using the stick puppets, have two students act out the story while the other students chant it.

Listening Center

Have students listen to Mother Goose nursery rhymes on a teacher-created audiotape and follow along in their own copies of the text.

Read-Aloud of Nursery Rhymes From *Tomie dePaola's Mother Goose* (dePaola, 1985c)

Materials

• a copy of the text

Procedure

When reading aloud familiar nursery rhymes, pause at the end of a line so students can complete the rhyme (e.g., "Hickory, dickory, dock, the mouse ran up the _____.").

Interactive and Scaffolded Writing

Materials

• a large dry-erase board or chalkboard for the teacher

• small dry-erase boards or chalkboards, or white paper on clipboards for students

• chalk or dry-erase markers for the teacher

• dry-erase markers, chalk, pencils, markers, or colored pencils for students

Procedure

Interactively write a play plan (see chapter 7, page 111) together with your students before they go to free-play centers. For example, have each student complete the sentence "I will play with _____" and add a picture of the center that he or she plans to attend after you model an illustration.

NURSERY RHYME LESSON 2

Shared Reading of *Little Miss Muffet* (Collins, 2003)

Materials

- a Big Book copy of the text
- a Big Book stand
- a stool
- a bowl
- a spoon
- a commercially or teacher-created spider puppet

Procedure

This activity focuses on reading with expression and using irregular past-tense verbs.

1. Before reading, revisit the concept of a nursery rhyme, reminding students that it is generally a poem or short story that rhymes. Cite other nursery rhymes that you previously have shared with the class. Briefly discuss the words *tuffet*, *curds*, and *whey* and their meanings in the context of the story.

2. During reading, have two students act out the nursery rhyme. The first student pretends to sit on a tuffet and eat curds and whey, while the second student plays the spider with a spider puppet. The other students should chant the nursery rhyme as the two students act it out.

3. After reading, ask relevant questions that prompt students to use irregular past-tense verbs correctly (e.g., "What did Miss Muffet do with the curds and whey? That's right; she *ate* the curds and whey."). Chant together, "Today I eat, yesterday I ate, and tomorrow I will eat!"

Learning Centers

Materials

- student copies of *Little Miss Muffet*
- teacher-created pictures from *Little Miss Muffet*
- journals
- black ink pads
- black crayons
- pencils
- black pipe cleaners or black construction paper
- a stool
- a bowl
- a spoon

- a commercially or teacher-created spider puppet

- scissors

- glue

ZPD Groups

This activity focuses on using irregular past-tense verbs such as *sat*, *came*, and *ate*. Each small ZPD group interacts with *Little Miss Muffet* student books. Provide all students with explicit instruction in language structures, phonological awareness, letter identification, writing, and concepts about print based on the ZPD of each group's members. Be sure to embed these brief prompts into instruction in a meaningful way.

Journal Writing Center

Have students make fingerprint spiders in their journals with a black ink pad and black crayons. Students put their index fingers in ink and press them on the journal paper to make a spider body, and then they use black crayons to draw spider legs. Have students write the word *spider* in pencil to label their fingerprint spiders.

Art and Drama Center

Have students make spiders with black pipe cleaners or construction paper, and using a stool, bowl, spoon, and a spider puppet have two students act out *Little Miss Muffet* while the other students chant.

Literacy and Language Center

Cut up teacher-created pictures from *Little Miss Muffet* and have students sequence and color them. Have students paste the pictures in order in their journals. Have students retell and rewrite the nursery rhyme in their own words if time allows. Some students may dictate their retellings to a parent volunteer or aide, who will record it for them.

Read-Aloud of More Nursery Rhymes From *Tomie dePaola's Mother Goose* (dePaola, 1985c)

Materials

- a copy of the text

Procedure

When reading aloud familiar nursery rhymes, pause at the end of a line so students can complete the rhyme (e.g., "Little Miss Muffet sat on a _____.").

Interactive and Scaffolded Writing

Materials

- a large dry-erase board or chalkboard for the teacher

- small dry-erase boards or chalkboards, or white paper on clipboards for students

- chalk or dry-erase markers for the teacher

- dry-erase markers, chalk, pencils, markers, or colored pencils for students

Procedure

1. Using your large dry-erase board or chalkboard and with students using their smaller boards or sheets of white paper, interactively write the words *Miss Muffet*. Be sure to model orally chunking the word *Muffet* into two parts—*Muff-et*—and stretching out the sounds in each part. Discuss capitalization.

2. Students may draw their own spiders on their boards or sheets of paper.

SONGBOOK LESSON 1

Shared Reading of *Down by the Bay* (Raffi, 1990)

Materials

- a Big Book copy of the text
- a Big Book stand
- a pointer
- an index card

Procedure

This activity focuses on reading fiction and looking for letter and word boundaries.

1. Before reading, introduce students to the concept of a songbook, explaining that it is a song accompanied by illustrations and print. Cite other songbooks that you previously have shared with the class, and ask students to name other songbooks that they know.

2. During reading, have students sing along as you read or sing the story.

3. After reading, inform students that nonfiction books tell readers about things that really have happened and fiction books such as this one tell readers about things that could not happen, such as a llama wearing pajamas. Have the students cite other events in the story that are fictitious.

4. Revisit the title, and have students count with you the number of letters and words in it. Use a pointer to point to the letters and an index card to place under the words.

Learning Centers

Materials

- student copies of *Down by the Bay*
- scissors
- cooking or home and garden magazines
- glue

- T-graph paper (paper with a horizontal line across the top and two vertical columns)
- multiple colors of tempera paint, including red, green, black, and yellow
- paintbrushes
- an easel
- large sheets of art paper
- watermelon seeds
- a muffin tin with a different number label in each hole

ZPD Groups
This activity focuses on concepts about print knowledge (e.g., letter and word boundaries, left-to-right directionality, and first and last). Each small ZPD group interacts with *Down by the Bay* student books. Provide all students with explicit instruction in phonological awareness, letter identification, writing, and concepts about print based on the ZPD of each group's members. Be sure to embed these brief prompts into instruction in a meaningful way.

Social Studies and Science Center
Have students cut out pictures of fruits and vegetables from magazines, sort fruits and vegetables separately, and glue the pictures on a teacher-created T-graph. Use one column of the graph for fruits and the other for vegetables. Adult assistance with this task may be necessary.

Art and Drama Center
Have each student paint a watermelon or other fruit or vegetable of his or her choice on sheets of art paper hung on an easel.

Mathematics Center
Have students count watermelon seeds and put the correct number of them into the muffin tin hole that is labeled with the same number.

Read-Aloud of *I'm a Little Teapot* (Trapani, 1997)

Materials
- a copy of the text

Procedure
Have students sing along, particularly with the song's first verse.

Interactive and Scaffolded Writing

Materials
- a large dry-erase board or chalkboard for the teacher
- small dry-erase boards or chalkboards, or white paper on clipboards for students
- chalk or dry-erase markers for the teacher
- dry-erase markers, chalk, pencils, markers, or colored pencils for students

Procedure

Using your large dry-erase board or chalkboard and with students using their smaller boards or sheets of white paper, interactively write the word *teapot*. Be sure to model chunking (with chin drops) or clapping the word into two parts—*tea...pot*—and stretching out the sounds in each part.

SONGBOOK LESSON 2

Shared Reading of *The Wheels on the Bus* (Raffi, 1998)

Materials

- a Big Book copy of the text
- a Big Book stand
- a pointer
- an index card

Procedure

This activity focuses on letter and word boundaries and one-to-one correspondence.

1. Before reading, revisit the concept of a songbook, explaining that it is a song accompanied by illustrations and print. Cite other songbooks that you previously have shared with the class, and ask students to name other songbooks that they know. Model one-to-one correspondence when reading the title.

2. During reading, have students sing along as you read or sing the story. Model and then have a student volunteer demonstrate with a pointer one-to-one correspondence, left-to-right directionality, and return sweep.

3. After reading, discuss other ways that people get around town in your community, or act out the song as students sing along, making up new verses with you.

4. Reread the title, and have students count with you the number of letters and words in it. Use a pointer to point to the letters and an index card to place under the words.

Learning Centers

Materials

- student copies of *The Wheels on the Bus*
- magazines
- scissors
- glue
- pie-graph paper
- multiple colors of tempera paint, including red, green, black, and yellow

- paintbrushes
- large sheets of art paper
- an easel
- vehicle stickers
- journals
- pencils and crayons

ZPD Groups

This activity focuses on concepts about print knowledge (e.g., letter and word boundaries, left-to-right directionality, and one-to-one correspondence). Each small ZPD group interacts with *The Wheels on the Bus* student books. Provide all students with explicit instruction in phonological awareness, letter identification, writing, and concepts about print based on the ZPD of each group's members. Be sure to embed these brief prompts into instruction in a meaningful way.

Social Studies and Science Center

Have students cut out vehicle pictures from magazines and categorize and glue different vehicles (e.g., cars, trucks, and buses) on a pie graph.

Art and Drama Center

Have students paint a bus and its passengers driving through town on sheets of art paper hung on an easel.

Journal Center

Have students write a "sticker story" by pasting vehicle stickers in their journals, and encourage students to use pencils or crayons to label the vehicles.

Read-Aloud of *Richard Scarry's Cars and Trucks and Things That Go* (Scarry, 1974) or *Miss Spider's New Car* (Kirk, 1997)

Materials

- a copy of the text

Procedure

Encourage students to make personal connections with the text such as discussing their own toy cars or their families' real cars.

Interactive and Scaffolded Writing

Materials

- a large dry-erase board or chalkboard for the teacher
- small dry-erase boards or chalkboards, or white paper on clipboards for students
- chalk or dry-erase markers for the teacher
- dry-erase markers, chalk, pencils, markers, or colored pencils for students

Procedure

Using your large dry-erase board or chalkboard and with students using their smaller boards or sheets of white paper, interactively write *bus*, *car*, *truck*, or all three, depending on the attention spans of your students.

WINTER BOOKS LESSON 1

Shared Reading of *The Snowy Day* (Keats, 1996)

Materials

- a Big Book copy of the text
- a Big Book stand
- a flannel board
- flannel story pieces (Make your own story pieces from felt, and have the students color them to match the activities in which Peter participates in the story.)

Procedure

This activity focuses on orally retelling stories in proper sequence.

1. Before reading, discuss what your students already know about snow and what they like to do on a snowy day.

2. During reading, make predictions about what Peter will do next in the snow before turning each page. Have students orally echo the prediction together.

3. After reading, use flannel story pieces on a flannel board to retell the story sequentially. Have students decide together which pictures come first, second, and so on. Then, have one student tell the rest of the class about his or her story piece.

Learning Centers

Materials

- student copies of *The Snowy Day* and *Peter's Chair* (Keats, 1998b)
- flannel story pieces
- a flannel board
- pieces of cardboard
- white sugar cubes
- white cake frosting
- plastic knives
- dark blue butcher paper
- black crayons

- paintbrushes
- Epsom salts mixed with water
- a teacher-created audiotape of *Peter's Chair*
- a tape recorder
- headphones

Procedure
This activity focuses on orally retelling a story. Provide all students with explicit instruction in phonological awareness, letter identification, writing, and concepts about print based on the ZPD of each group's members. Be sure to embed these brief prompts into instruction in a meaningful way.

ZPD Groups
Each small ZPD group interacts with *The Snowy Day* student books. Have students focus on retelling the story, using flannel story pieces on a flannel board.

Social Studies and Science Center
Have students build individual snow castles on a cardboard base with white sugar cubes that are held together with white cake frosting. Use plastic knives to spread the frosting.

Art and Drama Center
Have students draw on dark blue butcher paper with white crayons to make a class mural of each event depicted in *The Snowy Day*. Have students paint over the crayon drawings with Epsom salts dissolved in water to create a snowy look. Display the mural so students can retell the events in the story again.

Listening Center
Have students listen to *Peter's Chair* on a teacher-created audiotape. Provide a copy of the text so the students can follow along.

Read-Aloud of *Goggles!* (Keats, 1998a)

Materials
- a copy of the text

Procedure
Retell the story sequentially with your students.

Interactive and Scaffolded Writing

Materials
- a large dry-erase board or chalkboard for the teacher
- small dry-erase boards or chalkboards, or white paper on clipboards for students
- chalk or dry-erase markers for the teacher
- dry-erase markers, chalk, pencils, markers, or colored pencils for students

Procedure
Interactively stomp each word in the sentence "It is snowing," and then using your large dry-erase board or chalkboard and with students using their smaller boards or sheets of white paper, interactively write one word at a time.

WINTER BOOKS LESSON 2

Shared Reading of *Good Night, Moon* (Brown, 1991)

Materials
- Big Book copy of the text
- a Big Book stand
- a flannel board
- flannel story pieces (Make your own story pieces from felt, and have the students color them to match the events in the story.)

Procedure
This activity focuses on orally retelling stories in proper sequence.

1. Before reading, scan the pictures in the story and discuss what your students think is happening in the story.

2. During reading, make predictions about what is going to happen in the next picture before turning each page. Have students orally echo the predictions together.

3. After reading, use flannel story pieces on a flannel board to retell the story sequentially together with your students. Have your students decide together which flannel pictures come first, second, and so on. Then, have one child tell the rest of the class about his or her story piece.

Learning Centers

Materials
- student copies of *Good Night, Moon*
- moon pictures and shapes
- dark blue construction paper
- journals
- pencils
- glue
- scissors
- star stickers
- a teacher-created audiotape of *Happy Birthday, Moon* (Asch, 2000)

- a tape recorder
- headphones
- student copies of *Happy Birthday, Moon*

ZPD Groups
This activity focuses on the oral retelling of a story. Each small ZPD group interacts with *Good Night, Moon* student books. Provide all students with explicit instruction in phonological awareness, letter identification, writing, and concepts about print based on the ZPD of each group's members. Be sure to embed these brief prompts into instruction in a meaningful way.

Literacy and Language Center
Have students sequence various moon pictures (e.g., crescent, full, gibbous) and glue them onto dark blue construction paper in order. Then, have them draw the night sky in their journals with pencils and crayons.

Science Center
Make constellations—such as the Big and Little Dippers—with dark blue construction paper and star stickers.

Listening Center
Have students listen to a teacher-created audiotape of *Happy Birthday, Moon* while following along in their own copies of the text.

Read-Aloud of *Owl Moon* (Yolen, 1987)

Materials
- a copy of the text

Procedure
Have the students cup their hands around their mouths and hoot every time the owl in the story hoots.

Interactive and Scaffolded Writing

Materials
- a large dry-erase board or chalkboard for the teacher
- small dry-erase boards or chalkboards, or white paper on clipboards for students
- chalk or dry-erase markers for the teacher
- dry-erase markers, chalk, pencils, markers, or colored pencils for students

Procedure
Stomp the words in the sentence "It is a moon" as you and your students say it aloud together. Then, using your large dry-erase board or chalkboard and with students using their smaller boards or sheets of white paper, interactively write one word of the sentence at a time.

ALPHABET BOOKS LESSON 1

Shared Reading of *Chicka Chicka Boom Boom* (Martin & Archambault, 1989a)

Materials

- a Big Book copy of the text
- a Big Book stand
- plastic letters

Procedure

This activity focuses on oral recall of the alphabet and letter knowledge.

1. Before reading, chant or sing the Alphabet Song together, preview the book's illustrations, and discuss what students think is happening to the letters and coconut tree in the story.

2. During reading, give students plastic letters and have them match the appropriate letters to the letters in the text.

3. After reading, discuss why the tree fell over. Perhaps have the students form a few letters with their bodies. Chant or sing the Alphabet Song again.

Learning Centers

Materials

- student copies of *Chicka Chicka Boom Boom*
- tempera paint in multiple colors
- an easel
- large sheets of art paper
- paintbrushes
- Play-doh
- Kid Pix software on multiple computers

ZPD Groups

This activity's focus is on letter identification. Each small ZPD group interacts with *Chicka Chicka Boom Boom* student books. Provide all students with explicit instruction in phonological awareness, letter identification, writing, and concepts about print based on the ZPD of each group's members. Be sure to embed these brief prompts into instruction in a meaningful way.

Art Center

Have students paint their own coconut trees with letters on them using art paper hung on an easel.

Motor and Physical Activity Center

Have students make Play-Doh letters to write their names.

Computer Center

Have students begin their own alphabet books using Kid Pix software. Encourage students to make one illustration each for the letters *Aa, Bb, Cc,* and *Dd* if time allows.

Read-Aloud of *Animalia* (Base, 1987)

Materials

• a copy of the text

Procedure

Encourage students to echo the words in the story and listen for alliteration. They also may look for the hidden picture of the boy on each page.

Interactive and Scaffolded Writing

Materials

• a large dry-erase board or chalkboard for the teacher

• small dry-erase boards or chalkboards, or white paper on clipboards for students

• chalk or dry-erase markers for the teacher

• dry-erase markers, chalk, pencils, markers, or colored pencils for students

Procedure

Using your large dry-erase board or chalkboard and with students using their smaller boards or sheets of white paper, begin interactively writing a class alphabet chart. The first page might say *Aa.* Add additional letter pages as your students' attention spans allow. (See chapter 7 for an in-depth discussion of this activity.)

ALPHABET BOOKS LESSON 2

Shared Reading of *Eating the Alphabet: Fruits and Vegetables From A–Z* (Ehlert, 1989)

Materials

• a Big Book copy of the text

• a Big Book stand

• plastic letters

• individual alphabet cards

Procedure

This activity focuses on oral recall of the alphabet.

1. Before reading, scan the book's illustrations and discuss what your students think is happening in the story.

2. During reading, give students plastic letters and have them match the appropriate letters to the letters in the text.

3. After reading, sing the Alphabet Song and use individual student alphabet cards to match the sung letters to print during the song.

Learning Centers

Materials

- student copies of *Eating the Alphabet*
- magnetic letters
- a cookie sheet
- a variety of foods
- Kid Pix software on multiple computers

ZPD Groups
This activity focuses on letter identification and alliteration. Each small ZPD group interacts with *Eating the Alphabet* student books. Provide all students with explicit instruction in phonological awareness, letter identification, writing, and concepts about print based on the ZPD of each group's members. Be sure to embed these brief prompts into instruction in a meaningful way.

Mathematics, Science, or Literacy Center
Have students sort magnetic letters by shape (e.g., into letters that look round and letters that have sticks) into two columns on a cookie sheet.

Motor and Physical Center
Match real food to letters: F=fruit, G=grapes, H=ham, and C=crackers. Provide magnetic letters that students can use to associate with the foods that they are exploring. Try some foods with which students may not be as familiar—such as nectarines, cabbage, or rye bread—and then have students taste them.

Computer Center
Have students continue their own alphabet books using Kid Pix software. Encourage students to make one illustration each for the letters *Ee*, *Ff*, *Gg*, and *Hh* if time allows.

Read-Aloud of an Alphabet Book Such as *Alphabatics* (MacDonald, 1992)

Materials

- a copy of the text

Procedure
Have students form the letters with their bodies as you read.

Interactive and Scaffolded Writing

Materials

- a large dry-erase board or chalkboard for the teacher

- small dry-erase boards or chalkboards, or white paper on clipboards for students

- chalk or dry-erase markers for the teacher

- dry-erase markers, chalk, pencils, markers, or colored pencils for students

Procedure
Using your large dry-erase board or chalkboard and with students using their smaller boards or sheets of white paper, continue to interactively write a class alphabet chart, adding additional letter pages as students' attention spans allow. (See chapter 7 for an in-depth discussion of this activity.)

COLOR BOOKS LESSON 1

Shared Reading of the Lyrics to "Colors All Around" (Barney, 1999, track 4)

Materials

- *A Great Day for Learning* CD (Barney, 1999)

- CD player

- a pointer

- yellow, red, green, and blue cards

Procedure
This activity focuses on directionality, return sweep, one-to-one correspondence, rhyming, and color words.

1. Before reading, sing the song together once to practice it.

2. During reading, have one student use a pointer to track the print for the class and give the rest of the students color cards in yellow, red, green, and blue to use during the song. With students holding the color cards, have them follow the directions in the song: "Red stand up, green sit down, blue and yellow stand up!"

3. After reading, play a few color and rhyming games such as rhyming color words (e.g., *mellow* rhymes with _____) and clapping the syllables in color words.

Learning Centers

Materials

- student copies of "Colors All Around" lyrics

- teacher created songbook of "Colors" (Palmer, 1969, track 1)

- watercolors

- paint brushes

- paper
- Kid Pix software on multiple computers
- Candyland board game with its dice and color cards

ZPD Groups
This activity focuses on one-to-one correspondence, directionality, rhyming, and locating known color words. Each small ZPD group interacts with a teacher-created songbook of "Colors." Provide all students with explicit instruction in phonological awareness, letter identification, writing, and concepts about print based on the ZPD of each group's members. Be sure to embed these brief prompts into instruction in a meaningful way.

Art Center
Have students mix watercolors to experiment with making new colors (e.g., blue + yellow = green, and red + blue = purple).

Computer Center
Have students use the Kid Pix software to experiment with colors.

Mathematics Center
Play the Candyland board game with its dice and color cards.

Read-Aloud of *Brown Bear, Brown Bear, What Do You See?* (Martin, 1983)

Materials
- a copy of the text

Procedure
Encourage students to predict which animal will appear on the next page and to read along as they internalize the book's pattern.

Interactive and Scaffolded Writing

Materials
- a large dry-erase board or chalkboard for the teacher
- small dry-erase boards or chalkboards, or white paper on clipboards for students
- chalk or dry-erase markers for the teacher
- dry-erase markers, chalk, pencils, markers, or colored pencils for students

Procedure
Using your large dry-erase board or chalkboard and with students using their smaller boards or sheets of white paper, interactively write a class color chart or a Big Book about colors. For example, you may write, "It is red" or "It is yellow." If you have chosen to create a Big Book, have students draw illustrations that use the appropriate color for each page. Attempt only one page or chart entry per day.

COLOR BOOKS LESSON 2

Shared Reading of *Freight Train* (Crews, 2003)

Materials

- a Big Book copy of the text
- a Big Book stand
- pipe cleaners

Procedure

This activity focuses on letter and word boundaries, vocabulary development, and color words.

1. Before reading, count the letters and words in the book's title and discuss the author and illustrator. Preview the pictures, and predict where the train is going in this story.

2. During reading, encourage students to interact in a discussion about the different types of cars in the train and the colors used in the book.

3. After reading, revisit and discuss the vocabulary in this story such as *trestle, hopper car,* and *gondola car*. Use pipe cleaners to mark known color words.

Learning Centers

Materials

- student copies of *Freight Train*
- teacher-created sentence strips that read "It is yellow."
- scissors
- glue
- journals
- magazines
- large sheets of construction paper in various colors
- watercolors
- paintbrushes
- teacher-created *Freight Train* books
- Concentration card game with color cards

ZPD Groups

This activity focuses on one-to-one correspondence and locating known color words. Each small ZPD group interacts with *Freight Train* student books. Provide all students with explicit instruction in phonological awareness, letter identification, writing, and concepts about print based on the ZPD of each group's members. Be sure to embed these brief prompts into instruction in a meaningful way.

Journal Center
Provide teacher-created sentence strips that read "It is yellow." Have students cut out the words in the sentence and glue them into their journals in proper order. Also, have students glue yellow pictures cut from magazines onto the yellow page of the class's color Big Book, glue blue pictures from magazines onto a blue piece of construction paper, and so on.

Literacy and Art Center
Have students reread and color their own copies of teacher-created *Freight Train* books.

Mathematics Center
Play a Concentration card game with colors. Put the color cards face down on a table, and have students turn over two at a time, looking for two cards that are the same color. If the cards are the same color, the students keep them. If the cards are not the same color, the students turn the cards back over and watch others try to match cards until it is their turn again, all the while trying to remember where the matching color cards are. The student with the most pairs in the end is the color champion. It is helpful to have an adult monitoring this activity.

Read-Aloud of *My Many Colored Days* (Seuss, 1998)

Materials

• a copy of the text

Procedure
Link literacy to social and emotional development by incorporating a discussion about feelings into the read-aloud session.

Interactive and Scaffolded Writing

Materials

• a large dry-erase board or chalkboard for the teacher

• small dry-erase boards or chalkboards, or white paper on clipboards for students

• chalk or dry-erase markers for the teacher

• dry-erase markers, chalk, pencils, markers, or colored pencils for students

Procedure
Using your large dry-erase board or chalkboard and with students using their smaller boards or sheets of white paper, interactively write a class Big Book that combines colors and feelings (e.g., "I feel blue" and "I feel yellow"). Work on this interactively written book over several days.

Shared Reading of *One Potato, Two Potato, Three Potato, Four: 165 Chants for Children* (Colgin, 1990)

Materials

• a Big Book copy of the text

• a Big Book stand

Procedure

This activity focuses on introducing the meanings of punctuation marks and noticing how they look.

1. Before reading, teach students the "One potato, two potato" rhyme. A fun way to do this is to have two or three groups of students sit in a circle with their hands in fists (representing their potatoes). Touch students' fists one at a time while chanting "One potato, two potato, three potato, four. Five potato, six potato, seven potato, more!" After you have touched a student's fist, he or she should put that hand behind his or her back. Continue this process until all potatoes (fists) except one are behind the students' backs. The student whose fist remains in front of him or her is the great potato.

2. During reading, encourage students to interact with and notice the details of print on each page as much as possible. Now that the students know the rhyme so well, they may attend more closely to the print. As an example, say, "This mark is a comma. You will see it several times in this rhyme. Watch for more commas as I read the remainder of the rhyme."

3. After reading, show students how to hold out their hands when they see a period because it means *stop*, take a deep breath when they see a comma because it means *pause*, and throw their hands up in the air when they see an exclamation point because it means *excitement*. Reread the story while students use these responses when they see the punctuation marks.

Learning Centers

Materials

• student copies of *One Potato, Two Potato, Three Potato, Four*

• sentence strips

• scissors

• glue

• journals

• whole and halved potatoes

• tempera paints

• construction paper

- gumdrops

- toothpicks

ZPD Groups

This activity focuses on noticing and understanding the purpose of punctuation marks. Each small ZPD group interacts with *One Potato, Two Potato, Three Potato, Four* student books. Provide all students with explicit instruction in phonological awareness, letter identification, writing, and concepts about print based on the ZPD of each group's members. Be sure to embed these brief prompts into instruction in a meaningful way.

Journal Center

Have an aide write "It is a potato" on a sentence strip. Have students cut the words apart and put them back together with a buddy. Then, have students glue the reformed sentences in their journals.

Art Center

Have students make potato prints on construction paper by dipping the inside of a halved potato into tempera paint and pressing it onto a piece of construction paper. Adult assistance is advisable during this activity.

Motor and Physical Activity Center

Have students make potato men by using toothpicks and gumdrops to make faces on whole potatoes.

Read-Aloud of *Five Little Monkeys Jumping on the Bed* (Christelow, 1998)

Materials

- a copy of the text

- five monkey puppets

- a mat or small mattress

Procedure

Use five monkey puppets and a mat or small mattress to have students act out this number songbook.

Interactive and Scaffolded Writing

Materials

- a large dry-erase board or chalkboard for the teacher

- small dry-erase boards or chalkboards, or white paper on clipboards for students

- chalk or dry-erase markers for the teacher

- dry-erase markers, chalk, pencils, markers, or colored pencils for students

Procedure

Using your large dry-erase board or chalkboard and with students using their smaller boards or sheets of white paper, interactively write a class Big Book of number words. Students may draw illustrations to match the numbers. Interactively write one number word each day.

NUMBER WORD RHYMES AND SONGS LESSON 2

Shared Reading of *Five Little Ducks* (Raffi, 1999)

Materials

- a Big Book copy of the text
- a Big Book stand
- a teacher-created cardboard hill
- stairs or blocks
- duck masks
- pipe cleaners

Procedure

This activity focuses on activating prior knowledge, retelling stories in sequence, and locating known number words.

1. Before reading, sing the *Five Little Ducks* song together. Discuss what the students already know about ducks.

2. During reading, encourage students to echo the repetitive lines in this songbook, sing along, or both.

3. After reading, have students act out this rhyme using a cardboard hill in front of stairs or blocks so students can pretend to walk up and down the hill as you read. Have students sing while making appropriate motions (e.g., holding up five fingers when singing the words *five little ducks*) and act out the song with props (e.g., the hill and duck masks). Use pipe cleaners to circle known number words.

Learning Centers

Materials

- student copies of *Five Little Ducks*
- stairs or boxes
- a teacher-created cardboard hill
- duck masks
- small construction paper ducks of various colors

- construction paper
- glue
- a water table
- plastic ducks of various colors
- a large class graph
- clay or Play-Doh

ZPD Groups

This activity's focus is on reading comprehension and expression, one-to-one correspondence, and locating known number words. Each small ZPD group interacts with *Five Little Ducks* student books, acting out and retelling the story with props such as the duck masks and cardboard hill. Provide all students with explicit instruction in phonological awareness, letter identification, writing, and concepts about print based on the ZPD of each group's members. Be sure to embed these brief prompts into instruction in a meaningful way.

Mathematics Center

Model simple addition story problems with construction paper ducks (e.g., 2 ducks + 3 ducks = 5 ducks), and have students practice solving the problems by gluing the appropriate numbers of ducks onto construction paper.

Science Center

Have students pretend that a water table is a pond, and have them conduct duck races with plastic ducks. Students may propel their ducks through the water by blowing on them. Graph the winners of each race on the class graph to see which color duck wins the most races.

Motor and Physical Activity or Art Center

Have students mold ducks and other birds out of clay or Play-Doh.

Read-Aloud of *Make Way for Ducklings* (McCloskey, 1941)

Materials

- a copy of the text

Procedure

Explain to the students that the Mallard family is looking for a new home. Predict together where they may decide to settle.

Interactive and Scaffolded Writing

Materials

- a large dry-erase board or chalkboard for the teacher
- small dry-erase boards or chalkboards, or white paper on clipboards for students

- chalk or dry-erase markers for the teacher
- dry-erase markers, chalk, pencils, markers, or colored pencils for students

Procedure

Continue to interactively write a class Big Book of number words.

SPRING BOOKS LESSON 1

Shared Reading of *Jump, Frog, Jump* (Kalan, 1989)

Materials

- a Big Book copy of the text
- a Big Book stand
- a pointer

Procedure

This activity focuses on making predictions and locating and understanding the purpose of a book's title, author, and illustrator.

1. Before reading, discuss the book's title, author, and illustrator. Explain that the title says what the story will be about, the author is the person who wrote the story, and the illustrator is the person who drew the pictures. Talk about where this information is usually located in books. Preview the illustrations without giving away the end of the story. Have students make predictions about the story based on the title.

2. During reading, periodically pause and have students make predictions about the next part of the story based on the illustrator's drawings.

3. After reading, encourage students to interact in a discussion about how the author and illustrator work together to tell the story. Ask students questions such as, "Could you tell this story without the words?" and "Do the pictures help you to know what is happening?"

Learning Centers

Materials

- student copies of *Jump, Frog, Jump*
- a class aquarium with tadpoles
- journals
- pencils and crayons
- brown paper lunch bags
- construction paper
- scissors

- glue
- a teacher-created audiotape of *Days With Frog and Toad* (Lobel, 1984)
- a tape recorder
- headphones

ZPD Groups
This activity focuses on locating and understanding the purpose of a book's title, author, and illustrator. Each small ZPD group reads student copies of *Jump, Frog, Jump*.

Science and Social Studies Center
Students should discuss and listen to an adult helper read about the development of a tadpole into a frog. Have students observe tadpoles in a class aquarium and draw in their journals the changes that they observe each day.

Art Center
Have students make frog puppets from brown paper lunch bags, construction paper shapes, and glue, and then have them retell *Jump, Frog, Jump* in their own words to a classmate or adult helper.

Listening Center
Have students listen to *Days With Frog and Toad* on a teacher-created audiotape and use a student text to follow along.

Read-Aloud of *Frog and Toad Are Friends* (Lobel, 1970)

Materials
- a copy of the text

Procedure
Read the "Spring" chapter in *Frog and Toad Are Friends*, and predict and discuss observable signs of spring that the author and illustrator create in the story and pictures.

Interactive and Scaffolded Writing

Materials
- a large dry-erase board or chalkboard for the teacher
- small dry-erase boards or chalkboards, or white paper on clipboards for students
- chalk or dry-erase markers for the teacher
- dry-erase markers, chalk, pencils, markers, or colored pencils for students

Procedure
Pretend with your students to be authors and interactively write, "It is a frog." In addition, be illustrators and draw an illustration to match your story.

SPRING BOOKS LESSON 2

Shared Reading of *The Very Hungry Caterpillar* **(Carle, 1994)**

Materials

• a Big Book copy of the text

• a Big Book stand

• green, yellow, and red pieces of construction paper

Procedure

This activity focuses on retelling the beginning, middle, and end of a story.

1. Before reading, activate students' prior knowledge about caterpillars and butterflies. Acknowledge and affirm their thoughts and ideas.

2. During reading, encourage students to interact in a discussion about what is happening to the caterpillar throughout the story.

3. After reading, give groups of three students each pieces of construction paper to scaffold their retelling of this story. Give the first student a green piece of construction paper, the second student a yellow piece, and the third student a red piece. Before the students try this activity, model a retelling of the story with the green paper representing the beginning of the story, the yellow paper representing the middle of the story, and the red paper representing the end of the story. Initially, support the students a great deal in the activity, and after several days of practice, begin to release more and more of the responsibility to them.

Learning Centers

Materials

• Kid Pix software on multiple computers

• student copies of *The Very Hungry Caterpillar*

• small pieces of tissue paper in multiple colors

• glue

• a single-hole punch

• sheets of white paper

• journals

• pencils and crayons

• real butterflies or caterpillars

ZPD Groups

This activity focuses on retelling the beginning, middle, and end of a story. Each small ZPD group interacts with and "reads" *The Very Hungry Caterpillar* student books. Provide all students with explicit instruction in phonological awareness, letter identification, writing, and concepts about print based on the ZPD of each group's members. Be sure to embed these brief prompts into instruction in a meaningful way.

Creative Art
Have students design their own butterflies using glue and small pieces of tissue paper in multiple colors.

Literacy and Art Center
Have students create their own *The Very Hungry Caterpillar* books on sheets of white paper. Provide a single-hole punch so students can add holes to their books similar to the original if they wish.

Science and Social Studies Center
Have students observe real caterpillars, butterflies, or both and make written and/or pictorial records of their observations in their journals.

Read-Aloud of *Amanda's Butterfly* (Butterworth, 1991)

Materials

• a copy of the text

Procedure
Activate students' prior knowledge about butterflies before reading.

Interactive and Scaffolded Writing

Materials

• a large dry-erase board or chalkboard for the teacher
• small dry-erase boards or chalkboards, or white paper on clipboards for students
• chalk or dry-erase markers for the teacher
• dry-erase markers, chalk, pencils, markers, or colored pencils for students

Procedure
With students, orally chunk the syllables in *butterfly—but-ter-fly—* and then interactively write the word. Have students write the word on their own boards or sheets of paper and then draw their own butterflies if they wish.

Outcomes Framework, Checklists, and Assessment Forms

• • •

PRESCHOOL CURRICULUM FRAMEWORK

COGNITIVE DEVELOPMENT

- Motivation and curiosity
- Reasoning and problem solving
- Attention to task and continuance
- Representational thinking

LANGUAGE DEVELOPMENT AND LITERACY

Listening and Speaking

- Attending activities
- Oral structures of language
- Following directions
- Discussions and conversations
- Phonological awareness activities
- Show and tell participation

Phonological Awareness

- Rhyming
- Alliteration
- Segmenting
- Blending

Reading

- Enjoyment of and interaction with texts
- Print awareness and book handling
- Comprehension and meaning
- Variety in genres and cultures
- Alphabet knowledge
- Letter-sound relationships

Writing

- Function or purpose of written language
- Conveying a message
- Formation of symbols, letters, and words
- Audience and enjoyment
- Conventions of writing

MATHEMATICS, SCIENCE, AND SOCIAL STUDIES

- Explore number sense and concepts
- Explore cause-and-effect relationships
- Patterns
- Matching
- Sorting and classifications
- Shapes and colors
- Body parts
- Time, measurement, and money
- Communities
- Student environment
- Computers and technology
- Physical, earth, and life sciences

SOCIAL AND EMOTIONAL DEVELOPMENT

- Self-care
- Appropriate interactions for self and others
- Family and community relationships

MOTOR AND PHYSICAL DEVELOPMENT

- Gross motor skills
- Fine motor skills
- Health and safety

MUSIC, MOVEMENT, AND THE CREATIVE ARTS

- Response
- Creativity and initiative
- Enjoyment
- Cultural diversity
- Exploration

DRAMATIC PLAY

- Choices
- Variety

Teaching and Learning in Preschool: Using Individually Appropriate Practices in Early Childhood Literacy Instruction by Elizabeth Claire Venn
and Monica Dacy Jahn © 2004. Newark, DE: International Reading Association. May be copied for classroom use.

PRESCHOOL OUTCOMES

(These outcomes are designed for 3- to 6-year-old children. The boldface type highlights outcomes that are more typical for 5- to 6-year-olds.)

COGNITIVE DEVELOPMENT

Motivation and curiosity

    A. Participates willingly in a variety of activities.

    B. Uses imagination and inventiveness.

    C. Makes independent choices and decisions.

    D. Explores a variety of topics and activities.

Reasoning and problem solving

    A. Finds more than one solution to a task or question.

    B. Discovers solutions to problems through exploration or trial and error.

    C. Classifies, compares, and contrasts objects, events, and experiences.

Attention to task and continuance

    A. Persists in completing activities or tasks.

    B. Follows through with plans, directions, or goals.

    C. Maintains concentration on a task for a reasonable time, despite interruptions.

Representational thinking

    A. Explores representational thinking.

    B. Makes believe with objects.

    C. Engages in dramatic role-play.

LANGUAGE DEVELOPMENT AND LITERACY

Listening (receptive language)

    A. Follows simple directions with two to three steps.

    B. Participates appropriately in class discussions.

    C. Answers yes or no questions.

    D. Responds to presentations with appropriate questions or comments.

    E. Listens actively for 5–10 minutes to acquire new information.

    F. Listens actively for 10–15 minutes to acquire new information.

    G. Follows complex directions.

    H. For non–English-speaking children, listens to and begins to understand English.

(continued)

I. Discriminates between different environmental sounds.

J. Responds appropriately to "wh" questions.

Speaking (expressive language)

A. Expresses feelings and thoughts.

B. Speaks in simple sentences with an expanding vocabulary.

C. Speaks in complex sentences with an expanding vocabulary.

D. Initiates and leads a conversation.

E. Asks appropriate "wh" questions.

F. Is aware of conversational etiquette such as appropriate voice tones, responses, and manners.

G. Identifies common objects with correct vocabulary.

H. Uses speech in a variety of settings.

I. Explores the diversity and expressiveness of language.

J. For non–English-speaking children, attempts to speak in English.

K. Uses pronouns and irregular past-tense verbs.

Phonological awareness (oral language structures)

A. Understands oral word boundaries.

B. Understands that words may be segmented or blended into syllables.

C. Understands that compound words can be segmented and blended.

D. Understands that words may be segmented into phonemes.

E. Understands the concept of rhyme recognition.

F. Understands the concept of rhyme completion.

G. Understands the concept of rhyme production.

H. Understands the concept of alliteration.

I. Explores sentence and word structures.

J. Understands that speech contains separate phonemes.

Reading

A. Demonstrates basic concepts of print and book handling (front and back of book, directionality, letter and word boundaries, title, author, some punctuation, that print carries a message, etc.).

B. Understands the alphabetic principle.

C. Identifies some letters out of alphabetic sequence.

D. Explores letter recognition skills and sound-symbol relationships.

E. Knows the alphabet represents special visual symbols that can be individually named.

F. Reads some high-frequency words.

(continued)

G. Listens to a simple story and uses pictures to make predictions.

H. Retells a simple story sequentially with a beginning, middle, and end, using play, pictures, and/or illustrations.

I. Engages with a variety of genres and culturally diverse literature.

J. Recognizes own name.

K. Understands that print and pictures communicate meaning.

L. Recognizes common and familiar environmental print.

M. Self-selects materials based on personal interests and experiences.

N. Makes connections between text and self.

O. Understands that a book has a title, author, and illustrator.

P. Shows an awareness of print in a variety of settings.

Writing

A. Establishes an appropriate pencil grasp and uses one hand regularly.

B. Scribbles to convey a message.

C. Uses pictures, print, or both to convey a message, along the developmental continuum of writing.

D. Attempts appropriate conventions in writing.

E. Attempts appropriate directionality and return sweep.

F. "Reads" own writing.

G. Writes own name.

H. Writes interactively.

I. Writes with spaces between words.

J. Explores functions of language (e.g., environmental, aesthetic, and job related).

K. Understands that writing is a method of communicating.

L. Uses a variety of writing tools, such as crayons, pencils, and computers.

M. Writes a few known words and simple sentences independently.

N. Associates sounds with written words and letters.

MATHEMATICS, SCIENCE, AND SOCIAL STUDIES

A. Explores environment.

B. Explains or demonstrates explorations and predictions.

C. Sorts and classifies objects.

D. Constructs and explains patterns.

E. Discusses relationships between parts and the whole.

(continued)

F. Matches groups of objects with the corresponding numeral.

G. Demonstrates one-to-one correspondence.

H. Manipulates counters and other objects.

I. Counts objects to 20.

J. Identifies numerals.

K. Writes numerals 1–20.

L. Demonstrates conservation of numbers.

M. Demonstrates an understanding of basic mathematical language (e.g., *big, little, fewer,* and *greater*).

N. Arranges items in a sequence or series.

O. Explores basic problem-solving strategies.

P. Identifies own body parts.

Q. Explores a variety of shapes and colors.

R. Explores time (e.g., daytime, nighttime, **days of week, seasons, years, yesterday, today, and tomorrow**).

S. Explores the use of charts, graphs, and maps.

T. Explores basic measurement tools.

U. Explores the meaning and use of money.

V. Explores students' environments and interests.

W. Explores technology.

X. Explores cause-and-effect relationships.

Y. Explores topics in life, physical, and earth sciences.

Z. Explores different jobs and professions.

SOCIAL AND EMOTIONAL DEVELOPMENT

A. Knows own name and names of others in the home and school environments.

B. Interacts appropriately with adults and peers, acknowledging the rights of others and self.

C. Is familiar with and respectful of school environment.

D. Takes care of own personal needs.

E. Carries out classroom routines appropriately.

F. Expresses emotions appropriately.

G. Has a growing awareness of own abilities, characteristics, and preferences.

H. Demonstrates independence and self-direction.

I. Resolves conflicts appropriately.

(continued)

PRESCHOOL OUTCOMES (continued)

    J. Explores different cultures.

    K. Explores family and community similarities and differences.

MOTOR AND PHYSICAL DEVELOPMENT

Gross motor skills

    A. Engages in complex locomotor, manipulative, and stability movements (e.g., running, jumping, hopping, twisting, dodging, throwing, and catching).

    B. Demonstrates balance and coordination.

Fine motor skills

    A. Manipulates small objects effectively (e.g., buttons clothing, zips coat, and ties shoes)

    B. Uses fine motor skills to take care of personal needs.

    C. Uses scissors, pencils, and crayons correctly.

    D. Coordinates eye-hand movement.

Health and safety

    A. Demonstrates personal hygiene.

    B. Follows basic safety rules.

    C. Engages in activities that promote healthy living.

MUSIC, MOVEMENT, AND THE CREATIVE ARTS

A. Expresses self through movement and dancing to various musical tempos and styles.

B. Enjoys and/or interacts with a variety of music and instruments.

C. Responds to music by keeping the beat.

D. Chants or sings along with music.

E. Experiments and/or participates in a variety of art projects and creations.

F. Draws or paints simple pictures or creations with increasing capacity.

G. Shares art creations with others.

H. Appreciates a variety of artistic styles and mediums.

DRAMATIC PLAY

A. Participates in a variety of play.

B. Engages in the appropriate stages of play, cognitively and socially.

C. Explores real-life experiences through play (dramatic play).

PRESCHOOL OUTCOMES CHECKLIST

(These outcomes are designed for 3- to 6-year-old children. The boldface print highlights objectives that are more typical for 5- to 6-year-olds.)

Student Name _____ Birthday _____

M = Student has mastered this skill most of the time in class.

X = Student is still developing this skill.

NA = Not applicable at this time.

Pretest (/)	Midtest (/)	Posttest (/)	COGNITIVE DEVELOPMENT
			A. Motivation and Curiosity
_____	_____	_____	Uses imagination and inventiveness.
_____	_____	_____	Participates willingly in a variety of activities.
_____	_____	_____	Makes independent choices and decisions.
_____	_____	_____	Explores a variety of topics and activities.
			B. Reasoning and Problem Solving
_____	_____	_____	Finds more than one solution to a task or question.
_____	_____	_____	Discovers solutions to problems through exploration or trial and error.
_____	_____	_____	Classifies, compares, and contrasts objects, events, and experiences.
			C. Attention to Task and Continuance
_____	_____	_____	Persists in completing activities or tasks.
_____	_____	_____	Follows through with plans, directions, or goals.
_____	_____	_____	Maintains concentration on a task for a reasonable time, despite interruptions.
			D. Representational Thinking
_____	_____	_____	Explores representational thinking.
_____	_____	_____	Makes believe with objects.
_____	_____	_____	Engages in dramatic role-play.
			LANGUAGE DEVELOPMENT AND LITERACY
			A. Listening (Receptive Language)
_____	_____	_____	Follows simple directions with two to three steps.
_____	_____	_____	Participates appropriately in class discussions.
_____	_____	_____	Answers yes or no questions.

(continued)

PRESCHOOL OUTCOMES CHECKLIST (continued)

_____ _____ _____ Listens actively for 5–10 minutes to acquire new information.

_____ _____ _____ Responds to presentations with appropriate questions or comments.

_____ _____ _____ **Listens actively for 10–15 minutes to acquire new information.**

_____ _____ _____ **Follows complex directions.**

_____ _____ _____ Responds appropriately to "wh" questions.

_____ _____ _____ For non–English-speaking children, listens to and begins to understand English.

_____ _____ _____ Discriminates between different environmental sounds.

B. Speaking (Expressive Language)

_____ _____ _____ Expresses feelings and thoughts.

_____ _____ _____ Speaks in simple sentences with an expanding vocabulary.

_____ _____ _____ **Speaks in complex sentences with an expanding vocabulary.**

_____ _____ _____ Initiates and leads a conversation.

_____ _____ _____ **Identifies common objects with correct vocabulary.**

_____ _____ _____ Explores the diversity and expressiveness of language.

_____ _____ _____ Uses speech in a variety of settings.

_____ _____ _____ For non–English-speaking children, attempts to speak in English.

_____ _____ _____ Uses pronouns and irregular past-tense verbs.

_____ _____ _____ Is aware of conversation etiquette such as appropriate voice tone, responses, and manners.

_____ _____ _____ **Asks appropriate "wh" questions.**

C. Phonological Awareness (Oral Language Structures)

_____ _____ _____ Walks or stomps oral word boundaries in a simple sentence.

_____ _____ _____ Claps syllables in words.

_____ _____ _____ **Finger-taps phonemes in words.**

_____ _____ _____ **Segments and blends phonemes in words.**

_____ _____ _____ Recognizes when two words rhyme.

_____ _____ _____ Completes a rhyme independently.

_____ _____ _____ **Produces rhyming words.**

_____ _____ _____ Blends and segments compound words.

_____ _____ _____ Identifies an alliterative phrase.

(continued)

PRESCHOOL OUTCOMES CHECKLIST (continued)

Pretest Midtest Posttest
(/)   (/)   (/)

D. Reading

_____ _____ _____ Shows an interest in reading and self-selects materials.

_____ _____ _____ Recognizes common and familiar environmental print.

_____ _____ _____ Understands basic concepts of print and book handling (e.g., front and back of book, directionality, letter and word boundaries, title, author, some punctuation, that pictures and print carry a message, etc.).

_____ _____ _____ **Makes connections between text and self.**

_____ _____ _____ Uses one-to-one correspondence.

_____ _____ _____ Listens to a simple story and uses pictures to make predictions.

_____ _____ _____ Listens to a story and recalls at least one fact.

_____ _____ _____ **Retells a simple story sequentially, with a beginning, middle, and end, using play, pictures, and/or illlustrations.**

_____ _____ _____ **Reads some high-frequency words.**

_____ _____ _____ Recites the alphabet.

_____ _____ _____ **Matches some sounds to corresponding letters (alphabetic principle).**

_____ _____ _____ Recognizes own name.

_____ _____ _____ Identifies 10 letters out of alphabetic sequence.

_____ _____ _____ Knows letters in his or her own name.

E. Writing

_____ _____ _____ Establishes an appropriate pencil grasp and uses one hand regularly.

_____ _____ _____ Uses marks as letters.

_____ _____ _____ Attempts to write in recognizable letters.

_____ _____ _____ **Copies identical letters.**

_____ _____ _____ Scribbles to convey a message.

_____ _____ _____ Uses pictures, print, or both to convey a message, along the developmental continuum of writing.

_____ _____ _____ Uses temporary spelling to convey a message.

_____ _____ _____ Writes own name.

_____ _____ _____ **Writes a complete thought.**

_____ _____ _____ **Writes with spaces between words.**

_____ _____ _____ **Writes a simple story that corresponds with the illustrations.**

_____ _____ _____ **Expresses ideas using complex illustrations.**

(continued)

PRESCHOOL OUTCOMES CHECKLIST (continued)

Pretest   Midtest   Posttest
(/)   (/)   (/)

_____ _____ _____ **Uses letters to represent sounds in words.**

_____ _____ _____ Writes in all uppercase letters.

_____ _____ _____ **Writes in appropriate combination of lowercase and uppercase letters.**

_____ _____ _____ **Attempts capital letters appropriately.**

_____ _____ _____ **Attempts periods, question marks, and exclamation points.**

_____ _____ _____ Uses appropriate directionality and return sweep.

_____ _____ _____ Reads his or her own writing.

_____ _____ _____ **Writes a few known words and simple sentences independently.**

F. Letter Identification and **Sound Correspondence**

Fill in mastered upper- and lowercase letters for pre-, mid-, and posttest scores.

MATHEMATICS, SCIENCE, AND SOCIAL STUDIES

	Pre	Mid	Post		Pre	Mid	Post		Pre	Mid	Post		Pre	Mid	Post
Aa	___	___	___	Hh	___	___	___	Oo	___	___	___	Vv	___	___	___
Bb	___	___	___	Ii	___	___	___	Pp	___	___	___	Ww	___	___	___
Cc	___	___	___	Jj	___	___	___	Qq	___	___	___	Xx	___	___	___
Dd	___	___	___	Kk	___	___	___	Rr	___	___	___	Yy	___	___	___
Ee	___	___	___	Ll	___	___	___	Ss	___	___	___	Zz	___	___	___
Ff	___	___	___	Mm	___	___	___	Tt	___	___	___				
Gg	___	___	___	Nn	___	___	___	Uu	___	___	___				

Pretest   Midtest   Posttest   A. Exploration
(/)   (/)   (/)

_____ _____ _____ Explores his or her environment.

_____ _____ _____ **Explains or demonstrates explorations and predictions.**

_____ _____ _____ **Understands basic problem-solving strategies.**

_____ _____ _____ Explores cause-and-effect relationships.

_____ _____ _____ Explores own interests.

_____ _____ _____ Explores different jobs and/or professions.

_____ _____ _____ Explores physical, earth, and life sciences.

_____ _____ _____ Explores technology.

(continued)

PRESCHOOL OUTCOMES CHECKLIST (continued)

Pretest　Midtest　Posttest
（ / ）　（ / ）　（ / ）

B. Matching, Sorting, and Patterning

_____ _____ _____ Puts identical objects into a group.

_____ _____ _____ Sorts objects by one characteristic.

_____ _____ _____ **Sorts objects by two or more characteristics.**

_____ _____ _____ Can arrange items in a sequence or series.

_____ _____ _____ **Constructs and explains patterns.**

_____ _____ _____ **Matches a given sequence or pattern using three or more objects.**

C. Number and Numeration

_____ _____ _____ Demonstrates one-to-one correspondence.

_____ _____ _____ Identifies numbers 1–10.

_____ _____ _____ **Identifies numerals 1–20.**

_____ _____ _____ Counts objects to 10.

_____ _____ _____ **Counts objects to 20.**

_____ _____ _____ **Writes numerals 1–20.**

_____ _____ _____ **Demonstrates conservation of numbers.**

_____ _____ _____ Matches groups of objects with a corresponding numeral.

D. Mathematical Language

_____ _____ _____ **Understands terms such as _more, less, big, little, long, short_, and so on.**

_____ _____ _____ **Uses the above terms correctly.**

E. Time

_____ _____ _____ Knows daytime from nighttime.

_____ _____ _____ **Knows the difference between today, yesterday, and tomorrow.**

_____ _____ _____ **Knows the days of the week.**

_____ _____ _____ **Knows the months of the year.**

_____ _____ _____ **Knows the year.**

_____ _____ _____ **Knows the seasons.**

F. Measurement

_____ _____ _____ Explores the use of charts, graphs, and maps.

_____ _____ _____ Explores basic measurement tools.

_____ _____ _____ Explores the meaning and use of money.

(continued)

PRESCHOOL OUTCOMES CHECKLIST (continued)

G. Shapes

	Matches		Points to		Names	
	Pretest	Posttest	Pretest	Posttest	**Pretest**	**Posttest**
■ (square)						
△ (triangle)						
▭ (rectangle)						
○ (circle)						
◇ (diamond)						
⬭ (oval)						

H. Colors

	Matches	Points to	**Names**
Red			
Blue			
Yellow			
Green			
Orange			
Purple			
White			
Brown			
Black			

I. Identifying Body Parts

On each line, mark the date each part was identified.

____ fingernails	____ legs	____ thumbs	____ **wrists**
____ **jaw**	____ ears	____ **elbows**	____ **ankles**
____ back	____ head	____ **chin**	____ **hip**
____ toes	____ neck	____ **shoulders**	____ **waist**
____ fingers	____ **stomach**	____ chest	
____ arms	____ knees	____ **heels**	

Pretest (/)	Midtest (/)	Posttest (/)	SOCIAL AND EMOTIONAL DEVELOPMENT
			A. Adult and Peer Interactions and Cooperation
____	____	____	Knows classmates' names.
____	____	____	Makes a friend in class.
____	____	____	Interacts with adults appropriately.
____	____	____	Interacts with peers appropriately.
____	____	____	**Expresses emotions appropriately.**
____	____	____	Demonstrates familiarity with school environment.
____	____	____	Gains attention in appropriate ways.
____	____	____	Attempts to solve problems independently.
____	____	____	Follows directions and class rules.
____	____	____	Comes to class willingly.
____	____	____	Carries out class routines appropriately.
____	____	____	Demonstrates personal hygiene.
____	____	____	Respects rights of others.
____	____	____	Resolves conflicts appropriately.
			B. Self-Concept
____	____	____	Demonstrates self-confidence.
____	____	____	Knows his or her own name.
____	____	____	Knows his or her own age.
____	____	____	**Knows own birthday.**
____	____	____	**Knows own address.**
____	____	____	**Knows own phone number.**
____	____	____	Knows family members' names.

(continued)

PRESCHOOL OUTCOMES CHECKLIST (continued)

Pretest Midtest Posttest
(/)   (/)   (/)

        C. Family and Community Relationships

_____ _____ _____   Acknowledges personal, family, and community similarities and differences.

MOTOR AND PHYSICAL DEVELOPMENT

A. Gross Motor Skills

_____ _____ _____   Walking

_____ _____ _____   Running

_____ _____ _____   **Skipping**

_____ _____ _____   Hopping

_____ _____ _____   Maneuvers around obstacles in environment.

_____ _____ _____   **Tosses, catches, and kicks a ball.**

_____ _____ _____   Demonstrates balance and coordination.

B. Fine Motor Skills

_____ _____ _____   Manipulates small objects effectively (e.g., buttons clothing, zips coat, and ties shoes).

_____ _____ _____   Uses scissors, pencils, and crayons correctly.

_____ _____ _____   Cuts along a line.

_____ _____ _____   Coordinates eye-hand movement.

C. Health and Safety

_____ _____ _____   Demonstrates personal hygiene.

_____ _____ _____   Follows basic safety rules.

_____ _____ _____   Engages in activities that promote healthy living.

MUSIC, MOVEMENT, AND THE CREATIVE ARTS

_____ _____ _____   Engages in musical or rhythmical activities or both.

_____ _____ _____   Responds to music by keeping the beat.

_____ _____ _____   Chants or sings along with music.

_____ _____ _____   Draws or paints simple pictures, objects, or both and shares them with others.

_____ _____ _____   Explores a variety of art media.

DRAMATIC PLAY

_____ _____ _____   Engages in appropriate stages of play, cognitively and socially.

_____ _____ _____   Engages in cooperative play such as taking turns.

_____ _____ _____   Explores real-life experiences through play (dramatic play).

PRESCHOOL LITERACY CHECKLIST

Name of Child _____ Birth Date_____

Classroom Teacher _____ Phone_____

Phonological Awareness

___ word segmenting (compound words)   ___ rhyming production ("Tell me a rhyming word.")
___ word blending (compound words)   ___ oral word boundaries (clapping words)
___ rhyming recognition ("Do these words rhyme?") ___ rhyming completion/cloze
___ syllable blending (combining syllables to make words) ___ auditory discrimination (environmental sounds)
___ syllable segmenting (taking words apart by syllables) ___ uses appropriate oral language structures

Book Handling
___ front of book   ___ bottom of picture
___ print contains a message ___ left page before right

Directional Behavior
___ where to start   ___ return to the left
___ which way to go   ___ first and last concept

Oral Language: Concepts and Vocabulary
___ expands vocabulary to 4,000 words
___ understands similarities and differences
___ understands categorization
___ can follow 2–3-step verbal directions
___ can retell a simple narrative in sequence
___ can understand "wh" questions
___ uses pronouns and irregular past-tense verbs

Writing
___ scribbles
___ draws simples shapes (squares and circles)
___ uses marks as letters
___ expresses ideas using simple drawings
___ uses one hand regularly
___ knows writing is for communication
___ writes own name

Concepts About Print
___ understands concept of a word
___ understands concept of a letter

Printed Language
___ listens to stories
___ recognizes environmental print
___ understands different text forms
___ names and matches letters to their names

Can identify approximately 10 letters (including ones from own name) in any of the following ways:

Letter Identification (by name)
A a B b C c D d E e F f G g H h I i J j K k L l M m N n O o P p Q q R r S s T t U u V v W w X x Y y Z z

Letter Identification (by sounds)
A a B b C c D d E e F f G g H h I i J j K k L l M m N n O o P p Q q R r S s T t U u V v W w X x Y y Z z

Letter Identification (by describing formation)
A a B b C c D d E e F f G g H h I i J j K k L l M m N n O o P p Q q R r S s T t U u V v W w X x Y y Z z

Letter Identification (by label, such as *b* for *ball*)
A a B b C c D d E e F f G g H h I i J j K k L l M m N n O o P p Q q R r S s T t U u V v W w X x Y y Z z

Letter Identification (in context)
A a B b C c D d E e F f G g H h I i J j K k L l M m N n O o P p Q q R r S s T t U u V v W w X x Y y Z z

Adapted from La Dean Talcott/Manteca Unified School District by Shirla Loutas, Bonnie Bitner, and Claire Venn in 2001 as part of the "Literacy Consortium" in Natrona County School District, Casper, Wyoming.

KINDERGARTEN LITERACY CHECKLIST

Name of Child _____ Birth Date_____

Classroom Teacher_____ Phone_____

Phonological and Phonemic Awareness

___ rhyming recognition ("Do these words rhyme?")

___ phoneme blending ("C-a-t makes ___?")

___ phoneme segmenting (sounds in *cat* are _ _ _)

___ syllable blending (combining syllables to make words)

___ syllable segmenting (taking words apart by syllables)

___ rhyming production ("Tell me a rhyming word.")

___ oral word boundaries (clapping 4–6 words)

___ discrimination of initial and final sounds of words

___ uses appropriate oral language structures

Book Handling

___ front of book

___ print contains a message

___ bottom of picture

___ left page before right

Directional Behavior

___ where to start

___ which way to go

___ return to the left

___ first and last concept

___ line order altered

Writing

___ writes own name

___ uses letter strings to spell words

___ uses left-to-right directionality

___ writes with spaces between words

___ writes some upper- and lowercase letters

___ uses some letter-sound correspondence

___ writes several known words

___ uses some punctuation

Specific Concepts and Printed Language

___ knows meaning of question mark

___ knows meaning of period

___ knows meaning of comma

___ knows meaning of quotation marks

___ matching upper- and lowercase forms of same letter

___ knows capital letter from lowercase letter

Hierarchical Concepts

___ letters, letters within words, words within sentences

___ fluently reads familiar patterned texts

___ word-by-word matching

___ isolates one letter and then two letters

___ isolates one word and then two words

___ first and last letter of a word

Oral Reading

___ uses picture clues

___ locates a few known words in context

___ reads simple, familiar, patterned texts

Letter Identification (circle known)

A a B b C c D d E e F f G g H h I i J j K k L l M m N n O o P p Q q R r S s T t U u V v W w X x Y y Z z

Letter to Sound (decoding)

a b c d e f g h i j k l m n o p q r s t u v w x y z

Sound to Letter (encoding; document with writing samples)

a b c d e f g h i j k l m n o p q r s t u v w x y z

Known Words in Reading			Known Words in Writing		

Adapted from La Dean Talcott/Manteca Unified School District by Shirla Loutas, Bonnie Bitner, and Claire Venn in 2001 as part of the "Literacy Consortium" in Natrona County School District, Casper, Wyoming

PRESCHOOL ENVIRONMENT CHECKLIST

Teacher _____ Date _____

WARM, NURTURING ATMOSPHERE
____ teachers are warm, friendly, and enthusiastic
____ children are happy and engaged

CLASSROOM MANAGEMENT
____ clear expectations
____ smooth transitions
____ clearly defined routines
____ clean and organized room

LITERACY ENVIRONMENT
____ environmental print used
____ children's print and drawings displayed
____ children's names visible
____ theme is evident
____ poems and rhymes posted
____ management charts with icons
____ library (fiction, nonfiction, theme, and multicultural books)

ORAL LANGUAGE DEVELOPMENT
____ lots of adult-child interaction
____ small-group show and tells
____ children encouraged to engage in conversations with peers and adults

PLAY CENTERS
____ used daily and changed at least monthly
____ clear boundaries
____ management system in place
____ purposeful
____ real literacy artifacts in each center
____ variety of fun, realistic, and meaningful activities
____ writing materials evident
____ social interaction with adults and peers
____ no more than four children per center

OPENING AND CALENDAR
____ brief daily activity
____ greeting
____ calendar time
____ weather
____ interactive opening

READ-ALOUDS
____ large or small group
____ daily activity
____ interactive and lots of modeling
____ theme related
____ vocabulary enriching
____ schema development

LETTER KNOWLEDGE
____ name games
____ sing Alphabet Song with mini follow-along alphabet charts
____ personalized and meaningful letter wall
____ letter or word wall or both with children's names and pictures
____ manipulative letters
____ letter sorts

JOURNALS, WRITING, AND DRAWING
____ shared, interactive, guided, or scaffolded writing
____ daily opportunities for individual writing
____ class books
____ meaningful to children
____ daily activity
____ dated journal entries

LESSON PLANS
____ relevant theme
____ ZPD groups
____ shared reading
____ read-alouds
____ independent reading
____ play centers
____ content learning centers
____ opening and calendar activities
____ writing
____ show and tell

STUDENT PORTFOLIOS
____ one for every child
____ children's work included
____ anecdotal notes
____ ongoing assessments

PRESCHOOL AND KINDERGARTEN MATHEMATICS CHECKLIST

(The **boldface** type highlights outcomes that are more typical for kindergartners.)

Name of Child _____ Birth Date _____

Classroom Teacher _____ Phone _____

Patterns

___ locates a pattern
___ matches a pattern
___ copies a pattern
___ **extends a pattern**
___ **creates a pattern**
___ **explains a pattern**

Shapes

	Matches	Points to	**Names**
▢			
△			
▭			
◯			
◇			
⬭			

Time

___ knows daytime from nighttime
___ **names days of week**
___ **names seasons**
___ **names months**
___ **names year**
___ **names today, yesterday, and tomorrow**

Measurement

___ uses nonstandard units of measure to determine shorter or longer
___ **uses standard units of measure to determine shorter or longer**

Sorting

___ by color
___ by size
___ by shape
___ by use

___ sorts by one characteristic
___ **sorts by two or more characteristics**
___ **verbally describes sorted objects**

Seriation

___ orders objects in logical sequence (number, size, and so on)

Number Operations

___ counts to 10
___ **counts to 20**
___ makes groups of objects 1–10
___ **makes groups of objects 10–20**

___ matches a numeral with corresponding sets of objects
___ demonstrates one-to-one correspondence
___ **demonstrates conservation of number**

Can Identify Approximately 10 Numbers in Any of the Following Ways:

In Context (e.g., by counting)

1 2 3 4 5 6 7 8 9 10 11 12 13 14 15 16 17 18 19 20

By Describing Formation (e.g., around and around = 8)

1 2 3 4 5 6 7 8 9 10 11 12 13 14 15 16 17 18 19 20

By Name

1 2 3 4 5 6 7 8 9 10 11 12 13 14 15 16 17 18 19 20

By Value (e.g., 4 fingers = 4)

1 2 3 4 5 6 7 8 9 10 11 12 13 14 15 16 17 18 19 20

Write These Numbers

1 2 3 4 5 6 7 8 9 10 11 12 13 14 15 16 17 18 19 20

EARLY READING AND WRITING TEST SCORES AND RESULTS FORM

Record individual student scores for the Brigance screen; Clay's (1996) letter identification test, letter-sound correspondence test, and concepts about print test; and Floyd and Yates's (2001) phonological awareness test. For the Brigance screen, be sure to record whether the preschool or K–1 version was administered.

Student Name _____ Birth Date _____

Class and Year _____

	Pretest	**Midtest**	**Posttest**
Brigance	/100	/100	/100
Letter Identification	/54	/54	/54
Letter-Sound Correspondence	/26	/26	/26
Concepts About Print	/24	/24	/24
Phonological Awareness	/20	/20	/20

Pretest date _____

Midtest date _____

Posttest date _____

Teacher Comments:

Pretest _____

_____

_____

Midtest _____

_____

_____

Posttest _____

_____

_____

EARLY WRITING SURVEY

This form provides an informal opportunity to assess a child's ability to write his or her own name, draw a self-portrait, and write known letters and numbers. Use the form to record and monitor what the child produces on his or her own sheet of blank paper. Include the child's own work in his or her student portfolio, if desired.

Pretest Date_____

Student Name_____

Name

Self-Portrait

Letters

Numbers

Designed in 2002 by Raelene Shreve, Natrona County School District #1, Casper, Wyoming.

PRESCHOOL COMPREHENSIVE QUARTERLY REPORT

Teacher _____   Date Submitted _____

Child's Name	Cognitive Development				Language Development and Literacy				Mathematics				Science				Social Studies				Social and Emotional Development				Motor and Physical Development				Music, Movement, and the Creative Arts			
	Q1	Q2	Q3	Q4	Q1	Q2	Q3	Q4	Q1	Q2	Q3	Q4	Q1	Q2	Q3	Q4	Q1	Q2	Q3	Q4	Q1	Q2	Q3	Q4	Q1	Q2	Q3	Q4	Q1	Q2	Q3	Q4

1 = No (Child does not exhibit this skill or quality.)
2 = Rarely (Child has demonstrated part of the skill or must have assistance to complete it. Quality observed less than 50% of the time.)
3 = Sometimes (Child is practicing the skill but may make errors or not be able to complete the task without aid. Quality present more than 50% of the time but not 100% of the time.)
4 = Always (Child has mastered this skill, or the quality is present 100% of the time.)

Teaching and Learning in Preschool: Using Individually Appropriate Practices in Early Childhood Literacy Instruction by Elizabeth Claire Venn and Monica Dacy Jahn
© 2004. Newark, DE: International Reading Association. May be copied for classroom use.

Reproducible Prompt Cards

• • •

SHOW AND TELL PROMPT CARD

- That reminds me of...

- I wonder...

- One time,...

- Aha!

- Why did you...?

- I think...

- I remember when...

- When I was young...

READING PROMPT CARD

- I bet this book is about...

- Where should I start?

- Where do I go next?

- Point to the words while I read.

- Were there enough words?

- I wonder...

- What does the picture tell you?

- Maybe the...

- How do you think it will end?

- You know this letter...

- This is really important...

- This story reminds me of...

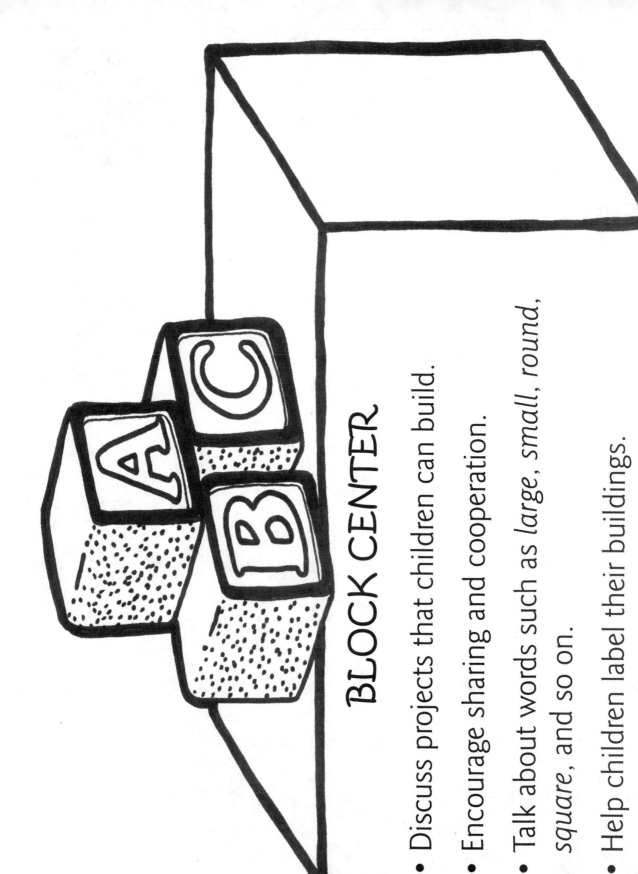

BLOCK CENTER

- Discuss projects that children can build.

- Encourage sharing and cooperation.

- Talk about words such as *large, small, round, square,* and so on.

- Help children label their buildings.

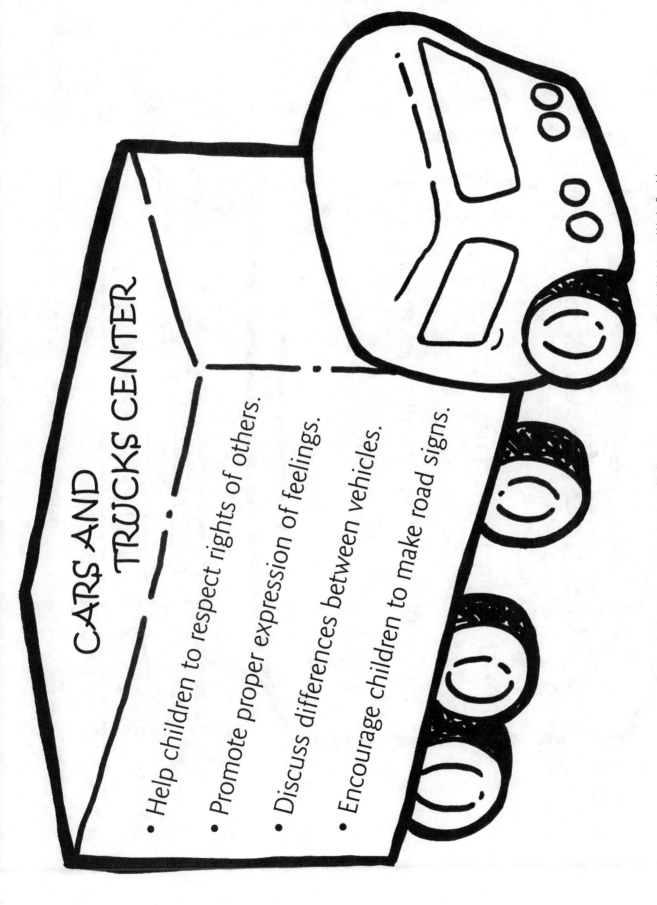

CARS AND TRUCKS CENTER

- Help children to respect rights of others.
- Promote proper expression of feelings.
- Discuss differences between vehicles.
- Encourage children to make road signs.

Teaching and Learning in Preschool: Using Individually Appropriate Practices in Early Childhood Literacy Instruction by Elizabeth Claire Venn and Monica Dacy Jahn. © 2004. Newark, DE: International Reading Association. May be copied for classroom use.

COMPUTER CENTER

- Help children with the equipment.
- Use computer language such as monitor and mouse.
- Encourage independent problem solving.
- Encourage creativity.

DRAMATIC PLAY CENTER

- Participate in the children's play.

- Encourage self-help skills.

- Encourage role-playing.

- Support turn taking and cooperating.

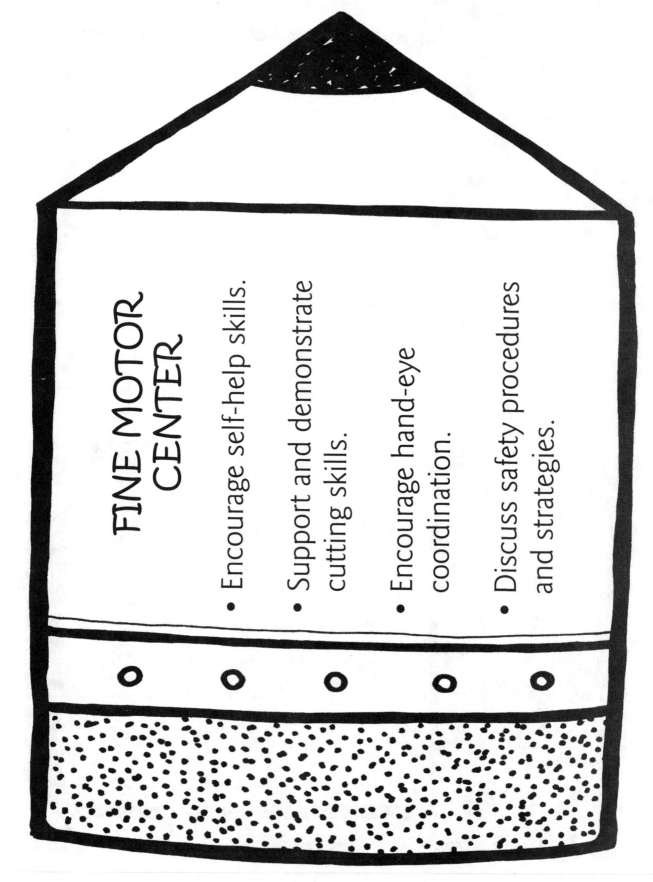

FINE MOTOR CENTER

- Encourage self-help skills.

- Support and demonstrate cutting skills.

- Encourage hand-eye coordination.

- Discuss safety procedures and strategies.

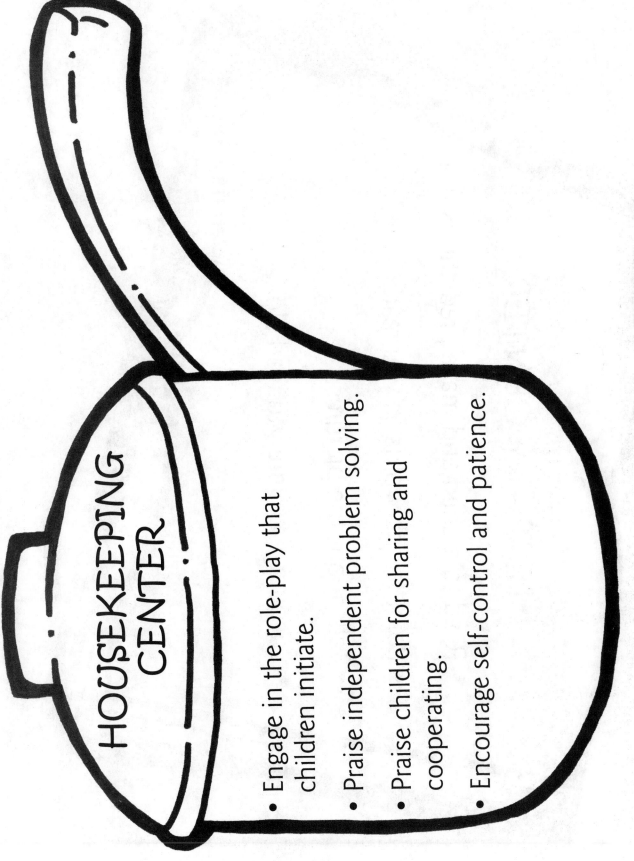

HOUSEKEEPING CENTER

- Engage in the role-play that children initiate.

- Praise independent problem solving.

- Praise children for sharing and cooperating.

- Encourage self-control and patience.

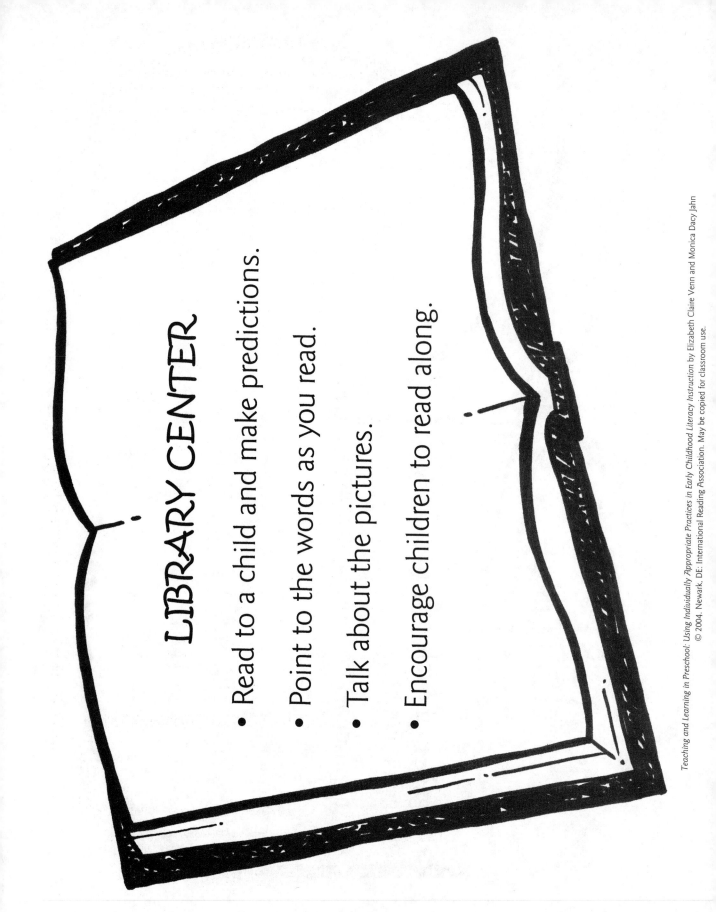

LIBRARY CENTER

- Read to a child and make predictions.

- Point to the words as you read.

- Talk about the pictures.

- Encourage children to read along.

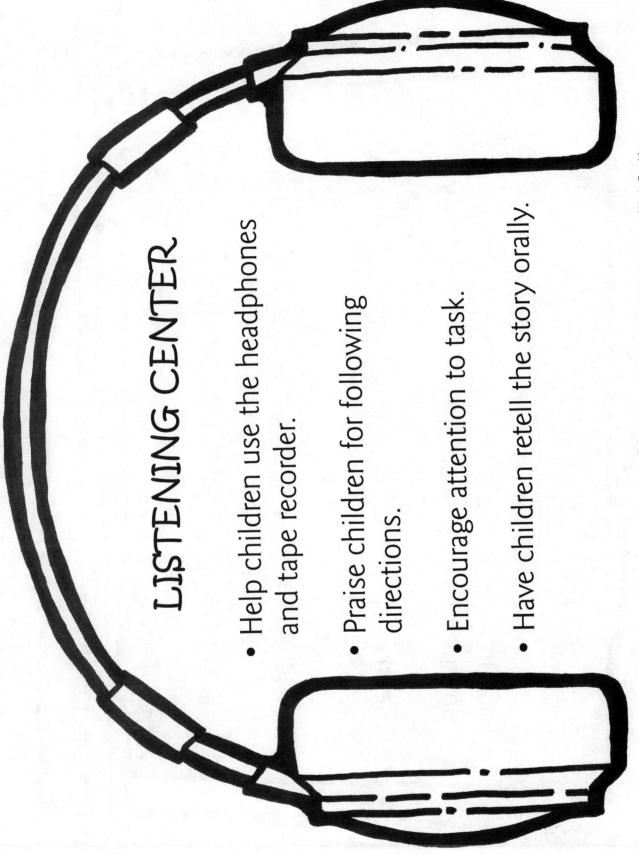

LISTENING CENTER

- Help children use the headphones and tape recorder.

- Praise children for following directions.

- Encourage attention to task.

- Have children retell the story orally.

MATHEMATICS CENTER

- Encourage counting and one-to-one correspondence (matching).

- Use mathematical language such as *bigger than*, *plus*, and *minus*.

- Praise independent problem solving.

- Help children create patterns and shapes.

Teaching and Learning in Preschool: Using Individually Appropriate Practices in Early Childhood Literacy Instruction by Elizabeth Claire Venn and Monica Dacy Jahn © 2004. Newark, DE: International Reading Association. May be copied for classroom use.

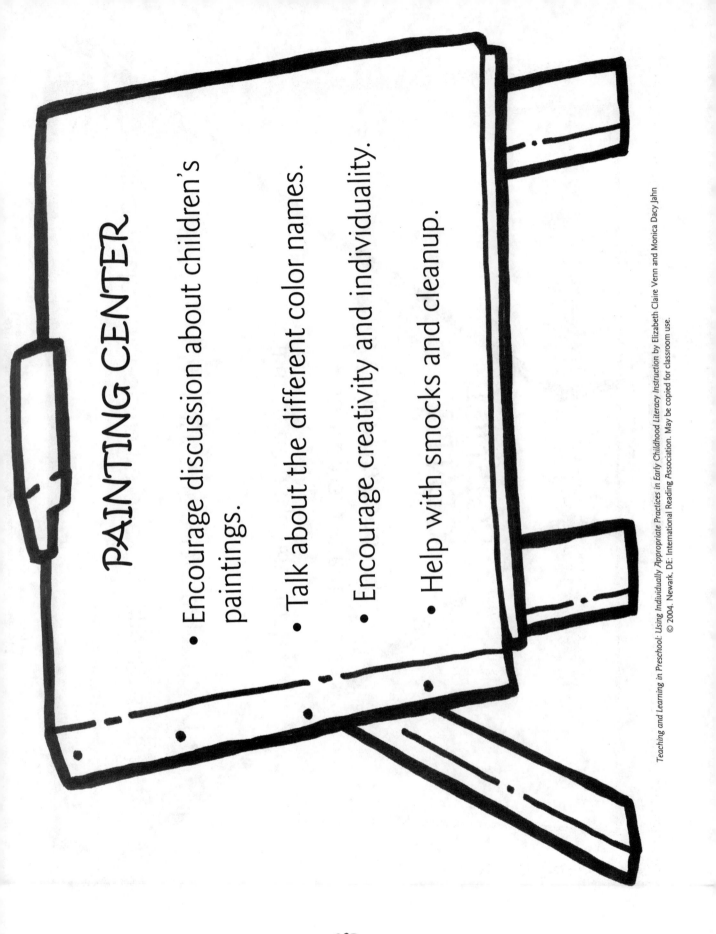

PAINTING CENTER

- Encourage discussion about children's paintings.

- Talk about the different color names.

- Encourage creativity and individuality.

- Help with smocks and cleanup.

SCIENCE CENTER

- Encourage children to make predictions.

- Encourage children to make generalizations.

- Discuss life cycles and habitats.

- Discuss similarities and differences in objects being explored.

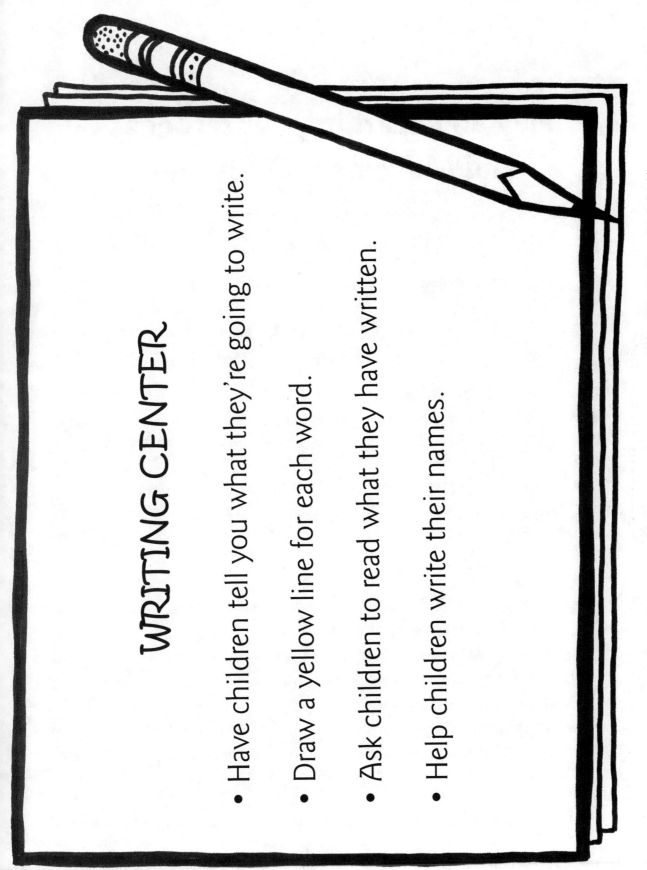

WRITING CENTER

- Have children tell you what they're going to write.

- Draw a yellow line for each word.

- Ask children to read what they have written.

- Help children write their names.

Play and Learning Center Ideas and Movement Activities

• • •

Literacy Play or Learning Center Ideas

Alphabet Knowledge Center

• Have students sort magnetic letters according to characteristics. For example, students should separate stick and circle letters, letters with short or long sticks, and upper- and lowercase letters.

• Have students dig for letters in the sand table and record the letters that they find.

• Have students match the first letters of their classmates' names to the appropriate pictures on a class pocket chart.

Early Writing Center

• Provide picture stamps with which students can illustrate and write a rebus.

• Have students write letters with several different writing tools.

• Have students write their own names, using different fonts, colors, or media.

• Supply racetrack letter cards and matchbox cars with which students can trace the letters.

Expressive Language Center

• Have students tell a story while using a wordless book or retell familiar nursery rhymes. Have them speak into a tape recorder with a microphone, and let them listen to their stories when they finish.

• Have students act out a familiar story, such as *The Three Little Pigs*, using props and costumes or puppets.

• Have students do show and tell with an aide or parent.

Phonological Awareness Center

- Have students play a segmenting syllables card game with a partner. One student draws a card with a picture on it (e.g., an antelope), claps the number of syllables in the represented word, and takes that number of markers or chips. The second child repeats the process with another card, and the game continues with the rest of the students in the center.
- Have students play a word-guessing game by listening to an audiotape and finding pictures of the objects named on the tape. For example, if the audiotape says *computer*, the students must find a picture of a computer.

Print Awareness and Concepts Center

- Provide a take-home book, and have students attach green sticky dots where they start reading on each page and red sticky dots where they stop reading on each page.
- Provide an appropriate text (with fewer or more words, depending on the student), and have the student circle each word or each letter.
- Have students listen to a teacher-created audiotape of instructions and find the designated environmental print. For example, if the audiotape says, "Find the sign that says *stop*," the students find this object in the classroom.

Print Knowledge and Appreciation Center

- Have students retell familiar nursery rhymes or stories by using flannel pieces on a flannel board.
- Provide a variety of books, magazines, newspapers, and comics in addition to copies of them on audiotapes so students can listen to and handle the texts.
- Have students do a text sort, putting nursery rhymes in one basket, magazines in a second basket, and nonfiction books in a third basket.

Receptive Language Center

- Supply teacher-created audiotapes with read-alongs that have simple, observable directions for students to follow. For example, before students turn to page 2, they should stand up and sit back down.
- Have students match pictures to environmental sounds that they hear on an audiotape.
- Have students pretend to have a telephone conversation about a 911 call, a doctor appointment, or a catalog order.

Movement Activities

Many commercial resources are available for games and movement activities. In what follows, we list a few of our favorite games and activities that often are requested by the children in our preschools. All of these games are very common throughout the United States, but they may be called by different names in different places.

Animal Pantomimes and Tag

Start out having the whole group move about like monkeys or elephants. Then, play tag and have children try to tag one another while imitating the animal movements.

Back to Back

Children move about the play area, following the teacher's command to run, hop, and so on. You or a selected child yells out "Back to back!" and each child finds a partner to stand with back to back. Rotate extra children so all get a turn to make partners, or participate in the game yourself to even the numbers. Also, try standing side to side and front to front.

Beanbag Toss and Catch

Each student has his or her own handheld beanbag and personal space. Call out directions for using the beanbag such as the following:

1. Place the beanbag on your palm, toss it up, and catch it on the back of your hand.

2. Toss the beanbag above your head, and jump up to catch it.

3. Toss the beanbag above your head, clap your hands, and catch it.

    a. Clap two times.

    b. See how many times you can clap before catching the beanbag.

4. Hold the beanbag in one hand, with your arm extended straight above your head. Let go of the beanbag, and try to catch it with the same hand before it reaches the floor.

5. Place the beanbag on your head. Tilt your head forward, and catch it in your hands.

    a. Repeat with hands at your waist.

    b. Repeat with hands behind your back.

Circle Kickout

Have children stand in two or three small circles, depending on the number of children present. They should stand 3 feet apart in the circle, and one player should stand in the middle with a foam ball. Choose the middle player by a random process such as picking whoever is wearing a certain color. That player tries to kick the ball so it goes past the children in the circle. The other children try to keep the ball in the circle by using their hands, feet, and bodies to stop it. When the ball gets through the circle or after a few minutes of play, a new child is the middle player.

Everybody's "It" Tag

All of the children are "It" and play tag. When a student is tagged, he or she must freeze in a straddle position and try to maintain his or her balance. The child becomes unfrozen when another child crawls through his or her straddled legs. After the first child says "Thank you," both children return to the game and try to tag more children.

Octopus

Select two children to be the octopus, and have them stand in the middle of the play area. Send the rest of the children to one end of the play area. On a predetermined signal, the children at the end of the play area will run to the other side of the play area while the two children playing the octopus try to tag as many children as possible. Children who are tagged become the octopus, along with the original two. This process is repeated until the last children are tagged, and then they become the octopus for a new game.

Simon Says

Children imitate the actions of a leader if the leader first says, "Simon says." Do not eliminate any children for imitating actions if the leader does not say "Simon says." Allow everyone to participate throughout the whole activity.

Target Throwing

Tape several pieces of construction paper (cut into any shape) to the exterior school wall beside the playground, and have each child throw a ball at his or her target, retrieve the ball, and repeat. After hitting the target three times in a row, the child may take a step backward and begin again.

Whistle Stop

Children move about the play area by running, hopping, jumping, leaping, or galloping, based on your directions. Everyone should be doing the same movement at one time. Blow the whistle for a given number of times, and the children stop to make groups with that number of children. For example, if you blow the whistle two times, the children arrange themselves into groups of two. For preschoolers, do not go above numbers 3 or 4 unless the children are very familiar with this activity.

Text and Music Resources

• • •

Having been literacy educators for more than two decades, we believe that it is important to provide preschool teachers with a relevant repertoire of children's literature related to the content areas. Although thematic units are typically filled with hands-on materials, realistic activities, and field trips, we believe that it is essential to demonstrate for our youngest students the power of books in exploration and new learning. Books can take children to new heights of adventure and elicit from them particular interests and opportunities for future study. We have provided the following booklists to help preschool teachers embellish and enhance their thematic resources in mathematics, social studies, science, music and movement, and the creative arts.

Suggested Books and Activities for Mathematics

Alborough, J. (1994). *Where's my teddy?* Cambridge, MA: Candlewick.

> This book teaches the concepts of size and making size comparisons, including the use of language such as *giant*, *tiny*, *large*, and *small*. Have children bring in their own stuffed animals (have extras available for children who do not bring any), and put them in order by size. Sort and classify by size and color and other attributes.

Bang, M. (2003). *Ten, nine, eight.* Glenview, IL: Scott Foresman.

> Children can predict the number that will be on the next page. Create a class book of counting backward, with each child making his or her own page.

Berger, S., & Chanko, P. (1999). *Big and little*. New York: Scholastic.

This book compares the different sizes that objects or animals can be. Provide students with objects or pictures of things that are different sizes and in different categories, and have children sort them in various ways.

Carle, E. (1994). *The very hungry caterpillar*. New York: Scholastic.

This classic book reinforces many mathematical, social studies, and science concepts. Children love to count the holes in the middle of the illustrated food items.

Christelow, E. (1998). *Five little monkeys jumping on the bed*. Boston: Houghton Mifflin.

This entertaining and silly book introduces counting backward and subtraction concepts in a fun and expressive manner. The book provides opportunities for children to role-play the act of subtraction as they eliminate one monkey at a time from "jumping on the bed."

Crews, D. (1986). *Ten black dots*. New York: William Morrow.

This counting book uses simple rhymes and large black dots to create images such as a snake or coat buttons. Give children black, round stickers to create their own image, and record how many dots they use. The students' work can be combined to form a class book.

Feelings, M.L. (1992). *Moja means one: Swahili counting book*. Ill. T. Feelings. New York: Puffin.

This counting book uses East African language and culture that correlates with numbers 1–10. Use this book as a model for creating a class book depicting your classroom or community's features, such as "one chalkboard" or "two rivers."

Hill, E. (2003). *Where's Spot?* New York: Puffin.

This simple flap book uses spatial words such as *in*, *under*, and *behind*.

Hoban, T. (1974). *Circles, triangles, and squares*. New York: Simon & Schuster.

This book presents photographs of common objects in a variety of shapes. Put children together in groups of three or four, and have them lie on the floor, making shapes with their bodies. Take a Polaroid snapshot of their shapes, and make a poster on which children can interactively label the shapes and write their own names under the appropriate pictures. Hang all the posters at the children's eye level.

Hoban, T. (1991). *Shapes and things*. New York: Simon & Schuster.

This book uses bright photographs to illustrate a variety of shapes. Have each child bring in a box of crackers, and keep the boxes separate from the ones used for snack time. Give each child a handful of crackers from different containers, and have the children sort the crackers however they would like. Circulate among the children, and have them explain their sorting choices. At another time, take one cracker from each package and make a real cracker graph.

Have the children find which shapes are the most and least common and count how many crackers of each shape there are. Make another tally graph, and have the children vote for their favorite cracker.

Hoban, T. (1997). *Is it larger? Is it smaller?* Glenview, IL: Scott Foresman.

Use this book to support children's understanding of mathematical terms and the concepts of *more* and *less*.

Hutchins, P. (1983). *You'll soon grow into them, Titch*. New York: William Morrow.

This book is perfect for talking with preschoolers about size relationships and words.

Hutchins, P. (1985). *Happy birthday, Sam*. New York: Puffin.

In this book, Sam finds out on his birthday that he is too short to do several things, but that changes when he receives a special birthday present. Measure students and adults, and compare their heights. List things that the preschoolers could do when they were babies and things that they can do now. Then, list what they are looking forward to doing when they are in first grade.

Lionni, L. (1995). *Inch by inch*. Glenview, IL: Scott Foresman.

This book can help children understand how to measure things by placing units of measure end to end. Many linear measurement activities could follow from a read-aloud of this book.

Lobel, A. (Ill.). (1970). *Frog and Toad are friends*. New York: HarperCollins.

In the "Lost Button" chapter of this book, Frog helps his friend Toad locate a lost button from his jacket. Give each child a container of 12–16 buttons, and have them sort the buttons by various attributes. Compare the attributes and sortings. Play Guess My Button, a game in which you describe a certain button and the children guess which one it is. The children take turns guessing, with your help if necessary.

Murphy, S.J. (2002). *One...two...three...sassafras!* Ill. J. Wallace. New York: HarperCollins.

This mathematics concept book illustrates number order in a fun way and has additional suggestions for related activities and books.

Nietzel, S. (1989). *The jacket I wear in the snow*. Ill. N.W. Parker. New York: Greenwillow.

This is a cumulative story and can get long unless children are involved in role-playing. The book is effective for teaching terms such as *under* and *over* and the concept of sequencing.

Pallotta, J. (1992). *The icky bug counting book*. Ill. R. Masiello. Watertown, MA: Charlesbridge.

This counting book has clear illustrations and interesting information about bugs. Select a page or two to read aloud to students.

Philpot, L., & Philpot, G. (1994). *Amazing Anthony Ant*. New York: Random House.

This flap book includes possibilities for songs, movement, and role-playing as it helps reinforce number names 1–5.

Sheppard, J. (1992). *The right number of elephants*. Ill. F. Bond. New York: HarperCollins.

Use this fantastical tale for children to practice counting backwards from 10 to 1.

Tang, G. (2002). *Math for all seasons*. Ill. H. Briggs. New York: Scholastic.

Bright illustrations on each page correlate with a mathematical riddle that can be solved by simple counting or another mathematics strategy.

Suggested Books for Social Studies

All About Me

Anholt, C., & Anholt, L. (1994). *All about you*. Ill. C. Anholt. New York: Puffin.

This book asks children what their preferences are for friends, play, food, and other things.

Canizares, S. (1999). *Feelings*. New York: Scholastic.

Photographs in this book show a variety of emotions that children experience.

Carlson, N.L. (1990). *I like me!* Upper Saddle River, NJ: Pearson Education.

This book shares what a pig likes about herself and is a great motivator for children to do the same.

Lionni, L. (1976). *A color of his own*. New York: Knopf.

A chameleon finds out what is special about himself.

McPhail, D.M. (1993). *Emma's pet*. New York: Dutton.

Emma wants a pet, but none of the pets she finds are just right. This book can trigger discussion about what pets children have and why certain animals are or are not good pets.

Tafuri, N. (1998). *I love you, little one*. New York: Scholastic.

Mothers tell their babies that they will always love them.

Zolotow, C. (1985). *William's doll*. Ill. W.P. du Bois. New York: HarperTrophy.

William really wants a doll, but everyone thinks he is a sissy.

Community Helpers

Bauld, J.S. (with Saunders-Smith, G., Ed.). (2000). *We need custodians*. Minnetonka, MN: Capstone.

Bauld, J.S. (with Saunders-Smith, G., Ed.). (2000). *We need principals*. Minnetonka, MN: Capstone.

Bauld, J.S. (with Saunders-Smith, G., Ed.). (2000). *We need teachers*. Minnetonka, MN: Capstone.
   Simple texts and clear pictures in this book series show how these school employees do their jobs.

Borass, T. (1999). *Plumbers* (Community Helpers series). Minnetonka, MN: Capstone.
   This book describes many aspects of being a plumber, how plumbers help people, and how people can help them.

Deedrick, T. (1998). *Bakers* (Community Helpers series). Minnetonka, MN: Capstone.
   Children who read this book will find out what bakers do every day and what equipment they use.

Frost, H. (with Saunders-Smith, G., Ed.). (1999). *Going to the dentist*. Minnetonka, MN: Capstone.
   This book depicts what a dentist does when children come for a checkup.

Hayward, L. (2001). *A day in the life of a doctor* (Jobs People Do series). London: Dorling Kindersley.
   This book is one in a series of books about real-life community helpers. All books in the series have bright photographs and simple text with key information about different occupations. Other titles are about a teacher, dancer, builder, firefighter, musician, police officer, and TV reporter.

Hutchings, A., & Hutchings, R. (1993). *Firehouse dog*. New York: Scholastic.
   This book explores the life of a firehouse dog and his days with busy firefighters.

Maass, R. (1989). *Fire fighters*. New York: Scholastic.
   Colorful photographs and text portray the many responsibilities of firefighters.

Ready, D. (1997). *Police officers* (Community Helpers series). Minnetonka, MN: Capstone.

Ready, D. (1998). *Mail carriers* (Community Helpers series). Minnetonka, MN: Capstone.
   These two books give important information about these professions and how they are essential in the community.

Smee, N. (2000). *Freddie visits the dentist*. New York: Barron's Educational Series.
   This book is one of a large series of books written for toddlers. In sturdy pages, this engaging story explains what happens during a dental checkup.

Diversity and Commonality

Baer, E. (1990). *This is the way we go to school: A book about children around the world*. Ill. S. Bjorkman. New York: Scholastic.

>This book is a worldwide tour of how children get to school.

Cheltenham Elementary School (Ill.). (2002). *We are all alike...We are all different*. New York: Scholastic.

>Kindergartners at Cheltenham Elementary School wrote the book and created paintings used for illustrations. Bright photographs of the children and their simple text combine to celebrate what things children have in common and what things are different. This book would be a wonderful starting point for studying the diversities and commonalities within a preschool classroom. Children can use drawings and writing to show where they live, who is in their family, and what they like to do.

Dorros, A. (1992). *This is my house*. New York: Scholastic.

>This is a straightforward book about houses all over the world.

Hamanaka, S. (1994). *All the colors of the earth*. New York: William Morrow.

>This beautiful picture book celebrates the diversity of children throughout the world.

Morris, A. (1989). *Hats, hats, hats*. Ill. K. Heyman. New York: Lothrop, Lee & Shepard.

>This book depicts different hats worn around the world.

Morris, A. (with Cohn, A., Ed.). (1990). *Loving*. Ill. K. Heyman. New York: Lothrop, Lee & Shepard.

>This multicultural book has large photographs and simple text that show how families all over the world do the same things in different ways to take care of their members.

Morris, A. (1993). *Bread, bread, bread*. Ill. K. Heyman. Glenview, IL: Scott Foresman.

Morris, A. (1994). *On the go*. Ill. K. Heyman. Glenview, IL: Scott Foresman.

>These multicultural books address the topics of food and transportation around the world.

Roca, N.B. (2002). *Boys and girls of the world: From one end to the other*. Ill. R.M. Cutto. New York: Barron's Educational Series.

>This book briefly describes life for children in nine different countries and gives adults additional information and activities to do with children.

Schaefer, L.M. (with Saunders-Smith, G., Ed.). (2000). *Some kids are blind*. Minnetonka, MN: Capstone.

Schaefer, L.M. (with Saunders-Smith, G., Ed.). (2000). *Some kids use wheelchairs*. Minnetonka, MN: Capstone.

These books describe the tools that physically challenged children use to complete daily tasks and the many things that they enjoy doing. The same publisher offers books on children who are deaf and children who wear leg braces.

Families

Blume, J. (1984). *The pain and the great one*. Ill. I. Trivas. New York: Simon & Schuster.

This funny story of sibling rivalry is told from two viewpoints—that of the older sister who is the "great one" and that of the younger brother who is the "pain."

Canizares, S., & Chanko, P. (1998). *Babies*. New York: Scholastic.

This multicultural board book is about babies' needs.

Canizares, S., & Chessen, B. (1999). *In the kitchen*. New York: Scholastic.

This book is about families working in the kitchen to prepare food.

Canizares, S., & Moreton, D. (1999). *Babies on the move*. New York: Scholastic.

This book is about how babies all over the world are carried by others.

Cole, B. (1984). *The trouble with Mom*. New York: Putnam.

In this book, a boy shares how his mother is very different from the other moms in the neighborhood: She is a witch!

Hoberman, M. (2001). *Fathers, mothers, sisters, brothers: A collection of family poems*. Ill. M. Hafner. Boston: Little, Brown.

This book includes many poems about families and common occurrences in family life.

Joosse, B. (2001). *Mama, do you love me?* Ill. B. Lavalee. San Francisco: Chronicle.

Beautiful illustrations support the simple story of the constancy of a mother's love through an exploration of Inuit culture. Facilitate a discussion about the constancy of family love, despite the inevitable mistakes that family members make.

Mayer, M. (2001). *Just Grandpa and me*. New York: Golden Books.

In this book, Little Critter tells all the things that he does with his grandpa. There are several titles in the family series that explore Little Critter's relationships with family members.

McPhail, D.M. (Ill.). (2003). *Sisters*. San Diego: Harcourt.

Pencil drawings in this book illustrate a simple text about two very different sisters who love each other very much.

Pellegrini, N. (Ill.). (1991). *Families are different*. New York: Holiday House.

This story is about an adopted girl and the different kinds of families that she notices.

Scott, A.H. (1992). *On Mother's lap*. Ill. G. Coalson. New York: Clarion Books.

In this book, an Inuit boy learns to share his mother's lap and love with his younger sister.

Tyler, L.W. (1989). *Waiting for Mom*. Ill. S. Davis. New York: Viking.

In this book, a small hippopotamus bravely waits after school for his tardy mother.

Weiss, N. (1987). *A family story*. New York: Greenwillow.

This story is about the love that cycles through generations as siblings grow up and have families of their own.

Wells, R. (Ill.). (1997). *Noisy Nora*. New York: Dial.

This classic story is about an older sibling who feels ignored by busy parents.

Willhelm, H. (1986). *Let's be friends again*. New York: Random House.

In this book, a boy who is upset with his younger sister learns that they can be friends.

Williams, V.B. (1990). *"More more more," said the baby*. New York: Greenwillow.

This book is about love and cuddling with babies.

Friends

Gomi, T. (1995). *My friends*. Cambridge, MA: Chronicle.

In this book, an Asian girl shares the things that she has learned to do from her animal and human friends. This book supports the concept that people are dependent on others in many ways.

Hale, I. (1992). *How I found a friend*. New York: Viking.

This simple text shows how sharing can help two children make friends.

Heine, H. (1986). *Friends*. New York: Simon & Schuster.

Teamwork and friends sticking together are the themes of this book. While reading this book, children can suggest the qualities of a good friend, and you can create a list of the qualities that can be referred to for community-building and conflict-resolution activities within the classroom.

Raschka, C. (Ill.). (1993). *Yo! Yes?* Danbury, CT: Orchard Books.

This simple book offers a profound message about making friends.

Roca, N.B. (2001). *Friendship: From your old friends to your new friends*. Ill. R.M. Curto. New York: Barron's Educational Series.

This book is about developing and maintaining friendships.

Nutrition

Frost, H. (with Saunders-Smith, G., Ed.). (2000). *The dairy group*. Minnetonka, MN: Capstone.

This book explains the different parts of the food pyramid, what foods are in each area, and how much of these foods should be eaten for a healthy diet. Other titles by the same author address eating right; fats, oils, and sweets; and the food groups.

Robinson, F. (1995). *Vegetables, vegetables*. San Francisco: Children's Book Press.

This book explains where vegetables come from and how people use them for a nutritious diet.

Places in the Community

Saunders-Smith, G. (1998). *The supermarket*. Minnetonka, MN: Capstone.

This book illustrates the various workers, areas, and equipment found in the supermarket. The same author offers books about the farm, fire station, and doctor's office.

Trumbauer, L. (with Saunders-Smith, G., Ed.). (2001). *At school*. Minnetonka, MN: Capstone.

This book describes what happens throughout the school day.

Safety

Raatma, L. (1999). *Safety at home*. Minnetonka, MN: Bridgestone.

This book shows how to be safe at home. Other titles by the same author explain safety around strangers, on the playground, and on the school bus.

Raatma, L. (1999). *Smoke alarms*. Minnetonka, MN: Bridgestone.

This book gives important home fire safety information. Other titles by the same author explain home fire drills and how to crawl low under smoke and stop, drop, and roll.

Suggested Books for Science

Animals and Insects

Barlowe, D., & Barlowe, S. (1980). *Who lives here? Animals of the pond, forest, prairie, desert, mountains, meadow, and swamp*. New York: Random House.

> This book depicts a variety of animal habitats.

Brown, M.W. (1995). *Big red barn* [Board book]. Ill. F. Bond. New York: Harper.

> This rhyming text explains life on a farm.

Chanko, P. (1998). *Baby animals learn*. New York: Scholastic.

> Colorful photographs in this book show mother animals teaching their babies how to survive.

Cousins, L. (Ill.). (2000). *Where does Maisy live? A lift-the-flap book* [Board book]. Cambridge, MA: Candlewick.

> This book is about the habitats in which different animals live and is a fun book to accompany a study of animals and their habitats.

Curran, E. (1989). *Hello, farm animals*. Ill. J. Goldsborough. New York: Troll.

> This simple text describes a busy day on the farm.

Dabcovich, L. (1988). *Busy beavers*. New York: Dutton.

> This book's descriptive text and illustrations show how beavers live.

Fowler, A. (1990). *It could still be a fish*. Chicago: Children's Press.

Fowler, A. (1990). *It could still be a mammal*. Chicago: Children's Press.

Fowler, A. (1990). *It's a good thing there are insects*. Chicago: Children's Press.

Fowler, A. (1991). *Please don't feed the bears*. Chicago: Children's Press.

Fowler, A. (1992). *The biggest animal ever*. Chicago: Children's Press.

Fowler, A. (1992). *Frogs and toads and tadpoles, too*. Chicago: Children's Press.

Fowler, A. (1992). *It's best to leave a snake alone*. Chicago: Children's Press.

Fowler, A. (1992). *Turtles take their time*. Chicago: Children's Press.

> This is a series of nonfiction books written for beginning readers, and the books are perfect for read-alouds. The clear photographs and simple text will answer children's questions and provide interesting information. The books' smaller size also makes them easy for children to handle.

Hockman, H. (Ed.). (1993). *What's inside? Animal homes.* London: Dorling Kindersley.

Large illustrations in this book depict animal homes, and the concise text gives important information about them.

Keats, E.J. (1999). *Over in the meadow.* New York: Puffin.

This classic counting book combines rhyme, rhythm, mathematics, and science. Children can act out the animal parts and sounds, count the animals, and use this book for reinforcing their knowledge of animal habitats.

Miller, J. (1988). *Seasons on the farm.* Englewood Cliffs, NJ: Prentice Hall.

Photographs in this book depict seasonal work on the farm.

Selsam, M.E., & Goor, R. (1981). *Backyard insects.* New York: Scholastic.

The text and pictures show children how to find common bugs in the backyard.

Shapiro, A.L. (2002). *Mice squeak, we speak: A poem by Arnold L. Shapiro.* Ill. T. dePaola. New York: Putnam.

This simple book addresses animals and the noises that they make. Children can imitate the animals and then play a guessing game in which one child makes an animal noise and the other children have to name the animal.

Turner, G. (1994). *Over on the farm.* New York: Penguin.

This is a counting book of farm animals.

Tuxworth, N. (1996). *Let's look at animals.* New York: Lorenz.

This book shares important facts about various animals' body parts and habitats.

Wildsmith, B. (1992). *Squirrels.* New York: Oxford University Press.

The watercolor illustrations and concise text in this book describe the lives of squirrels.

Construction, Machines, and Vehicles

Barton, B. (1990). *Building a house.* Glenview, IL: Scott Foresman.

This book's pictures and simple text demonstrate from start to finish how a house is built.

Barton, B. (1997). *Machines at work* [Board book]. New York: HarperCollins.

This book depicts how machines help in construction.

Canizares, S. (1999). *Where does it park?* New York: Scholastic.

Bright photographs in this book show where vehicles park.

Crews, D. (1980). *Truck*. New York: William Morrow.

Crews, D. (1984). *School bus*. New York: William Morrow.

Crews, D. (2003). *Freight train*. New York: Mulberry Paperbacks.

These books are about special vehicles.

Freeman, M.S. (with Saunders-Smith, G., Ed.). (1999). *Ambulances* (Community Vehicles series). Minnetonka, MN: Capstone.

Other titles in the Community Vehicles series are about fire boats, fire engines, and police cars.

Gibbons, G. (1990). *How a house is built*. New York: Holiday House.

This book offers a detailed description of different kinds of houses and how they are built.

Hill, L.S. (1999). *Get around in the city*. Minneapolis, MN: Carolrhoda.

Hill, L.S. (1999). *Get around in the country*. Minneapolis, MN: Carolrhoda.

These books describe how people all over the world use a variety of transportation.

Hoban, T. (1999). *Construction zone* [Board book]. New York: Greenwillow.

This book has clear and colorful photographs depicting the different large machines and vehicles used in construction projects.

Maestro, B., & DelVecchio, E. (1984). *Big city port*. New York: Simon & Schuster.

This book describes what happens in a big city port.

Earth, Water, and Air

Beers, B. (with Saunders-Smith, G., Ed.). (2000). *Earth's land and water*. Minnetonka, MN: Capstone.

This book explains in simple terms topographical features such as rivers, mountains, and valleys.

Butterfield, M., Calder, S., & Calder, S. (1999). *Where am I? The desert*. Mankato, MN: Thameside.

This book depicts desert plants and animals.

Butterfield, M., Calder, S., & Calder, S. (1999). *Where am I? Ocean*. Mankato, MN: Thameside.

In this book, children discover sea creatures and try to guess where they live.

Fowler, A. (1993). *It could still be a rock*. Chicago: Childrens' Press.

In this book, simple text and pictures explain many facts about rocks.

Halpern, S. (1995). *My river*. New York: Scholastic.

This book's simple text and bright illustrations show what lives in a river.

Hoban, T. (2000). *I wonder*. San Diego: Harcourt.

This book's simple text and vivid pictures encourage children to ask questions about the physical world around them.

Marzollo, J. (1996). *I am water*. Ill. J. Moffatt. New York: Scholastic.

In this book, a simple patterned text shows how water is invaluable in everyday life.

The Human Body and Health

Carle, E. (1999). *From head to toe* [Board book]. New York: HarperCollins.

In this book, animals move parts of their bodies and ask kids to do the same. This text is fun for movement activities and naming body parts.

Frost, H. (with Saunders-Smith, G., Ed.). (1999). *Brushing well*. Minnetonka, MN: Capstone.

Frost, H. (with Saunders-Smith, G., Ed.). (1999). *Food for healthy teeth*. Minnetonka, MN: Capstone.

Frost, H. (with Saunders-Smith, G., Ed.). (1999). *We need water*. Minnetonka, MN: Capstone.

Frost, H. (with Saunders-Smith, G., Ed.). (2000). *Drinking water*. Minnetonka, MN: Capstone.

These books discuss the elements needed for healthy, strong bodies.

Frost, H. (with Saunders-Smith, G., Ed.). (2001). *The skeletal system*. Minnetonka, MN: Capstone.

This book explains the basic functions of the skeletal system and how bones, joints, and muscles are connected and work together.

Ross, T. (2000). *Wash your hands*. La Jolla, CA: Kane/Miller.

This book is a fun story that encourages hand washing.

Royston, A. (1999). *Clean and healthy* (Safe and Sound series). Portsmouth, NH: Heinemann.

Germs, washing hands, and visiting the doctor and dentist are just some of the topics discussed in this book.

Royston, A. (1999). *Eat well* (Safe and Sound series). Portsmouth, NH: Heinemann.

This book discusses how nutritious foods keep our bodies healthy and strong.

Royston, A. (1999). *A healthy body*. Portsmouth, NH: Heinemann.

This book focuses on the importance of exercising to keep healthy.

Royston, A. (1999). *Safety first*. Portsmouth, NH: Heinemann.

This book discusses basic rules for crossing the street, playing, and cycling safely.

Thomas, P. (2002). *My amazing body: A first look at health and fitness*. Ill. L. Harker. New York: Barron's Educational Series.

This book is about all the amazing things a body can do and how to take care of the body.

Plants

Hall, Z. (2002). *It's pumpkin time!* Ill. S. Halpern. New York: Scholastic.

Large, vibrant illustrations in this book describe how a pumpkin seed grows into a mature plant in the fall. This is a good support book for plant investigations.

Royston, A. (1998). *Life cycle of a bean*. Portsmouth, NH: Heinemann.

Royston, A. (1998). *Life cycle of a sunflower*. Portsmouth, NH: Heinemann.

These books cover the life cycles of different plants.

Royston, A. (2000). *How plants grow*. Portsmouth, NH: Heinemann.

Topics covered in this book include roots, stems, and evergreen leaves and food storage.

Saunders-Smith, G. (1998). *Flowers*. Minnetonka, MN: Capstone.

Saunders-Smith, G. (1998). *From bud to blossom*. Minnetonka, MN: Capstone.

Saunders-Smith, G. (1998). *Leaves*. Minnetonka, MN: Capstone.

Saunders-Smith, G. (1998). *Seeds*. Minnetonka, MN: Capstone.

These four books present important facts about plants.

Schaefer, L.M. (with Saunders-Smith, G., Ed.). (2000). *What grows from a tree?* Minnetonka, MN: Capstone.

This book depicts the parts of a tree and the different types of trees.

Weather and the Seasons

Branley, F. (2000). *Snow is falling*. Ill. H. Keller. New York: HarperCollins.

This book describes how snow can be both helpful and hazardous.

Franco, B. (1994). *Fresh fall leaves*. Ill. S. Halpern. New York: Scholastic.

In this book, children enjoy playing in the fall leaves. This book is also good for movement activities and artistic expression.

Hutchings, A., & Hutchings, R. (1994). *Picking apples and pumpkins*. New York: Scholastic.

This book depicts a family outing to the pumpkin patch and apple orchard in the fall.

Kalan, R. (1991). *Rain*. Ill. D. Crews. New York: Mulberry.

This book's interesting illustrations explore how rain changes what the world looks like.

Maestro, B. (1992). *Snow day*. Ill. G. Maestro. New York: Scholastic.

This book shows how a forceful snowstorm has an impact on people in a variety of ways and how community helpers save the day.

Maestro, B. (1994). *Why do leaves change color?* Ill. L. Krupinski. New York: HarperCollins.

Although this nonfiction book is written for primary-grade children, portions of the text can be shared with preschoolers to help explain what occurs when leaves change their colors. The beautiful illustrations portray the lovely scenery as summer leads into fall.

Palazzo, J. (1989). *Rainy day fun*. Ill. G. Ulrich. New York: Troll.

In this book, children play dress-up when it rains.

Pulver, R. (1990). *Mrs. Toggle's zipper*. Ill. R.W. Alley. New York: Simon & Schuster.

In this humorous book, Mrs. Toggle is stuck in her winter coat and everyone at school tries to get her out of it.

Rockwell, A. (1989). *Apples and pumpkins*. Ill. L. Rockwell. New York: Simon & Schuster.

In this book, a family visits an apple orchard and pumpkin patch.

Schaefer, L.M. (with Saunders-Smith, G., Ed.). (1999). *What kind of a day is it? A cold day*. Minnetonka, MN: Capstone.

Schaefer, L.M. (with Saunders-Smith, G., Ed.). (1999). *What kind of a day is it? A hot day*. Minnetonka, MN: Capstone.

These books describe what happens on a cold day and a hot day, respectively. Other titles by the same author address rainy, snowy, sunny, and windy days.

Spier, P. (1982). *Peter Spier's rain*. New York: Doubleday.

This wordless picture book conveys the fun of playing in the rain.

Wallace, K. (1999). *Whatever the weather*. London: Dorling Kindersley.

This book is written to help preschoolers and kindergartners learn about weather phenomena such as thunder, lightning, and icicles.

The Way Things Move

Schaefer, L.M. (with Saunders-Smith, G., Ed.). (1999). *Back and forth*. Minnetonka, MN: Capstone.

Schaefer, L.M. (with Saunders-Smith, G., Ed.). (1999). *Circular movement*. Minnetonka, MN: Capstone.

Schaefer, L.M. (with Saunders-Smith, G., Ed.). (1999). *Push and pull*. Minnetonka, MN: Capstone.

Schaefer, L.M. (with Saunders-Smith, G., Ed.). (1999). *Start and stop*. Minnetonka, MN: Capstone.

Schaefer, L.M. (with Saunders-Smith, G., Ed.). (1999). *Vibrations*. Minnetonka, MN: Capstone.

Schaefer, L.M. (with Saunders-Smith, G., Ed.). (1999). *Zigzag movement*. Minnetonka, MN: Capstone.

These books illustrate how things can move in different ways.

Suggested Resources for Music and Movement Activities

Instrumental Music

Bach, J.S. (n.d.). [Recorded by Baby Einstein]. *Baby Bach* [CD]. Burbank, CA: Buena Vista Records. (2002)

Bartels, J. (1980). *Sillytime magic* [CD]. New York: BMG Records. (1994)

Beethoven, L. (n.d.). [Recorded by various artists]. *Fantasia 2000: An original Walt Disney Records soundtrack* [CD]. Burbank, CA: Walt Disney Records. (1999)

Palmer, H. (1978). *Sea gulls* [LP]. Northridge, CA: Hap-Pal Music.

Vocal Music

CJ. (1995). Farmer in the dell. On *FUNdamentals* [CD]. Hilmar, CA: Suite A Records.

CJ. (1995). Five little monkeys. On *FUNdamentals* [CD]. Hilmar, CA: Suite A Records.

CJ. (1995). On top of spaghetti. On *FUNdamentals* [CD]. Hilmar, CA: Suite A Records.

CJ. (2000). Drivin' a car. On *Move it!* [CD]. Hilmar, CA: Suite A Records.

CJ. (2000). The giggle wiggle. On *Move it!* [CD]. Hilmar, CA: Suite A Records.

CJ. (2000). Jungle jazz (the clean-up song). On *Move it!* [CD]. Hilmar, CA: Suite A Records.

CJ. (2000). The shape shake. On *Move it!* [CD]. Hilmar, CA: Suite A Records.

CJ. (2000). Stop & go. On *Move it!* [CD]. Hilmar, CA: Suite A Records.

CJ. (2001). *FARMdamentals* [CD]. Hilmar, CA: Suite A Records.

Diamond, C. (1986). Four hugs a day. On *Ten carrot diamond* [cassette]. Vancouver, BC: Hug Bug Records.

Diamond, C. (1986). I wanna be a dog. On *Ten carrot diamond* [cassette]. Vancouver, BC: Hug Bug Records.

Family Folk Festival [cassette]. (1993). Redway, CA: Music for Little People.

Grammer, R. (1983). Counting song. On *Can you sound just like me?* [CD]. Brewerton, NY: Smilin' Atcha Music.

Grammer, R. (1983). Finger plays. On *Can you sound just like me?* [CD]. Brewerton, NY: Smilin' Atcha Music.

Grammer, R. (1986). Barnyard Boogie. On *Teaching peace* [CD]. Brewerton, NY: Smilin' Atcha Music.

Grammer, R. (1986). Shake your brain. On *Teaching peace* [CD]. Brewerton, NY: Smilin' Atcha Music.

Grammer, R. (1986). Teaching peace. On *Teaching peace* [CD]. Brewerton, NY: Smilin' Atcha Music.

Greg and Steve. (1998). ABC rock. On *We all live together, Vol. 1* [CD]. Cypress, CA: Youngheart.

Greg and Steve. (1998). Brown bear, brown bear, what do you see? On *Playin' favorites* [CD]. Cypress, CA: Youngheart.

Greg and Steve. (1998). Buckle my shoe. On *We all live together, Vol. 3* [CD]. Cypress, CA: Youngheart.

Greg and Steve. (1998). Creative dramatics. On *We all live together, Vol. 4* [CD]. Cypress, CA: Youngheart.

Greg and Steve. (1998). Days of the week [English and Spanish]. On *We all live together, Vol. 4* [CD]. Cypress, CA: Youngheart.

Greg and Steve. (1998). Down on the farm. On *We all live together, Vol. 5* [CD]. Cypress, CA: Youngheart.

Greg and Steve. (1998). Freeze. On *We all live together, Vol. 2* [CD]. Cypress, CA: Youngheart.

Greg and Steve. (1998). Good morning. On *We all live together, Vol. 2* [CD]. Cypress, CA: Youngheart.

Greg and Steve. (1998). Head, shoulders, knees, & toes. On *Big fun* [CD]. Cypress, CA: Youngheart.

Greg and Steve. (1998). If you're happy and you know it. On *We all live together, Vol. 3* [CD]. Cypress, CA: Youngheart.

Greg and Steve. (1998). Itsy bitsy spider. On *Big fun* [CD]. Cypress, CA: Youngheart.

Greg and Steve. (1998). Just like me (mirror movements). On *We all live together, Vol. 4* [CD]. Cypress, CA: Youngheart.

Greg and Steve. (1998). Listen and move. On *We all live together, Vol. 2* [CD]. Cypress, CA: Youngheart.

Greg and Steve. (1998). Magic of reading. On *Big fun* [CD]. Cypress, CA: Youngheart.

Greg and Steve. (1998). Months of the year. On *We all live together, Vol. 2* [CD]. Cypress, CA: Youngheart.

Greg and Steve. (1998). Number game. On *We all live together, Vol. 5* [CD]. Cypress, CA: Youngheart.

Greg and Steve. (1998). Number rock. On *We all live together, Vol. 2* [CD]. Cypress, CA: Youngheart.

Greg and Steve. (1998). Question. On *We all live together, Vol. 1* [CD]. Cypress, CA: Youngheart.

Greg and Steve. (1998). Rock and roll rhythm band. On *We all live together, Vol. 5* [CD]. Cypress, CA: Youngheart.

Greg and Steve. (1998). Round in a circle. On *We all live together, Vol. 1* [CD]. Cypress, CA: Youngheart.

Greg and Steve. (1998). Shapes. On *We all live together, Vol. 3* [CD]. Cypress, CA: Youngheart.

Greg and Steve. (1998). This old man. On *Playin' favorites* [CD]. Cypress, CA: Youngheart.

Greg and Steve. (1998). Zip-a-dee-do-dah. On *Playin' favorites* [CD]. Cypress, CA: Youngheart.

Greg and Steve. (2000). Bop 'til you drop. On *Kids in action* [CD]. Cypress, CA: Youngheart.

Greg and Steve. (2000). Can't sit still. On *Kids in action* [CD]. Cypress, CA: Youngheart.

Greg and Steve. (2000). Can you leap like a frog? On *Kids in action* [CD]. Cypress, CA: Youngheart.

Greg and Steve. (2000). Goin' on a bear hunt. On *Kids in action* [CD]. Cypress, CA: Youngheart.

Palmer, H. (1993). Parade of colors. On *Can a cherry pie wave goodbye?* [CD]. Northridge, CA: Hap-Pal Music.

Palmer, H. (1993). Say the opposite. On *Can a cherry pie wave goodbye?* [CD]. Northridge, CA: Hap-Pal Music.

Raffi. (1996). Down by the bay. On *Singable songs for the very young: Great with a peanut-butter sandwich* [CD]. Cambridge, MA: Rounder Records.

Raffi. (1996). The more we get together. On *Singable songs for the very young: Great with a peanut-butter sandwich* [CD]. Cambridge, MA: Rounder Records.

Raffi. (1996). The sharing song. On *Singable songs for the very young: Great with a peanut-butter sandwich* [CD]. Cambridge, MA: Rounder Records.

Raffi. (1996). Wiloughby wallaby woo. On *Singable songs for the very young: Great with a peanut-butter sandwich* [CD]. Cambridge, MA: Rounder Records.

Ultimate kids song collection: 101 favorite sing-alongs [CD]. (2000). Montreal, QC: Madacy Records.

Suggested Books for the Creative Arts

Adams, P. (Ill.). (1989). *There was an old lady who swallowed a fly.* Swindon, UK: Child's Play.

Adams, P. (Ill.). (2000). *Old MacDonald had a farm.* Swindon, UK: Child's Play.

Brett, J. (Ill.). (1999). *Gingerbread baby.* New York: Putnam.

Brown, M.T. (Ill.). (1993). *Play rhymes.* New York: Puffin.

Calmenson, S. (1997). *Engine, engine, number nine*. Ills. P. Meisel & S. Schett. New York: Hyperion.

Carle, E. (1981). *I see a song*. New York: HarperCollins.

Carle, E. (with Gauch, P., Ed.). (1996). *Little cloud*. New York: Philomel.

Carlstrom, N. (1991). *Wild, wild sunflower child Anna*. Ill. J. Pinkney. Glenview, IL: Scott Foresman.

Cauley, L. (2001). *Clap your hands*. New York: Putnam.

Cowen-Fletcher, J. (1996). *Mama zooms*. New York: Scholastic.

Fleming, D. (Ill.). (1998). *In the small, small pond*. New York: Henry Holt.

Franco, B. (1994). *Fresh fall leaves*. Ill. S. Halpern. New York: Scholastic.

Hoban, L. (1980). *Harry's song*. New York: William Morrow.

Isadora, R. (1979). *Ben's trumpet*. New York: Greenwillow.

Locker, T. (1997). *Water dance*. San Diego: Harcourt.

Martin, B., Jr., & Archambault, J. (1989). *Chicka chicka boom boom*. Ill. L. Ehlert. New York: Simon & Schuster.

Peek, M. (Ill.). (1985). *Mary wore her red dress, and Henry wore his green sneakers*. New York: Clarion.

Raffi. (1989). *Tingalayo*. New York: Crown.

Raffi. (1990). *Down by the bay*. Ill. M.B. Westcott. New York: Crown.

Raffi. (1990). *Shake my sillies out*. Ill. D. Allender. New York: Crown.

Raffi. (1998). *The wheels on the bus* [Board book]. Ill. S.K. Wickstrom. New York: Crown.

Rosen, M. (1989). *We're going on a bear hunt*. Ill. H. Oxenbury. New York: Margaret K. McElderry.

Rosen, M. (1990). *Little Rabbit Foo Foo*. Ill. A. Robins. New York: Simon & Schuster.

Spier, P. (Ill.). (1989). *London bridge is falling down*. New York: Doubleday.

Trapani, I. (Ill.). (1994). *Twinkle, twinkle, little star*. Watertown, MA: Charlesbridge.

Trapani, I. (Ill.). (1995). *Oh where, oh where has my little dog gone?* Watertown, MA: Charlesbridge.

Trapani, I. (Ill.). (1997). *I'm a little teapot*. Watertown, MA: Charlesbridge.

Westcott, N. (Ill.). (1992). *Peanut butter and jelly: A play rhyme*. New York: Dutton.

Westcott, N. (Ill.). (1998). *The lady with the alligator purse* [Board book]. Boston: Little, Brown.

Williams, R.L. (1994). *The bear went over the mountain*. Huntingdon Beach, CA: Creative Teaching Press.

Williams, V.B. (1988). *Music, music for everyone*. New York: William Morrow.

Preschool Parent Materials

• • •

This appendix includes the Preschool Parent Handbook, the Sign-Up Sheet for Parent Volunteers, and the Sign-Up Sheet for Preparing Play and Learning Center Materials.

The Preschool Parent Handbook can be explained and disseminated to parents during an open house or home visit early in the school year. The handbook clearly delineates the preschool's goals and objectives, activities, and expectations and parent responsibilities. In many cases, it may be beneficial to read aloud each page to parents in a one-on-one setting.

The Sign-Up Sheet for Parent Volunteers is designed to ascertain parents' special talents and interests. Teachers can use this information to invite parents to participate in preschool activities of interest to them. The sign-up sheet also may enhance and encourage parents' volunteer efforts in addition to augmenting their instruction and support of students' learning.

The Sign-Up Sheet for Preparing Play and Learning Center Materials may encourage parent involvement in center planning and preparation as parents become more familiar with preschool procedures and activities. Supporting this level of parent participation at school may have an impact on parent-child interactions that subsequently occur at home.

PRESCHOOL PARENT HANDBOOK

Welcome to preschool! We are so excited to be involved with you and your child as you begin school together. Your participation in this program is so important to your child's future school success. We look forward to getting to know you here at our school. All supplies, such as crayons, pencils, and markers, will be provided by the preschool program.

Philosophy

The philosophy of the preschool framework is incorporated in the following beliefs:

- All children can learn to read and write effectively.
- Parents want to help their children succeed.
- All children begin school with diverse backgrounds and experiences.
- All children have the right to receive a quality early childhood education from a highly skilled instructor.
- All children deserve the opportunity to participate in an individually appropriate classroom that provides a nurturing, comfortable, and brain-compatible environment.
- Early intervention programs are the key to long-term school achievement for many children.
- Many young children require explicit teaching and instruction to become successful readers and writers.
- Parents benefit from opportunities to observe appropriate adult-child interactions in order to ensure their children's school success.
- All children will be more successful in school when their parents are involved in their education.
- All children need opportunities to apply what they have been taught.
- An effective way to break the cycle of school failure is to provide families with early cognitive, social, emotional, and physical support.
- Effective instruction is based on and meets individual student needs.

Goal

This preschool is an early intervention framework designed to give preschoolers and their families the support and guidance that they need as they enter their elementary school years together.

Objectives

- To increase significantly the literacy acquisition of young children as they enter their formal years of education.
- To model and provide for children and their families individually appropriate practices in all cognitive, social, emotional, and physical interactions.
- To transition students and families comfortably into the public school setting.
- To increase parental awareness and involvement in all school activities.

Activities

Your child will be participating in activities and tasks such as the following:

Calendar activities

Read-alouds

Shared reading (with Big Books and follow-up activities)

Partner and cross-age reading

Independent reading (looking through books independently)

Phonological awareness activities (playing with the sounds of language)

Oral language development activities

Writing activities

Small-group literacy and language activities

Print awareness activities (learning to look at letters and symbols)

Large- and small-group mathematics lessons

Social studies and science projects

Music and movement activities

Physical development activities (using large muscle groups, coordination, and balance)

Computer labs

Library and media center activities

Snacks and recess

Playtime

Art

Making friends and getting along with others

Play and learning centers

Mathematics	Writing
Reading	Listening
Language	Book knowledge and appreciation
Games, puzzles, and puppets	Housekeeping
Fine motor	Art
Science	Computer
Water and sand table	Post office
Blocks	Dramatic play

Teaching and Learning in Preschool: Using Individually Appropriate Practices in Early Childhood Literacy Instruction by Elizabeth Claire Venn and Monica Dacy Jahn © 2004. Newark, DE: International Reading Association. May be copied for classroom use.

Is Your Child Ready for Preschool?

Place check marks by the completed items.

_____ 1. My child will be 3 years old by _____.

_____ 2. My child is toilet trained.

_____ 3. My child has complete immunization records.

_____ 4. My child has completed screening activities.

_____ 5. My child has visited the preschool.

Are You Ready for Your Child to Start Preschool?

Place check marks by the completed items.

_____ 1. I have returned necessary permission forms.

_____ 2. I have labeled all of my child's personal items (backpack, coat, and so on).

_____ 3. I have made transportation arrangements.

_____ 4. I have met with the preschool director and various school staff.

_____ 5. I have signed up on the parent volunteer sheet.

Preschool Parent Requirements

• Personally accompany your child to and from the classroom, and sign in and out daily.

• Adhere to school rules and regulations, including the discipline policy.

• Participate in the preschool classroom one hour per week.

• Participate in the school at large one hour per week. (This hour also may be spent in the preschool.)

• Help your child meet minimum daily attendance requirements for students (90% daily attendance).

• Contact the school when you or your child will be absent.

• Sign and return all permission slips and other forms.

• Actively participate in activities.

Discipline Policy

Preschool participants are expected to abide by the elementary school rules and regulations in order to provide a consistent set of guidelines both for parents and children throughout the elementary school years.

In addition, the preschool and the elementary school in which it is housed expect families to comply with the following guidelines:

• Children will be kind and courteous to their peers and adults.

• Children will keep their hands and feet to themselves.

• Children will follow directions.

• Children will share materials.

• Children will be good listeners.

• Parents will follow the examples of the school personnel when interacting with students.

• Parents will model appropriate listening skills during class lessons.

• Parents will direct all questions and concerns to school personnel.

Health and Safety Issues

• All children are required to have up-to-date immunizations as defined by current state law.

• Parents are required to call the school if their children will be absent or tardy.

• Children should be kept at home if they have fevers or other contagious illnesses.

• Staff members will contact the parents if a child gets sick at school and needs to be taken home.

• In the event of inclement weather, we will follow the regular school dismissal policy.

• Participants will follow the teacher's directions for any emergency situation.

• Students should be dressed for the weather conditions because we will be going outside for recess.

• Students will be participating in any annual health screenings provided by the school.

• We will follow the school's medication distribution policy.

Tips for Parent Volunteers

- Follow directions given by the classroom teacher.

- Physically bend down to be at the height of students when speaking to them.

- Avoid baby talk.

- Be positive and cheerful.

- When speaking with students, consider using the following language:

    - "Tell me about your (picture, story, painting, building, blocks, or other project)."

    - "You're *talking*, and you need to be *listening*." (State the inappropriate behavior, and tell the child the appropriate behavior.)

    - "What else can you try? Is there another way to do it?"

    - "Tell me more about...."

    - "Let's all listen to...."

- Feel free to ask questions or express concerns.

- Dress comfortably for activities.

- Get acquainted with other parents in the preschool program.

- Check the calendar frequently to make sure you can attend on the days for which you have signed up to participate.

- If an illness or emergency prevents you from attending, please call the school office to let the staff know that you will not be in class that day.

Preschool Parent Contract

I understand that for my child, _____, to participate in preschool, I am responsible for volunteering at school two hours per week. I acknowledge that the success of this early childhood intervention and my child's future education is based upon ongoing home-school collaboration and communication. I know that my weekly participation is valued and is a fundamental component of this preschool, and I understand my responsibility to fulfill this commitment.

I plan to volunteer on the following days and times:

Mondays from_____ to_____ o'clock

Tuesdays from_____ to_____ o'clock

Wednesdays from _____ to_____ o'clock

Thursdays from _____ to_____ o'clock

Fridays from_____ to_____ o'clock

Parent signature_____

Student name_____

Date_____

Teacher signature_____

Date_____

Teaching and Learning in Preschool: Using Individually Appropriate Practices in Early Childhood Literacy Instruction by Elizabeth Claire Venn and Monica Dacy Jahn © 2004. Newark, DE: International Reading Association. May be copied for classroom use.

Parent Volunteer Form

Please complete this form, and return it to your child's classroom teacher.

Parent name _____

Student name _____

1. Please check the items below that you would be able to help with at preschool.

_____ driving for field trips _____ helping with classroom celebrations

_____ sharing a job or hobby through a field trip or classroom visit

What job or hobby will you share? _____

_____ other (explain)_____

2. Please check the areas in which you feel comfortable assisting the children.

_____ cooking _____ sewing _____ computers _____ art activities

_____ typing dictation _____ story reading _____ publishing student books

_____ small-group activities _____ science explorations _____ music and movement

3. Please check the items that you could help with at home.

_____ making games and materials (involves cutting, coloring, and pasting)

_____ word-processing student books

_____ cutting out laminated items

_____ assembling and binding student or class books

Thank you! Your help and support are invaluable!

SIGN-UP SHEET FOR PARENT VOLUNTEERS

Please sign your name under the days on which you are going to volunteer your time. In addition, please supply the times that you plan to be working in the preschool itself.

For the week of _____

Monday _____

    1. _____   5. _____
    2. _____   6. _____
    3. _____   7. _____
    4. _____   8. _____
    Snacks _____

Tuesday _____

    1. _____   5. _____
    2. _____   6. _____
    3. _____   7. _____
    4. _____   8. _____
    Snacks _____

Wednesday _____

    1. _____   5. _____
    2. _____   6. _____
    3. _____   7. _____
    4. _____   8. _____
    Snacks _____

Thursday _____

    1. _____   5. _____
    2. _____   6. _____
    3. _____   7. _____
    4. _____   8. _____
    Snacks _____

Friday _____

    1. _____   5. _____
    2. _____   6. _____
    3. _____   7. _____
    4. _____   8. _____
    Snacks _____

SIGN-UP SHEET FOR PREPARING PLAY AND LEARNING CENTER MATERIALS

I have listed the materials that our preschoolers will need for the following centers. Please locate (or create) and organize the necessary items prior to the time and date indicated. Thank you for your help!

Center	Items Needed	Location	Time and Date

REFERENCES

Adams, M.J. (1990). *Beginning to read: Thinking and learning about print*. Cambridge, MA: MIT Press.

Adams, M.J., Foorman, B.R., Lundberg, I., & Beeler, T. (1997). *Phonemic awareness in young children: A classroom curriculum*. Baltimore: Paul H. Brookes.

Allington, R.L., & Walmsley, S.A. (1995). *No quick fix: Rethinking literacy programs in America's elementary schools*. New York: Teachers College Press; Newark, DE: International Reading Association.

Barnett, W.S. (2002). Preschool education for economically disadvantaged children: Effects on reading achievement and related outcomes. In S.B. Neuman & D.K. Dickinson (Eds.), *Handbook of early literacy research* (pp. 421–443). New York: Guilford.

Barnett, W.S., & Hustedt, J. (2003). Preschool: The most important grade. *Educational Leadership, 60*, 54–57.

Berk, L.E., & Winsler, A. (1995). *Scaffolding children's learning: Vygotsky and early childhood education*. Washington, DC: National Association for the Education of Young Children.

Bodrova, E., & Leong, D.J. (1996). *Tools of the mind: The Vygotskian approach to early childhood education*. Englewood Cliffs, NJ: Prentice Hall.

Bodrova, E., Leong, D.J., Paynter, D., & Hensen, R. (2001). *Scaffolding literacy development in the preschool classroom*. Aurora, CO: Mid-Continent Research for Education and Learning.

Bowman, B.T., Donovan, M.S., & Burns, M.S. (Eds.). (2001). *Eager to learn: Educating our preschoolers*. Washington, DC: National Academy Press.

Bradley, L., & Bryant, P. (1983). Categorizing sounds and learning to read: A causal connection. *Nature, 301*, 419–421.

Bradley, L., & Bryant, P. (1985). *Rhyme and reason in reading and spelling*. Ann Arbor, MI: University of Michigan Press.

Bredekamp, S., & Copple, C. (Eds.). (1997). *Developmentally appropriate practice in early childhood programs*. Washington, DC: National Association for the Education of Young Children.

Bricker, D., & Squires, J. (with Mounts, L., Potter, L., Nickel, R., Twombly, E., & Farrell, J.). (1999). *Ages and stages questionnaire: A parent-completed, child-monitoring system* (2nd ed.). Baltimore: Paul H. Brookes.

Burns, M.S., Griffin, P., & Snow, C.E. (Eds.). (1999). *Starting out right: A guide to promoting children's reading success*. Washington, DC: National Academy Press.

Calkins, L.M. (2000). *The art of teaching reading*. New York: Longman.

Clay, M.M. (1975). *What did I write? Beginning writing behavior*. Portsmouth, NH: Heinemann.

Clay, M.M. (1991). *Becoming literate: The construction of inner control*. Portsmouth, NH: Heinemann.

Clay, M.M. (1993). *Reading recovery: A guidebook for teachers in training*. Portsmouth, NH: Heinemann.

Clay, M.M. (1996). *An observation survey of early literacy achievement*. Portsmouth, NH: Heinemann.

Clay, M.M. (1998). *By different paths to common outcomes*. York, ME: Stenhouse.

Clay, M.M. (2001). *Change over time in children's literacy development*. Portsmouth, NH: Heinemann.

D'Arcangelo, M. (2003). On the mind of a child: A conversation with Sally Shaywitz. *Educational Leadership, 60*, 6–10.

Dixon-Krauss, L. (1996). *Vygotsky in the classroom: Mediated literacy instruction and assessment*. Reading, MA: Addison-Wesley Higher Education.

Dorn, L.J., French, C., & Jones, T. (1998). *Apprenticeship in literacy: Transitions across reading and writing*. York, ME: Stenhouse.

Dwyer, M.C., Chait, R., & McKee, P. (2000). *Building strong foundations for early learning: The U.S. Department of Education's guide to high-quality early childhood education programs*. Washington, DC: U.S. Department of Education.

Epstein, A. (2001). Thinking about art: Encouraging art appreciation in early childhood settings. *Young Children,* 56(3), 38–43.

Erickson, H.L. (1995). *Stirring the head, heart, and soul: Redefining curriculum and instruction.* Thousand Oaks, CA: Corwin Press.

Floyd, S., & Yates, W. (2001). *Curriculum-aligned thematic phonological awareness treatment.* Lake City, SC: Susan Floyd.

Gallahue, D.L. (1993). *Developmental physical education for today's children.* Dubuque, IA: Brown & Benchmark.

Gersten, R., & Geva, E. (2003). Teaching reading to early language learners. *Educational Leadership, 60,* 44–49.

Goldenberg, C. (2002). Making schools work for low-income families in the 21st century. In S.B. Neuman & D.K. Dickinson (Eds.), *Handbook of early literacy research* (pp. 211–231). New York: Guilford.

Haight, W. (2003). *Parenting: Babies and Toddlers Newsletter, 1.*

Hart, B., & Risley, T.R. (1995). *Meaningful differences in the everyday experience of young American children.* Baltimore: Paul H. Brookes.

Hart, B., & Risley, T.R. (1999). *The social world of children learning to talk.* Baltimore: Paul H. Brookes.

Holdaway, D. (1984). *The foundations of literacy.* Portsmouth, NH: Heinemann.

International Reading Association, & National Association for the Education of Young Children. (1998). *Learning to read and write: Developmentally appropriate practices for young children.* A joint position statement of the International Reading Association (IRA) and the National Association for the Education of Young Children (NAEYC). Newark, DE: Author; Washington, DC: Author.

Jensen, E. (1996). *Brain-based learning.* Del Mar, CA: Turning Point.

Jensen, E. (1998). *Teaching with the brain in mind.* Alexandria, VA: Association for Supervision and Curriculum Development.

Jensen, E. (2000). *Learning with the body in mind.* San Diego: The Brain Store.

Jordano, K., & Callela, T. (Eds.). (1998). *Fall phonemic awareness songs and rhymes, Vol. 2340: Fun lyrics sung to familiar tunes.* Cypress, CA: Creative Teaching Press.

Keene, E.O., & Zimmermann, S. (1997). *Mosaic of thought: Teaching comprehension in a reader's workshop.* Portsmouth, NH: Heinemann.

Klenschy, M., & Hoge, S. (1991, January/February). *Kindergarten programs for four-year-olds: An early intervention strategy.* Paper presented at the annual meeting of the California Association for Bilingual Education, Anaheim, CA. (ERIC Document Reproduction Service No. 333976)

Knoff, H.M. (2001). *The stop and think social skills program: Teacher's manual for PreK–1.* Longmont, CO: Sopris West.

Kovalik, S.J., & Olsen, K.D. (2001). *Exceeding expectations: A user's guide to implementing brain research in the classroom.* Covington, WA: Books for Educators.

McDevitt, T.M., & Ormrod, J.E. (2001). *Child development and education.* Englewood Cliffs, NJ: Pearson Education.

Morrow, L.M. (2001). *Literacy development in the early years: Helping children read and write.* Boston: Allyn & Bacon.

National Institute of Child Health and Human Development. (2000). *Report of the National Reading Panel. Teaching children to read: An evidence-based assessment of the scientific research literature on reading and its implications for reading instruction* (NIH Publication No. 00-4769). Washington, DC: U.S. Government Printing Office.

Neuman, S.B., & Dickinson, D.K. (Eds.). (2002). *Handbook of early literacy research.* New York: Guilford.

Owocki, G. (1999). *Literacy through play.* Portsmouth, NH: Heinemann.

Paulson, L., Noble, L., Jepson, S., & van den Pol, R. (2001). *Building early literacy and language skills.* Longmont, CO: Sopris West.

Phillips, D., McCartney, K., & Scarr, S. (1987). Child care quality and children's social development. *Developmental Psychology, 23,* 537–543.

Pianta, R., & La Paro, K. (2003). Improving early school success. *Educational Leadership, 60,* 24–29.

Pikulski, J. (1994). Preventing reading failure: A review of five effective programs. *The Reading Teacher, 48,* 30–39.

Roskos, K.A., Christie, J.F., & Richgels, D.J. (2003). The essentials of early literacy instruction. *Young Children, 58*(2), 52–60.

Sanders, S.W. (2002). *Active for life: Developmentally appropriate movement programs for young children.* Washington, DC: National Association for the Education of Young Children.

Smith, M.W., & Dickinson, D.K. (2002). *Early language and literacy classroom observation (ELLCO) toolkit.* Baltimore: Paul H. Brookes.

Snow, C.E., Burns, M.S., & Griffin, P. (Eds.). (1998). *Preventing reading difficulties in young children.* Washington, DC: National Academy Press.

Spiegel, D.L. (1999). Meeting each child's literacy needs. In L.B. Gambrell, L.M. Morrow, S.B. Neuman, and M. Pressley (Eds.), *Best practices in literacy instruction.* New York: Guilford.

Sprenger, M.B. (1999). *Learning and memory: The brain in action.* Alexandria, VA: Association for Supervision and Curriculum Development.

Stahl, S.A. (2002). Teaching phonics and phonological awareness. In S.B. Neuman & D.K. Dickinson (Eds.), *Handbook of early literacy research* (pp. 333–347). New York: Guilford.

Stanovich, K.E. (1986). Matthew effects in reading: Some consequences of individual differences in the acquisition of literacy. *Reading Research Quarterly, 21,* 360–407.

Stanovich, K.E. (1991). The psychology of reading: Evolutionary and revolutionary developments. *Annual Review of Applied Linguistics, 12,* 3–30.

Temple, C., Nathan, R., Burris, N.A., & Temple, F. (1992). *The beginnings of writing* (3rd ed.). Boston: Allyn & Bacon.

U.S. Centers for Disease Control and Prevention. (n.d.). *Promoting better health: A Report to the President.* Retrieved September 12, 2003, from http://www.cdc.gov/nccdphp/dash/physicalactivity/promoting_health/index.htm.

U.S. Department of Health and Human Services. (1998). *Head Start program performance standards.* Washington, DC: Author.

Venn, C., Jahn, M., & Shreve, R. (1997). *All ready reading and writing preschool guidebook.* Casper, WY: All Ready LLC.

Venn, C., Jahn, M., & Shreve, R. (2002). *All ready reading and writing preschool guidebook* (Rev. ed.). Casper, WY: All Ready LLC.

Vygotsky, L.S. (1978). *Mind in society: The development of higher psychological processes* (M. Cole, V. John-Steiner, S. Scribner, & E. Souberman, Eds. and Trans.). Cambridge, MA: Harvard University Press. (Original work published 1934)

Wolfe, P., & Brandt, R. (1998). What do we know from brain research? *Educational Leadership, 56,* 8–13.

Wood, D.J., Bruner, J., & Ross, G. (1976). The role of tutoring in problem solving. *Journal of Child Psychology and Psychiatry, 17,* 89–100.

Wyoming Early Childhood Standards Task Force. (2002). *Wyoming Department of Education early childhood readiness standards.* Cheyenne, WY: Wyoming Department of Education.

CHILDREN'S LITERATURE AND MUSIC REFERENCES

Adams, P. (Ill.). (1995). *This old man.* Swindon, UK: Child's Play.

Ahlberg, J., & Ahlberg, A. (1999). *Each peach pear plum.* New York: Penguin.

Asch, F. (Ill.). (2000). *Happy birthday, moon.* New York: Simon & Schuster.

Barney. (1999). Colors all around. On *A great day for learning* [CD]. Richardson, TX: The Lyons Group.

Base, G. (1987). *Animalia.* Waterbury, CT: Abrams.

Bayer, J. (1992). *A my name is Alice.* Ill. S. Kellogg. New York: Dutton.

Berenstain, S., & Berenstain, J. (1997). *The Berenstain bears: Inside, outside, upside down* [Board book]. New York: Random House.

Berenstain, S., & Berenstain, J. (2000). *The Berenstain bears and baby makes five.* New York: Random House.

Brown, M.W. (1991). *Good night, moon* [Board book]. Ill. C. Hurd. New York: Harper.

Butterworth, N. (1991). *Amanda's butterfly.* New York: Doubleday.

Carle, E. (1987). *The tiny seed.* New York: Scholastic.

Carle, E. (1994). *The very hungry caterpillar.* New York: Scholastic.

Carlstrom, N. (1996). *Jesse Bear, what will you wear?* New York: Simon & Schuster.

Catalanotto, P. (2002). *Matthew A.B.C.* New York: Atheneum.

Cauley, L. (Ill.). (1992). *Goldilocks and the three bears.* New York: Putnam.

Christelow, E. (1998). *Five little monkeys jumping on the bed.* Boston: Houghton Mifflin.

Cole, J. (1986). *This is the place for me.* Ill. W.C. Van Horne. New York: Penguin.

Colgin, M.L. (1990). *One potato, two potato, three potato, four: 165 chants for children.* Mt. Rainier, MD: Gryphon House.

Collins, H. (Ill.). (2003). *Little Miss Muffet.* Toronto: Kids Can Press.

Cousins, L. (Ill.). (1996). *Jack and Jill: And other nursery rhymes* [Board book]. New York: Dutton.

Crews, D. (1986). *Ten black dots.* New York: William Morrow.

Crews, D. (2003). *Freight train.* New York: Mulberry Paperbacks.

Day, A. (1989). *Carl goes shopping.* New York: Farrar, Straus & Giroux.

dePaola, T. (Ill.). (1985a). Humpty Dumpty. In T. dePaola, *Tomie dePaola's Mother Goose* (p. 62). New York: Putnam.

dePaola, T. (Ill.). (1985b). Old King Cole. In T. dePaola, *Tomie dePaola's Mother Goose* (p. 37). New York: Putnam.

dePaola, T. (Ill.). (1985c). *Tomie dePaola's Mother Goose.* New York: Putnam.

Eastman, P.D. (Ill.). (1960). *Are you my mother?* New York: Random House.

Ehlert, L. (1989). *Eating the alphabet: Fruits and vegetables from A–Z.* San Diego: Harcourt.

Guarino, D. (1997). *Is your mama a llama?* Ill. S. Kellogg. New York: Scholastic.

Hague, K. (1999). *Alphabears: An ABC book.* Ill. M. Hague. New York: Henry Holt.

Hoban, T. (1992). *Look up, look down.* New York: Greenwillow.

Hutchins, P. (1968). *Rosie's walk.* New York: Simon & Schuster.

Hutchins, P. (1986). *The doorbell rang.* New York: William Morrow.

Kalan, R. (1989). *Jump, frog, jump.* Ill. B. Barton. New York: Mulberry.

Kalan, R. (1991). *Rain.* Ill. D. Crews. New York: Mulberry.

Keats, E.J. (1996). *The snowy day.* New York: Viking.

Keats, E.J. (1998a). *Goggles!* New York: Puffin.

Keats, E.J. (1998b). *Peter's chair.* New York: Puffin.

Kimmel, E. (1994). *Hershel and the Hanukkah goblins.* Ill. T.S. Hyman. New York: Holiday House.

Kirk, D. (Ill.). (1997). *Miss Spider's new car.* New York: Scholastic.

Kraus, R. (1994). *Leo the late bloomer.* Ill. J. Aruego. New York: HarperCollins.

Lionni, L. (1987). *The biggest house in the world.* New York: Knopf.

Lobel, A. (Ill.). (1970). *Frog and Toad are friends.* New York: HarperCollins.

Lobel, A. (Ill.). (1984). *Days with Frog and Toad.* New York: HarperCollins.

Locker, T. (1997). *Water dance.* San Diego: Harcourt.

Locker, T. (2001). *Mountain dance.* San Diego: Harcourt.

Locker, T. (2003). *Cloud dance.* New York: HarperCollins.

MacDonald, S. (Ill.). (1992). *Alphabatics.* New York: Simon & Schuster.

MacDonald, S. (2000). *Look whooo's counting.* New York: Scholastic.

Marshall, J. (1993). *Red riding hood.* New York: Puffin.

Martin, B., Jr. (1983). *Brown bear, brown bear, what do you see?* [Board book]. Ill. E. Carle. New York: Henry Holt.

Martin, B., Jr. (1997). *Polar bear, polar bear, what do you hear?* Ill. E. Carle. New York: Henry Holt.

Martin, B., Jr., & Archambault, J. (1989a). *Chicka chicka boom boom.* Ill. L. Ehlert. New York: Simon & Schuster.

Martin, B., Jr., & Archambault, J. (1989b). *White Dynamite and Curly Kidd.* Ill. T. Rand. New York: Henry Holt.

Mayer, M. (Ill.). (1968). *There's a nightmare in my closet.* New York: Dial.

McCloskey, R. (1941). *Make way for ducklings.* New York: Viking.

McQueen, L. (Ill.). (1987). *The little red hen.* New York: Scholastic.

Mendez, P. (1991). *The black snowman.* Ill. C. Byard. New York: Scholastic.

Miranda, A. (1997). *To market, to market*. Ill. J. Stevens. San Diego: Harcourt.

Mosel, A. (1988). *Tikki Tikki Tembo*. Ill. B. Lent. New York: Henry Holt.

Numeroff, L. (2000). *If you give a mouse a cookie*. Ill. F. Bond. New York: HarperCollins.

Palmer, H. (1969). Colors. On *Learning basic skills through music, Vol. 1* [CD]. Northridge, CA: Hap-Pal Music.

Parkinson, K. (Ill.). (1987). *The enormous turnip*. Morton Grove, IL: Whitman.

Peek, M. (Ill.). (1985). *Mary wore her red dress, and Henry wore his green sneakers*. New York: Clarion.

Perkins, L.R. (1995). *Home lovely*. New York: Greenwillow.

Philpot, L., & Philpot, G. (1994). *Amazing Anthony Ant*. New York: Random House.

Raffi. (1990). *Down by the bay*. Ill. M.B. Westcott. New York: Crown.

Raffi. (1998). *The wheels on the bus* [Board book]. Ill. S.K. Wickstrom. New York: Crown.

Raffi. (1999). *Five little ducks* [Board book]. Ills. J. Aruego & A. Dewey. New York: Crown.

Ransom, C. (2001). *Little Red Riding Hood*. Ill. T. Lyon. New York: McGraw-Hill.

Rosen, M. (1989). *We're going on a bear hunt*. Ill. H. Oxenbury. New York: Margaret K. McElderry.

Rosen, M. (1990). *Little Rabbit Foo Foo*. Ill. A. Robins. New York: Simon & Schuster.

Royston, A. (1998). *Life cycle of a bean*. Portsmouth, NH: Heinemann.

Scarry, R. (1974). *Richard Scarry's cars and trucks and things that go*. New York: Golden Books.

Seuss, Dr. (1960a). *Green eggs and ham*. New York: Random House.

Seuss, Dr. (1960b). *One fish, two fish, red fish, blue fish*. New York: Random House.

Seuss, Dr. (1998). *My many colored days*. Ills. S. Johnson & L. Fancher. New York: Knopf.

Shannon, D. (2002). *Duck on a bike*. New York: Blue Sky.

Spier, P. (1982). *Peter Spier's rain*. New York: Doubleday.

Trapani, I. (Ill.). (1994). *Twinkle, twinkle, little star*. Watertown, MA: Charlesbridge.

Trapani, I. (Ill.). (1997). *I'm a little teapot*. Watertown, MA: Charlesbridge.

Viorst, J. (1987). *Alexander and the terrible, horrible, no good, very bad day*. Ill. R. Cruz. New York: Aladdin.

Yolen, J. (1987). *Owl moon*. Ill. J. Schoenherr. New York: Philomel.

INDEX

Note: Page numbers followed by *f* indicate figures.

D

E

F

K

L

and, 168–170; stability movement in, 168, 171; suggestions for, 272–273; in writing instruction, 116–117

Mueller, V., 190*f*

Munsch, R., 190*f*

Murphy, S., 146

music, 152–156; resources for, 289–292. *See also* songs

N

name puzzles, 127

names: letter, 130; in letter learning, 125, 125*f*, 126*f*, 127–128, 128*f*; in print awareness, 123; in songs, 155

Nathan, R., 97

National Association for the Education of Young Children (NAEYC), 2, 3, 7, 16, 79, 194

National Institute of Child Health and Human Development, 8, 82

National Reading Panel, 8, 82

neuroscientific research, 8–11

nonfiction, 139–141

norm-referenced tests, 34

numerical concepts, 143

Numeroff, L., 85*f*

nursery rhymes: acting out, 50–51; in oral language development, 70; in phonological awareness, 72. *See also* children's literature

O

observation: teacher, 25–26

An Observation Survey of Early Literacy Achievement (Clay), 36, 95, 118, 132

occupational print, 121

Olsen, K.D., 9, 11, 46

one-on-one assessments, 25

on-task behavior: fostering of, 54

opening activities, 141

oral language development, 10, 61–71; amount of talking and, 62, 71; cultural aspects of, 69; dramatic play in, 65; explicit instruction in, 65, 70; expressive language in, 62; flexibility in, 68–70; pragmatics in, 67–68; prosody in, 70–71; read-alouds in, 69, 70; receptive language in, 62; reciprocal discourse in, 67–68; for second-language learners, 76; semantics in, 64–67; show and tell in, 65–67; singing and, 161–162; social interaction in, 67–68; structural aspects of, 68–70; syntax in, 68–70; vocabulary development in, 64–67; wordless books in, 71; ZPD groups in, 86–94, 88*f*

oral language structures, 68–70

orienting behaviors: in print awareness, 123

Ormrod, J.E., 11, 14

Owocki, G., 121

P